Innovating to Learn, Learning to Innovate

Centre for Educational Research and Innovation

OECD

ORGANISATION FOR ECONOMIC CO-OPERATION AND DEVELOPMENT

The OECD is a unique forum where the governments of 30 democracies work together to address the economic, social and environmental challenges of globalisation. The OECD is also at the forefront of efforts to understand and to help governments respond to new developments and concerns, such as corporate governance, the information economy and the challenges of an ageing population. The Organisation provides a setting where governments can compare policy experiences, seek answers to common problems, identify good practice and work to co-ordinate domestic and international policies.

The OECD member countries are: Australia, Austria, Belgium, Canada, the Czech Republic, Denmark, Finland, France, Germany, Greece, Hungary, Iceland, Ireland, Italy, Japan, Korea, Luxembourg, Mexico, the Netherlands, New Zealand, Norway, Poland, Portugal, the Slovak Republic, Spain, Sweden, Switzerland, Turkey, the United Kingdom and the United States. The Commission of the European Communities takes part in the work of the OECD.

OECD Publishing disseminates widely the results of the Organisation's statistics gathering and research on economic, social and environmental issues, as well as the conventions, guidelines and standards agreed by its members.

> *This work is published on the responsibility of the Secretary-General of the OECD. The opinions expressed and arguments employed herein do not necessarily reflect the official views of the Organisation or of the governments of its member countries.*

Foreword

In recent decades, OECD economies have experienced a rapid transformation from their traditional industrial base to knowledge-based societies in which learning (over lifetimes with highly-developed "learning-to-learn skills"), creativity, and innovation capacities are central. Such capacities are important not only for a successful economy, but also for effective community and social engagement, participatory democracy, and for living fulfilling meaningful lives. At the same time, too many of today's schools are not adequately fostering deep knowledge, creativity and understanding: they are not well aligned with the knowledge economy and society of the 21st Century.

The reflections arising from these observations define a new OECD/CERI project *Innovative Learning Environments*, which has grown out of the near-completed work on "Schooling for Tomorrow". The shift between the two is from schooling to learning, from futures thinking to innovation, and towards a stronger base in the research findings of learning and related sciences. The further aim is to stimulate reflection on the potential of innovative forms of learning arrangements to enrich mainstream practice and reform. It promises to complement the system-level evidence gathered by the major OECD surveys such as PISA (Programme for International Student Assessment) and TALIS (Teaching and Learning International Survey) with the close focus on the micro "proximal" factors of education and learning.

These concerns have moved ever closer to the heart of the OECD's Centre for Educational Research and Innovation (CERI) agenda. The main conference event recently marking CERI's 40th anniversary was entitled "Learning in the 21st Century: Research, Innovation and Policy" (it was held in Paris on 15-16 May 2008).

The focus on learning and innovation is also integral to broader OECD-wide preoccupations. In 2007, the OECD *Innovation Strategy* was launched as a far-reaching horizontal and multi-disciplinary exercise. Its goal is to address countries' needs for a more comprehensive understanding of how to promote, measure and assess innovation and its underlying dynamics of change.

In preparing this volume, particular mention needs to be made of the part played by Mexico in the lead role in the first phase of the work on Innovative Learning Environments. The generous support and input culminated in the OECD-Mexico International Conference: "Emerging Models of Learning and Innovation", held on 14-16 June 2006 in Mérida, Yucatán. The analysis and inputs from the Mexico study are amply reflected in this report.

Within the OECD Secretariat, Francisco Benavides and David Istance were responsible for putting this report together, with substantial input from Hanna Dumont. The main editorial preparation of this volume for publication was made by Delphine Grandrieux, with Vanessa Shadoian.

ACKNOWLEDGEMENTS

This publication and the launch of the OECD/CERI Innovative Learning Environments project would not have been possible without the support of Mexico and of many individuals and institutions, only some of whom can be acknowledged by name below.

We would like first to extend our thanks to the Mexican Ministry of Public Education (SEP) for their support of the launch study, to the then-Minister Reyes Tamez-Guerra, and to Rafael Freyre and Silvia Schmelkes for their key roles in the initiative. Very special thanks go to Silvia Ortega, former Federal Administrator of Educational Services at Mexico Federal District, for her energetic leadership of the Mexican team and of the different activities and events involved. Our collective thanks go to all members of her team, in particular for Maricarmen Verdugo. FLACSO-Mexico (Latin American Faculty of Social Sciences) generously supported several of the preparatory meeting and events.

We give our special appreciation to the education leaders, authorities, students and families from the four initiatives which participated so valuably as case studies in Mexico:

- The Cerro del Judío Friendship Centre (Magdalena Contreras District, Mexico City); in particular Verónica González and Concepción Arista.

- Regular Education Support Services Unit No. 8 (Iztapalapa District, Mexico City); in particular Lucero Azpeitía and Sonia Navarrete.

- Intelligent Classroom for Migrants (different farms in Culiacan and Elota municipalities, Sinaloa State); in particular Patricia Inzunza and Berta Gómez.

- Ayuujk Polyvalent Integral Community High School (BICAP) (Community of Santa Maria Tlahuitoltepec, Mixe Region, Oaxaca State); in particular Fidel Perez y Crisóforo Vargas

We would like to thank Carmen Solis (former Yucatan Minister of Education), Silvia Paredes (then Director of Strategic Programmes), and their team in co-hosting the Mérida conference, in June 2006. We thank too the different conference partners: the Autonomous University of Yucatán, the CICY (Yucatán Centre for Scientific Research), and CINVESTAV-Merida Unit (Research and Advanced Studies Centre of the National Polytechnic Institute).

This volume would not, of course, be possible without the intellectual contributions of the individual chapter authors: Inés Aguerrondo, Tom Bentley, Carl Bereiter, Juan Cassassus, María Cecilia Fierro-Evans, María de Ibarrola, Lilia Pérez-Franco, Mar Rodríguez-Romero, Juana M. Sancho-Gil, Marlene Scardamalia, Anne Sliwka, MarcelaTovar-Gómez and Margarita Zorrilla.

Our OECD colleagues in Mexico played an extremely valuable role throughout the study and during the Mérida conference; special thanks go to Gabriela Ramos, former Head of the OECD Mexico Centre, and to the OECD Centre team, in particular Adriana Montejano and Adriana Ruiz.

Finally, our thanks to our Paris-based OECD colleagues (other than those referred to in the Foreword), especially Francesc Pedro, Henno Theisens, Tracey Burns, Bruno della Chiesa, Delia Rodrigo, Paulo Santiago, Sue Lindsay, Jennifer Gouby and Patricia Nilsson.

Table of Contents

Executive Summary

OECD economies have experienced the transformation from their traditional industrial base to the knowledge era in which learning and innovation are central. Yet, many of today's schools have not caught up as they continue to operate as they did in the earlier decades of the 20th Century. How can learning within and outside schools be reconfigured in environments that foster the deeper knowledge and skills so crucial in our new century? To succeed in this is not only important for a successful economy, but also for effective cultural and social participation and for citizens to live fulfilling lives.

This book summaries and discusses key findings from the learning sciences, shedding light on the cognitive and social processes that can be used to redesign classrooms to make them really effective learning environments. It explores concrete examples in OECD countries, from alternative schools to specific case studies in Mexico, that are seeking to break the mould and realise the principles emerging from learning science research. It asks how these insights can inspire educational reform for the knowledge era, in which optimising learning is the driving aim and in which innovation is both the widespread catalyst of change and the defining result.

Innovating to Learn, Learning to Innovate will be of particular interest to policy makers, researchers, teachers, students and families. It is published by the OECD Centre for Educational Research and Innovation (CERI).

The search for innovative learning environments

The opening chapter by the OECD Secretariat (Francisco Benavides, Hanna Dumont and David Istance) starts with the core competences and knowledge that OECD education systems aim to develop in their students for the 21st Century to argue that the current organisation of OECD education systems may well not provide the optimal environments to facilitate the acquisition of these skills. The chapter analyses four sources to enrich the reform agenda: a) findings and principles derived from the learning sciences; b) research-based innovations; c) the experience and lessons of alternative schooling; and d) innovative cases in the field. It concludes that these offer the basis of a new paradigm at the centre of the educational reform agenda.

Optimising learning: implications of learning sciences research

Keith Sawyer's starting point in Chapter 2 is the transformation in recent decades of many OECD member countries from industrial to knowledge economies, which emphasises the importance of creativity, innovation, and ingenuity. Learning scientists have shown that far too many schools are not teaching the deep knowledge that underlies knowledge work. Cognitive scientists have studied how children retain material better and are able to generalise it to a broader range of contexts, when they learn deep rather than surface knowledge and when they learn how to use that knowledge in real-world settings. Thus, learning science is seen as providing the basis to argue that standard model schools are not well aligned with the knowledge economy.

Educated workers now need a conceptual understanding of complex concepts, and the ability to work with them. They need to be able critically to evaluate what they read, be able to express themselves clearly both verbally and in writing, and understand scientific and mathematical thinking. They need to learn integrated and usable knowledge, rather than the sets of compartmentalised and de-contextualised facts. They need to be able to take responsibility for their own continuing, lifelong learning.

The most effective learning environments will have the following characteristics:

- *Customised learning:* Each child receives a customised learning experience.

- *Availability of diverse knowledge sources:* Learners can acquire knowledge whenever they need it from a variety of sources: books, web sites, and experts around the globe.

- *Collaborative group learning:* Students learn together as they work collaboratively on authentic, inquiry-oriented projects.

- *Assessment for deeper understanding:* Tests should evaluate the students' deeper conceptual understanding, the extent to which their knowledge is integrated, coherent, and contextualised.

The "standard model" of schooling is seen to align poorly with these. While some of these characteristics can be implemented within the standard model (*e.g.* collaborative learning tasks as many schools are doing today), others are much more difficult to implement (for example, customised learning is inconsistent with a high degree of standardisation).

Research-based innovation and alternative approaches to constructivism

Research-based innovation is the particular interest of Carl Bereiter and Marlene Scardamalia (Chapter 3). It allows future-oriented educators to identify approaches that offer the promise of making qualitative leaps beyond current outcomes, helping education systems to identify approaches that are worth working to develop as new directions. Its focus on *fruitfulness* is seen as different from all the approaches in education based on "effect size". It also contrasts with *basic* research, aimed at understanding the phenomenon or problem of interest, and with *decision-oriented* research, aimed at identifying "best practice" and guiding policy decisions. "Design research" has been applied as a term to research aiming to create and improve innovations; each major advance opens up novel possibilities for future advances. While standard in the applied sciences and engineering, it is still a novelty in education and marks a significant departure from "evidence-based" or "best" practice.

Research-based innovation in the learning sciences has given rise to a number of promising pedagogical avenues, which belong to the broad family of social-constructivist approaches. They propose five dimensions of different educational practice to distinguish among recent research-based innovations:

- *Degree of directedness:* This dimension ranges from extreme directedness, at one end, to collaborative inquiry at the other in which students work together to understand something. "Self-directed learning", "co-operative learning", "self-regulated learning" and "guided discovery" apply in the intermediate range.

- *Emphasis on ideas versus activities:* The sustained and well-directed effort at idea improvement is often lacking in many areas of human activity. Initiating students into this process is among the single most important contributions of schools in the Knowledge Age.

- *Emphasis on the individual versus community:* Many progressive forms of education emphasise the individual. There is, however, a growing recognition of the importance of dialogue in the education process which, if sustained and meaningful, translates into a community.

- *Design versus beliefs:* Design is about the usefulness, adequacy, improvability, and developmental potential of ideas and may be contrasted with normative beliefs. Different approaches to learning mix the normative and design modes in different combinations – both are important.

- *Accommodation to external constraints:* When innovations are put into practice, compromises have to be made, which almost always involve some sacrifice of effectiveness, clarity, and integrity.

Lessons from alternative schooling

Anne Sliwka (Chapter 4) surveys alternative education giving an overview of some of the main currents and examples. While it is a "fragmented landscape" in some respects, it also has some core common features and alternative schooling often confirms the directions suggested by the learning sciences. Many teaching practices developed in alternative schools, such as student-centred and independent learning, project-based and cooperative learning and authentic assessment have become increasingly mainstream through their influence on public education.

The learner: most of the alternative models of education perceive and organise learning as an active process based on the needs and interests of individual students. *The learning environment:* the traditional classroom set-up has been deliberately discontinued by most alternative schools; instead their learning environments tend to put the learner centre stage, to provide a wide array of learning resources and to facilitate individual as well as collaborative learning. They often use the "community" as a deliberate extension of the classroom. *Teachers:* the teacher role ranges from being a coach that students may draw on if they so choose through to a provider, organiser and manager of customised learning in experiential learning environments.

Curricula and content of learning: most alternative schools enjoy considerable freedom in the design of their curricula. A notable feature of most alternative schools is their aim to teach an integrated curriculum that does not strictly separate traditional subject areas but rather emphasises the interconnections between the disciplines. *Assessment:* alternative schools share the conviction that children and adolescents learn most effectively when they are interested and motivated which shapes the form, function and culture of assessment. They tend to focus on individual and criterion-referenced forms of assessment, such as learning reports, learning logs and portfolios, in which students document and reflect on their own learning.

Democratic pedagogies, curricula and teaching

Mar Rodríguez-Romero (Chapter 5) argues that we cannot afford to waste the wealth of knowledge which is hidden in a myriad of anonymous initiatives. For her, these "local innovations" are essential in order to discover new forms and dynamics of teaching and learning to guide the difficult renovation of pedagogical practices that have characterised schools up to now. Rodríguez suggests this should lead to radical not incremental change around three main orientations: situated pedagogies, curricular justice, and democratic teaching and learning.

Situated pedagogies are strategic, diversified and emancipatory, taking advantage of grassroots educational experiences and local commitment. Situated teaching seeks to promote authentic – *i.e.* significant – educational practices in relation to a particular culture and community. *Curricular justice* is about mitigating the effects and reproduction of both socio-economic and cultural inequalities. A common learning programme is necessary, which should extend access to both the advantaged and the disadvantaged the experiences and knowledge that are habitually ignored but which are essential for widening social participation. *Democratic teaching and learning* is about the creation of democratic structures and processes within the school, along with a democratic curriculum. Democracy in school has a clear link with community action in that the school should form part of the cultural practices in which students and their families are involved.

In the process of community construction, an essential role is played by those intermediary social structures such as neighbours, family, voluntary associations, non-governmental organisations, by teachers' associations and by the school itself, situated between people's private lives and depersonalised public institutions. The state, through different administrations including educational structures, should encourage the appearance of these intermediary channels of participation.

The construction of learning environments:
lessons from the Mexico study[1]

The authors of Chapter 6 were all in the network of experts in the Mexico study, 2005-2006. Juana Sancho-Gil sets the current push to innovate and reform against the historical backcloth of progressive movements during the 20th Century. She argues for more radical approaches given the disappointing results of reforms – learning outcomes are still limited and schools and teachers continue to work in highly traditional ways – and she stresses the need to search for new models or structures of learning with learners and their needs at their centre.

Juan Cassasus adopts an *interactionist* perspective and proposes that the driving forces of most innovations are needs and emotions. In what he calls the *needs-emotions-action*s dynamic, the extent of satisfaction of certain needs sets off emotional responses which in turn drive individuals or groups to react or innovate to respond to their needs.

Marcela Tovar-Gómez and Lilia Pérez-Franco use the four Mexico study cases extensively for their analyses. Tovar-Gómez argues for the creation of new learning structures that recognise the heterogeneous nature of education and its contexts, which call for more flexible instruments and for more participative and structured methods. She suggests *inter alia* revising the certification processes and explicitly encouraging counselling and research activities among teachers. Pérez-Franco notes that the innovations examined have survived while following different "building routes". Some started as on-the-ground responses to local needs; others were created in the system's middle tiers in response to top-down reforms, articulated by public servants who were sensitive to the needs, abilities and requests of local actors. She outlines different profiles for the actors of innovation which survive.

Margarita Zorrilla highlights and discusses urgent outstanding questions: how can recent learning science outcomes be translated into practice? How can teachers' understanding of these findings be facilitated

---

[1] As explained in the foreword to this publication, the OECD Centre for Educational Research and Innovation (CERI) started in 2005 the analytical work on models of learning. The core of this analysis was co-ordinated with Mexico and was based on intensive consultations and discussions with different groups of experts, as well as on fieldwork. This period, from July 2005 to June 2006, was known as the *exploratory phase* and concluded with the OECD-Mexico International Conference: "Emerging Models of Learning and Innovation" held between 14-16 June 2006 in Mérida, Yucatán.

and how can they be helped to apply them? How could teachers and other actors become real mediators between learners and the knowledge they need and want to acquire? How can a broader and more equitable concept of quality education be fostered?

For María de Ibarrola, innovations need to be understood historically in context. She observes that recent reforms and education initiatives in Mexico have sought to improve the education system but have fallen short. Thus she exhorts national and international analysis to "make visible" ground-level experiences that have obtained successful learning outcomes as one means to facilitate the transition towards more flexible education policies and systems.

An executive summary of the four Mexico study cases is included as Annex A of this publication.

What makes educational innovations work on the ground?

For María Cecilia Fierro-Evans (Chapter 7), innovation is a managerial process with the purpose of responding to practical needs or problems. It involves a critical review of practices influencing performance which can then build legitimacy and support. It can be understood in terms of: i) a model of intervention; ii) agents of change and political processes; and iii) the cultural, institutional and educational context.

The *intervention model* refers to the content and scope of the proposed changes, the structure and context of the intervention, its expected evolution, the size of the target population; and whether is local or wider in origin. While micro-level innovations might seem to have "limited relevance", paradoxically, they are usually the most permanent and make the deepest impact on practice.

The *role of agents and the change process*: an innovation's development is determined by the social interaction of group members through the successive stages of: awareness, expression, interest, trial and evaluation, trial period, and adoption. The problem-resolution model of innovation insists that target populations must themselves generate the innovation and its implementation will depend on the ability to solve problems and establish spaces for participation.

As regards *context*, changing practices embedded in strong historical and cultural roots is always problematic – the clearer the philosophical and psycho-pedagogical underpinnings, the greater are their possibilities in inspiring change. Insufficient training is a frequently-reported weakness in innovation projects, sometimes only amounting to the provision of information about expected changes. Open and constant dialogue among teachers, students and experts may foster the energy and creativity to stimulate innovation, reinforcing innovative attitudes, creative participation and a willingness to expose established practices to critical analysis.

The phases and functioning of educational innovation

For Inés Aguerrondo in Chapter 8 a new paradigm of learning and teaching will require both re-thinking the micro-level configurations of learning and education ("the didactic triangle") and the larger processes and dynamics of education. She analyses the dynamics of innovation in terms of four phases.

The first phase may be described as *Genesis or Gestation*, after the innovation has been triggered by a perceived problem or gap that needs to be addressed. There must be the political and administrative space for the innovation to happen, agents and actors to launch it, and sufficient buy-in from others. The second phase is about *setting the innovation in motion*. It is at this stage that difficulties and any resistance will become apparent which will demand strategies to address them. These strategies may be termed "feasibilities" and divided into: i) to want to do (politico-cultural feasibility); ii) to know what to do (feasibility of knowledge); and iii) to be able to do (concrete feasibility and resources available).

The third phase is about *implementation* and the dynamics of the process. Innovation takes place inside a complex system, both within the educational context and in interaction with external factors. After being set in motion, the three main processes are: (1) *consolidation*, when the innovation strengthens and enriches itself, (2) *bureaucratisation,* when the innovation transforms itself internally, keeping its shape but not its innovating content; (3) *interruption* happens when a formal decision is taken to end the experience. The fourth phase is about the *sustainability and functionality*. Functionality depends on the enhancement of "performance" as regards the problem the innovation has addressed. Sustainability is both about ensuring, while avoiding the problems of, routine and institutionalisation and meeting the challenge of expansion.

Open learning: a systems-driven model of innovation

Tom Bentley (Chapter 9) argues that the basic approach to educational reform across OECD countries revolves around the same governance paradigm and the on-going dominance of public bureaucracies. For him this focus has not resulted in the replacement of the traditional bureaucratic model of schooling. Bureaucracy is usually characterised as rigid, rule-based, and internally focused. Instead, education resilience lies in its flexibility in permitting an ordered, incremental process of adjustment within its own organisational parameters.

These organisational structures may thus be functional but they limit the possibilities of learning. They limit the scope of inquiry, interaction and information flow in teaching and learning activities and they limit the transfer of innovation by maintaining fragmented organisational units, largely insulated from the pressures of competition and market incentive. Schooling also tends to be insulated from innovation because of the perceived risks of responding to the younger generations without losing the socialising role that society expects of education.

Given the sway of bureaucratic systems, new reform strategies for improvement need to harness them in the relentless, open-ended pursuit of better learning outcomes. For Bentley, open systems offer greatest potential for education system reform. Open source educational repositories, seeking to share learning resource and design learning environments through open collaboration, are now rapidly growing. Organising these at scale requires open systems of co-ordination and development, with clear design rules and hierarchies of decision-making and their rigorously tested by users.

Chapter 1
The Search for Innovative Learning Environments
by
Francisco Benavides, Hanna Dumont and David Istance
(OECD Secretariat)

This chapter starts with the core competences and knowledge that OECD education systems aim to develop in their students for the 21st Century to argue that the current organisation of OECD education systems may well not provide the optimal environments to facilitate the acquisition of these skills. It analyses four sources to enrich the reform agenda: a) findings and principles derived from the learning sciences; b) research-based innovations; c) the experience and lessons of alternative schooling; and d) some highly innovative cases in the field. It concludes that these offer the basis of a new paradigm at the centre of the educational reform agenda.

1.1. Introduction

The increasing interest in OECD countries in how people learn and in different learning environments responds to the need to prepare all for contemporary knowledge economies and societies. It stems also from the concern with those who succeed least well, for whom the conventional educational offer fails. Existing educational arrangements are often far from optimal as regards the learning which is taking place. Hence the need for research and perspectives which go beyond "effective practice" (which assume that existing institutional arrangements will continue and the challenge is to find solutions within those arrangements). The reform agenda needs to build on and be inspired by different possible learning arrangements, now and in the future.

This was summed up by one commentator during the OECD "Schooling for Tomorrow" project – which has been the forerunner for this work on learning and innovation – in the following terms:

"...reforms have ultimately come up against a wall, or rather a ceiling, beyond which further progress seems impossible, leading increasing numbers of school administrators and educators to wonder whether schools do not need to be reformed but to be reinvented." (OECD, 2006a, pp. 187-188)

If there is to be "reinvention" and not just "reform" it is likely that more profound change will still be needed which goes right into the nature of teaching and learning themselves. The reform agenda can be built on and informed by at least three key pillars: a) robust research on learning and teaching; b) consideration of innovative learning experiences and environments in the field; and, c) the broader educational and non-educational trends that set the context for the immediate and longer-term future.

Firstly this chapter introduces the case for seeking new learning environments in the core competences and knowledge that OECD education systems should aim to develop for the worlds of today and tomorrow. It argues that the current organisation of OECD education systems may well not generate the optimal environments to facilitate the acquisition of these skills. Secondly, it analyses four sources for change to be considered in the 21st Century reform agenda: a) principles emerging from recent research on learning and teaching; b) research-based innovations and the development of different learning models and approaches; c) the experience of the alternative schooling; and d) innovative cases in the field. The last section discusses briefly the reform agenda that may generate a paradigm based on knowledge creation rather than transmission, where the learning principles define the main educational aims and where systemic innovation is both the trigger and a principal outcome for OECD countries.

1.2. Why looking for new learning approaches and environments?

What are the reasons to suppose that school systems really do need radical change? In recent decades, OECD (and many other) countries have invested significant resources aimed at transforming their education systems. These efforts have included, among other things: major teacher training programmes; the widening access to and use of digital hardware and software; large curriculum change; and system restructuring to give more autonomy to schools and local communities. Underlying all these strategies has been the common goal of providing students with the cognitive and meta-cognitive knowledge and the skills to be competitive in the 21st Century. This raises immediately the definition of the abilities, knowledge and skills that learners are intended to acquire at school.

One framework for the key competencies needed to function in today's complex demanding society, which goes well beyond any particular level or educational setting, was elaborated through the OECD DeSeCo project.[1] This came up with three broad clusters, each further divided into three components:

- *Using tools interactively*: a) the ability to use language, symbols and text interactively; b) the ability to use knowledge and information interactively; c) the ability to use technology interactively.

- *Interacting in heterogeneous groups*: a) the ability to relate well to others; b) the ability to co-operate; c) the ability to manage and resolve conflicts.

- *Acting autonomously*: a) the ability to act within the big picture; b) the ability to form and conduct life plans and personal projects; c) the ability to assert rights, interests, limits and needs.

With similar intent, the European Parliament and Council recommended eight key competences for lifelong learning. These competences are: (1) Communication in the Mother Tongue; (2) Communication in Foreign Languages; (3) Mathematical Competence and Basic Competence in Science and Technology; (4) Digital Competence; (5) Learning to Learn; (6) Interpersonal, Intercultural and Social competences, Civic Competence; (7) Entrepreneurship; and (8) Cultural Expression. The abilities of critical thinking, creativity, initiative-taking, problem-solving, risk assessment, decision-taking, and managing feelings constructively are seen as playing a role in all eight key competences.[2]

The new OECD Programme for the International Assessment of Adult Competencies (PIAAC) also has defined "literacy" broadly, in this case as "the interest, attitude, and ability of individuals to appropriately use socio-cultural tools, including digital technology and communication tools, to access, manage, integrate and evaluate information, construct new

---

[1] For further information on the DeSeCo (The Definition and Selection of Key Competences) see: *www.oecd.org/document/17/0,3343,en_2649_39263238_2669073_1_1_1_1,00.htm*

[2] See the Official Journal of the European Union of the 30 December 2006. *http://eur-lex.europa.eu/LexUriServ/site/en/oj/2006/l_394/l_39420061230en00100018.pdf*

knowledge, and communicate with others in order to participate effectively in society".[3]

Flexibility, creativity, communication with peers, problem-solving, and deep thinking are at the centre to all these concepts. They are focused not on the acquisition of a specific set of tools relevant for a certain point in time, but on a lifelong dynamic capacity of analysis and skills acquisition. These fundamental competences are about the nature of culture, society, and socialisation in the broadest terms, and they are shaped by much more than schools and education systems. It is nevertheless relevant to know how well such systems are contributing in the development of these skills, and how able and flexible they are to adapt new principles and dynamics that facilitate their acquisition. If schools are not the only places where these 21st Century skills and knowledge are nurtured, it is necessary to understand how their learning can be assured and if the role of schooling is an optimal one.

As reviewed next, available indicators such as those generated through PISA show that education systems are far from providing the learning environments that would facilitate students to achieve to their full potential. Many aspects of schooling are not consistent with many of the recent findings from the research on effective learning and teaching.

Competences and PISA – the argument for more successful learning of wider competence sets

The "PISA argument" for changing school systems is that even in terms of some their own parameters and cognitive goals, schools are not outstandingly successful.[4] For instance, in only five OECD countries do more than two-thirds of young people reach or surpass PISA Level 3 in reading literacy – the level which involves comprehension and interpretation of moderately complex text. The five countries in question are: Canada, Finland, Ireland, Korea and New Zealand. The average across OECD countries is 57.1% attaining Level 3 or above. In 17 OECD countries, 40% or more do not achieve at the Level 3 threshold in reading literacy. The countries which have 40% or more achieving at best at Levels 2 are Austria, the Czech Republic, Denmark, France, Germany, Greece, Hungary, Iceland, Italy, Luxembourg, Mexico, Norway, Portugal, the Slovak Republic, Spain,

---

[3] See *www.oecd.org/edu/piaac*

[4] PISA has measured the outcomes of education systems at the end of compulsory schooling and related factors every three years since 2000, involving well over 1 million 15-year-olds surveyed and over 60 countries.

Turkey and the United Kingdom. These students are the majority in Greece, Italy, Mexico, Portugal, the Slovak Republic, Spain and Turkey (OECD, 2007b).

PISA assessments are based on a dynamic model "in which new knowledge and skills necessary for successful adaptation to a changing world are continuously acquired throughout life" (OECD, 2003b), rather than measuring achievement in terms of specific curricula. With its focus on reading, mathematical and scientific *literacy*, PISA emphasises the mastery of processes, the understanding of concepts, and the ability to function in different situations in each domain, rather than the possession of specific knowledge. Beyond these domains, the assessment of *cross-curricular competencies* such as ICT and problem-solving skills is an integral part of PISA.

Regarding problem-solving and taking all OECD countries together, around a fifth of the students in 2003 could be considered "reflective, communicative problem-solvers", who are able to analyse a situation, make decisions and manage multiple conditions simultaneously, with just under a third being "reasoning, decision-making problem-solvers" and a third counted as "basic problem solvers". This leaves around 16% considered as "weak or emergent problem-solvers", who are generally unable to analyse situations or solve problems that call for more than the direct collection of information. There are large differences between countries on problem-solving but still larger variation within countries. This again raises the question of the effectiveness of education systems in core respects.

In sum PISA results highlight that too many students are not well prepared for the knowledge society in terms of the different literacies and problem-solving abilities. And, as discussed above, the ambitious definitions of contemporary learning needs increase the challenges even higher since they go far beyond academic, cognitive competence, to the meta-cognitive and even socio-emotional development.

Learning sciences and contemporary societies and economies – the arguments for change

Analysts have made much of the transformation in recent decades of many OECD countries from industrial to knowledge economies, with dominant activities based on the production and distribution of knowledge and information rather than the production and distribution of things (*e.g.* Drucker, 1993). Many analysts have come to emphasise the importance of creativity, innovation, and ingenuity in the knowledge economy so connecting back to the key competences reviewed above; indeed, some scholars now characterise today's economy as the *creative economy* (Florida, 2002).

This is the backdrop of Sawyer's analysis in Chapter 2. When learning scientists first went into classrooms (Sawyer, 2006), they discovered that most schools were not teaching the deep knowledge that underlies knowledge work. By the 1980s, cognitive scientists had discovered that children retain material better, and are able to generalise it to a broader range of contexts, when they learn deep knowledge rather than surface knowledge, and when they learn how to use it in real-world social and practical settings. Thus, learning scientists began to argue that standard model schools were not aligned with the knowledge economy.

An underlying theme of the learning sciences is that students learn deeper knowledge when they engage in activities that are similar to the everyday activities of professionals who work in a discipline. Knowledge workers tend to apply their expertise in complex social settings, with a wide array of technologically advanced tools. These observations have led to a *situated* view of knowledge (Greeno, 2006). This means that knowledge is not just a static mental structure inside the learner's head but instead knowing is a process that involves the person, the tools and other people in the environment, and the activities in which that knowledge is being applied. This active, embedded conception moves beyond the transmission and acquisition conception of learning implicit in the traditional model.

The knowledge economy calls for much more than the memorisation of facts and procedures. Educated workers need a conceptual understanding of complex concepts, and the ability to work with them creatively to generate new ideas, new theories, new products, and new information. They need to be able critically to evaluate what they read, be able to express themselves clearly both verbally and in writing, and understand scientific and mathematical thinking. They need to learn integrated and usable knowledge, rather than the sets of compartmentalised and de-contextualised facts. They need to be able to take responsibility for their own continuing, lifelong learning. These abilities are important to the economy, to the continued success of participatory democracy, and to living a fulfilling, meaningful life.

Many of today's schools are not teaching the deep knowledge that underlies innovative activity, as suggested *inter alia* by the PISA results described in the previous section. Sawyer suggests that the current structural configurations of the standard schooling model make it very hard to create learning environments that result in deeper understanding and the development of critical problem-solving capacities for most students. While the "standard model" of schooling described by Sawyer may be something of a caricatured heuristic device, it helps make clear the scale of the educational enterprise ahead.

Sliwka (see Chapter 4) also suggests that the learning sciences demonstrate the shortcomings of the traditional transmission and acquisition model of schooling. She reminds us, however, that there are different "school models" in the field. Those which are further removed from the principles identified by the learning sciences are not able to create rich learning environments and will not be successful in preparing their students with the appropriate skills for the future.

It might be tempting, if misguided, for educationists to marginalise such an economic focus for defining key features and competences. But social, cultural and personal goals in today's knowledge society are very much in line with the economic arguments: to succeed in community and family challenges, for instance, calls for very similar capacities for co-operation, analysis, creativity, entrepreneurialism and innovation.

Schools as organisations – weak knowledge management and innovative capacity

Many studies have argued for more flexible, open forms of learning and of school organisation. But while it is not difficult to identify numerous promising examples, it is not so easy to find evidence of more sustained and widespread change. A variety of the factors inhibiting fundamental change to traditional practices has been analysed in OECD/CERI work on knowledge management (OECD, 2000a; OECD, 2004a).

This work suggests that, in general, schools have weak networking and knowledge-sharing among teachers. Spending on educational research and development is very low in contrast to other sectors of activity characterised by the intensive creation and use of knowledge and the application of the R&D is quite limited. Most of the professional knowledge that teachers use in their daily work is tacit: it is rarely made explicit or shared with colleagues. Schools and classrooms are normally isolated one from another rather than interlinked. In short, the message is that too many schools still tend to have only rudimentary knowledge management practices, despite knowledge being education's explicit business.

OECD/CERI analysis of knowledge management in education (2004) identifies four key "pumps of innovation" that may be found in different sectors of economic and social activity. The problem identified in this report regarding the effective operation of all four sources or "pumps" of innovation is that traditional arrangements and organisation of education have tended to inhibit their application compared with many other sectors.

Box 1.1 identifies the "innovation pumps" that the OECD education systems have difficulties to implement.

Box 1.1. "Innovation pumps"

- *The "science-based" innovation pump*: education has not traditionally made enough direct use of research knowledge, and there is often cultural resistance to doing so. This is increasingly being targeted in OECD reform efforts.

- *The "horizontally-organised" innovation pump*: there are obvious benefits in terms of teachers pooling their knowledge through networks, but incentives to do so remain underdeveloped. There is need to tighten the "loose coupling" between the individual units – single teachers, individual classrooms, individual schools as units – that characterises so many school systems.

- *The "modular structures" pump:* this is about building a complex process or system from smaller subsystems that can be designed independently but function together. Education is accustomed to working in modules, but much that takes place has schools or teachers operating separately from each other.

- *The "information and communication technologies" pump*: there is a powerful potential for digital technologies to facilitate the transformation of education, but its use in schools remains underdeveloped, partly because the main *modus operandi* of school administration and instruction are resistant to change.

1.3. Different approaches to re-designing learning environments

There are different approaches to rearranging the learning environments. One is to closely focus on research and identify the "learning principles" emerging on how people learn and the different processes that this implies. This takes concrete form when (research-based) innovation is built on different theories and research findings. Another is to examine the philosophies and practices of the different learning arrangements known as "alternative education". Yet another is to look at innovations in order to identify education initiatives and learning environments in the field, and to understand their dynamics, successes and difficulties. This section takes each in turn, drawing on the chapters of this volume.

Building on learning science research

Learning science is an interdisciplinary field that studies teaching and learning from different scientific perspectives. It has clarified some key features about learning. For instance, learning always takes place against a backdrop of *existing knowledge*. *Reflection* or meta-cognition – thinking about the process of learning and thinking about knowledge – is fundamental; so is *deeper conceptual understanding* and the *tailored help to learn* ("scaffolding"). Learning sciences researchers have as one of their main goals to design more effective learning environments including schools and classrooms based on their findings.

Drawing on the research findings, Sawyer in Chapter 2 identifies a set of conclusions that should guide the design of learning environments, which can in turn be used to guide the development of new models of schooling:

- *Customised learning*: more effective learning will occur if each learner receives a customised learning experience.

- *Diverse knowledge sources*: students gain expertise from a variety of sources as well as the traditional ones – from the Internet, at the library, or through e-mail exchange with a working professional – and the teacher is far from being the only source of classroom expertise.

- *Distributed knowledge*: collaborating student groups can accelerate learning.

- *Curriculum*: what seems simpler to an adult professional is not necessarily simpler to a learner; the curriculum has to take into account children's theories and their (mis-) conceptions.

- *The role of the teacher*: teachers should be highly-trained professionals, comfortable with technology, with a deep pedagogical understanding of the subject matter, able to respond and improvise to the uniquely emerging flow of each classroom.

- *Assessment*: customised learning sits awkwardly with requirements for every student to learn the same thing at the same time and assessment is too often of the relatively superficial as compared with deep knowledge.

As Marcela Tovar-Gómez (Chapter 6) reminds us, however, it is not enough simply to grasp the main findings of the learning sciences; it is necessary to link theory and practice into the organisational aspects of teaching. One way to do this she suggests is to foster "Counselling-Research-Actions Circuits" among teachers, which are cycles of different activities to help teachers put theoretical knowledge into practice and to become ever more expert at doing so.

Comparing learning models and approaches

Research-based innovation is the particular interest of Carl Bereiter and Marlene Scardamalia (Chapter 3). This research aims at creating innovations in which the guiding criterion is *fruitfulness* – does the idea have potential? Is it worth developing further? They contrast this with *basic* research, aimed at understanding the phenomenon or problem of interest, and with *decision-oriented* research, aimed at identifying "best practice" and guiding policy decisions. The focus on fruitfulness is seen as different from the whole stratum of research in education that takes "effect size" as coin of the realm. It allows future-oriented educators to identify approaches that offer the promise of making qualitative leaps beyond current outcomes, helping education systems to identify approaches that are worth working to develop as new directions.

"Design research" has been applied as a term to research aiming to create and improve innovations (Bereiter, 2002; Collins, Joseph and Bielaczyc, 2004); each major advance opens up novel possibilities for future advances. A good example relates to the many present-day uses of computers, hardly any of which were foreseen by the pioneer computer scientists years ago. In the applied sciences and engineering, the term is largely superfluous because virtually all the research is of this sort, with research feeding back into further design decisions. But, argue Bereiter and Scardamalia, it is still a novelty in education. It marks a significant departure from "evidence-based" or "best" practice.

Research-based innovation in the learning sciences has given rise to a number of promising pedagogical avenues, which belong to the broad family of social-constructivist approaches. Bereiter and Scardamalia propose five dimensions of different educational practice to distinguish among recent research-based innovations:

- *Degree of directedness – from instruction to epistemic agency*: this dimension ranges from extreme directedness, at one end, to collaborative inquiry at the other in which students work together to understand something. "Self-directed learning", "co-operative learning", "self-regulated learning" and "guided discovery" are terms applicable to the intermediate range.

- *Extent of emphasis on ideas versus activities*: what makes science progressive is the sustained and well-tooled effort at idea improvement, something notably lacking in many other areas of human life focused on the successful accomplishment of activities. Initiating students into this process and trusting that progress will result is among the single most important things that schools can do to prepare students for the Knowledge Age.

- *Extent of emphasis on the individual versus community*: in contrast with the strong focus on the individual, there is a growing recognition of the importance of dialogue in the education process. The forms of interactions include teacher-mediated dialogue, teacher-managed argument or debate, and independent group discussion. Sustained and meaningful discourse creates a community which, if it is oriented toward cognitive goals, is a learning- or knowledge-building community enlisting students' natural motives to belong to the service of educational goals.

- *"Design mode" versus "belief mode"*: in belief mode, the focus is on what we and others believe or ought to believe. When in design mode, we are concerned with the usefulness, adequacy, improvability, and developmental potential of ideas. Different approaches to learning may mix the normative and design modes differently – both are important.

- *Extent of accommodation to external constraints*: when innovations are put into practice, compromises have to be made, which almost always involve some sacrifice of effectiveness, clarity, and integrity. A general issue of accommodation is the extent to which scientific language should be translated in terms that are more accessible to practitioners to find the right balance of integrity and accessibility.

The lessons provided by "alternative schooling"

Can alternative schools serve as models for a broader renewal of mainstream education? Anne Sliwka responds positively to this question (Chapter 4), noting that many features of alternative schools make sense from a learning sciences perspective. She argues that alternative schooling has already been influential in recent years as the instructional strategies and assessment techniques they have developed have impacted on teaching and learning in many public school systems across the world. As we have just noted, the landscape of alternatives in education varies along a number of dimensions; Sliwka nevertheless identifies several lessons useful for mainstream education that are also coherent with the principles of learning sciences.

- *The conception of the learner:* most of the alternative models of education perceive and organise learning as an active process based on the needs and interests of individual students. Different types of alternative schools provide a considerable range of freedom to their students within reasonable limits of appropriate behaviour fostering the intrinsic motivation to learn. Many alternative schools try to ensure that children work to their individual level of mastery and competence.

- *The learning environment:* the traditional classroom set-up – with desks arranged in rows, an exposed teacher's desk, and a board in the front of the room – has been deliberately discontinued by most alternative schools. Their learning environments tend to put the learner centre stage, to provide a wide array of learning resources and to facilitate individual as well as collaborative learning. As alternative models of education tend to emphasise the interrelation between effective learning and the learner's emotional well-being, they often also pay special attention to the aesthetic side of learning environments. As students are given considerable freedom to choose learning activities they wish to engage in, alternative forms of education often use the "community" as a deliberate extension of the classroom, and students use various in-school and community resources including people, natural resources and cultural institutions to enrich their own learning.

- *The role of teachers:* as alternative education is learner-focused, teachers are not regarded as mere agents of curriculum delivery. With varying degrees of intervention, the teacher role ranges from being a coach that students may draw on if they so choose through to a provider, organiser and manager of customised learning in experiential learning environments. At many alternative schools, teachers spend more time mentoring and facilitating the learning process of individuals or small groups than directly giving lessons. Where customised learning for individual children is realised, teachers require significant diagnostic skills as they have to present individual students with new challenging material based on the competence level they have achieved.

  Many alternative schools make room for experiential education in larger projects; for this, a key teacher competence lies in recognising authentic learning opportunities. As the possibility to learn from natural consequences, mistakes and successes is one of the main reasons to engage in authentic experience and problem-solving, teachers need to be able to deal professionally with ambiguity, uncertainty, risk, and failure.

- *Curricula and content of learning:* most alternative schools enjoy considerable freedom in the design of their curricula. The older the students that they teach, however, the more schools tend to align core content of their teaching with central examinations and state requirements. A notable feature of most alternative schools is their aim to teach an integrated curriculum that does not strictly separate traditional subject areas but rather emphasises the interconnections between the disciplines.

- *The function and culture of assessment:* alternative schools share the conviction that children and adolescents learn most effectively when they are interested in and motivated towards a topic or a project. This orientation towards fostering intrinsic rather than extrinsic motivation influences the design of learning environments and the devolution of freedom, choice and responsibility to students. It powerfully shapes the form, function and culture of assessment.

Alternative schools focus on individual children and their specific talents, interests, learning styles and speeds. Social comparison between children is discouraged and for that reason so are traditional forms of testing and summative assessments. Instead, they tend to focus on individual and criterion-referenced forms of assessment, such as learning reports, learning logs and portfolios, in which students document and reflect their own learning. The overall principle underlying the culture of assessment in most alternative schools is to support the individual child on the basis of a "credit" not a "debit" model.

In sum, Sliwka concludes: "wherever educational alternatives combine customised learning with collaborative group learning in authentic, inquiry-oriented projects, provide their students with access to diverse knowledge sources and assess them for deeper understanding and further learning, alternative schools seem to be ahead of mainstream education and can serve as meaningful models for the renewal of mainstream education across the globe".

The inspiration of practice

The inspiration provided by innovative practices themselves may also serve as a guide to new learning environments. Lilia Pérez-Franco (Chapter 6) argues that the goal of the education system should be to accompany those actors who have found "new routes" to respond to their learning needs, and to design with them realistic policies that can guarantee these routes. Mar Rodríguez (Chapter 5) similarly argues that we cannot afford to waste the wealth of knowledge which is hidden in a myriad of anonymous initiatives. For her, these "local innovations" are essential in order to discover new forms and dynamics of teaching and learning to guide the difficult renovation of pedagogical practices that have characterised schools up to now. Rodríguez suggests this should lead to radical not incremental change around three main orientations: *situated pedagogies, curricular justice, and democratic teaching and learning.*

Situated pedagogies are strategic, diversified and emancipatory, taking advantage of grassroots educational experiences and local commitment and working against exclusion. Situated teaching is contextualised and seeks to promote authentic – *i.e.* significant – educational practices in relation to a particular culture and community. The teaching is sensitive to cultural difference and to the cultural and linguistic base of students from often-excluded social groups.

Curricular justice is about mitigating the effects and reproduction of both socio-economic and cultural inequalities. For Rodríguez, a common learning programme is necessary, with methods and contents that reflect the experiences and cultural habits of disadvantaged populations. These should extend to both the advantaged and the disadvantaged, permitting all access to experiences and knowledge that are habitually ignored but which are essential for widening social participation and understanding. Competitive assessments should also, for Rodríguez, be replaced by equity-based or descriptive assessments.

Democratic teaching and learning is about the creation of democratic structures and processes within the school, along with a democratic curriculum. Like situated pedagogy and curricular justice, this is about the dignity and rights of minorities and individuals; the use of critical reflection and analysis to evaluate ideas, problems and policies; the free circulation of ideas; and concern for the welfare of others. Democracy in school has a clear link with community action in that the school should form part of the cultural practices in which students and their families are involved.

In the process of community construction, an essential role is played by those intermediary social structures such as neighbours, family, voluntary associations, non-governmental organisations, by teachers' associations and by the school itself, situated between people's private lives and depersonalised public institutions. These structures act as bridges, facilitating the participation of teachers in the educational policy of the local society and, by extension, in the wider social fabric. The state, through different administrations including educational structures, should encourage the appearance of these intermediary channels of participation.

Concrete innovative examples

The examples presented in this section serve to provide concrete references for the different theoretical arguments. They are not individual isolated cases but have already provided some evidence of scalability or at least of inspiration to others. Based on the design of The Met (*www.themetschool.org*) (see Box 1.2), The Big Picture Company has developed a US network of more than 54 Big Picture Schools and others located internationally in Australia, the Netherlands, and Israel (*www.bigpicture.org*).

Box 1.2. The MET

The learning environment

The Metropolitan Regional Career & Technical Center (MET) is a network of six small high schools in Providence, Rhode Island, United States. In 1996 it was co-founded by "The Big Picture Company", a non-profit educational change organisation whose mission is to catalyse changes in American education.

The learning process

- *The learners:* there are 690 students in the MET. The student population is ethnically diverse and 65% of the students come from low-income families.

- *The facilitators:* the staff at the MET comes from diverse fields. Every school at the MET has at least two social work interns.

- *The content of learning:* MET aims to teach students empirical reasoning, quantitative reasoning, communication, social reasoning and personal qualities. MET addresses the whole learner, including the student's physical, mental and emotional well-being.

- *The organisation of learning:* students are organised into advisories: groups of 15 individuals in the same grade level and led by an advisor, who stays with them for all four years of high school. Students are also paired with adult mentors who share their career interests. This is because school-based learning is blended with outside experience through an internship programme. For each student, a challenging and personalised learning plan is developed every quarter by the students themselves, their advisors and their parents. Instead of multiple choice tests and exams, each student defends his/her work in exhibitions each quarter in front of advisors, parents, mentors and peers. Instead of grades, students receive quarterly narratives from their advisors, in which the advisor describes the student's academic and personal growth in detail. There are no standard fixed-time classes.

The learning context

The MET is not just a school but also a community centre where community members are involved in the daily workings of the school. In addition, parents are involved in the development of their children's learning plan and in assessing their child's work. A health centre is also part of the MET.

Learning outcomes

The MET has been very successful: on average, 98% of the graduates are accepted to college, the graduation rate is 94 % (the city's average is 54%) and the attendance rate is 92% (the city's average is 80%). According to the "Rhode Island's School Accountability for Learning and Teaching Surveys", the MET has consistently ranked among the state's top high schools for parent involvement, school climate, and quality of instruction.

There have been about 100 internal and external publications in German on the Laboratory School (*www.uni-bielefeld.de/LS*) in the past 25 years (see Box 1.3). Its teaching and learning materials are made available for the public (through publications, workshops, teacher training and presentations), after they have been tested and evaluated.

Box 1.3. The Laboratory School[5]

The learning environment

The Laboratory School is an experimental comprehensive school in Bielefeld, Northrhine-Westfalia, Germany. It was founded in 1974 to develop new forms of teaching, learning and living in school and making the results available to the public. Its work is both practical and theoretical, as the school is linked with a research institution evaluating the work of the school.

The learning process

- *The learners:* 660 from pre-school to 10th grade assist the Laboratory School.

- *The facilitators:* the school has approximately 90 facilitators, including 60 teachers, 25 kindergarten teachers and 5 teachers for special education and psychologists. In addition, researchers take part in the development of the organisation of learning.

- *The content of learning:* alongside the basic subjects, special emphasis is placed on social learning and on how to take responsibility for one's own learning.

- *The organisation of learning:* the Laboratory School is an all-day school. It is structured corresponding to the age of the students: students from grades 0 to 2, 3 to 5, 5 to 7, and 8 to 10 are placed in the same learning group. Thus, the Laboratory School has ability-mixed and age-mixed groups. There is both individualised and project-based learning, which is always blended with real-world experiences. Learning moves from very open forms with no time structures and an integrated, cross-subject curriculum at early grades to more structured forms and a more detailed curriculum at higher grades. In regard to this, marks are not introduced until the end of 9th grade.

The learning context

The neighbourhood, the community and the physical environment of the school are integrated in the learning process. Also, parental involvement is expected and parents are informed about the learning process of their children in detail. The school is linked with a research institution.

---

[5] This description was done mainly using the information and data from the Laboratory School webpage.

Box 1.4. Notschool.net

The learning model

Notschool.net is a national, internet-based "Virtual Online Community", offering an alternative to traditional education for young people who for various reasons can no longer cope with school. Notschool.net was originally a research project developed with a UK university department. Today due to its results, it has become a charity: the Inclusion Trust.

The learning process

- *The learners:* Notschool.net is aimed at teenagers aged 14 to 16. A person is only eligible for Notschool.net if the traditional educational alternatives have failed.

- *The facilitators:* there are approximately 130 mentors and 20 experts. The latter run areas of content closely related to the traditional curriculum and develop opportunities for accreditation. Sometimes, experienced students act as role models for the new students.

- *The content of learning:* Notschool.net aims to provide students with a bespoke pathway into further education, lifelong learning and further qualifications. Its goal is to rebuild the student's confidence, self-esteem and social skills.

- *The organisation of learning:* when joining Notschool.net, each student is required to attend an induction session. At these sessions, there are no restrictions: students are encouraged to play music, move around freely or eat. Once all the equipment is set up at home, all young people follow their own pattern of learning and their own specialised interest. Each mentor develops a learning plan with each of their students, which is reviewed at least every six weeks. At the end of attending Notschool.net, work experience and college tasters are very common and students are encouraged to develop e-portfolios.

The learning context

Local teams of the Netschool.net are expected to be in regular contact with families, celebrating successes and supporting the learner. The families are also encouraged to use the computer system.

Learning outcomes

Research from the first year pilot showed that over 98% achieved formal accreditation. Self-esteem and confidence was built along with literacy improvement. After attending Notschool.net, students' standard ICT and creativity related skills have much improved.

From 2001, the then UK Department for Education and Skills (DfES) extended the pilot Notschool.net (*www.notschool.net*) project eventually to cover over 30 local authorities and the project developed a model for engaging disaffected teenagers (see Box 1.4). The DfES decided that Notschool.net and its inclusion model showed wider potential and extended it beyond being a university research project to a charity, the Inclusion Trust. Up to summer 2007, over 3 500 young people have taken part.

One conclusion to be drawn from this brief consideration of cases is the need to avoid an exaggerated contrast between what goes on in *formal schools* and the learning which takes place in a host of *out-of-school learning environments*. Assuming that all which goes on in schools fits a traditional stereotype – transmission pedagogy, preoccupation with the reproduction of facts and recall, strong binary precepts (correct vs. incorrect, pass vs. fail) and uni-dimensional intelligence, negligible co-operation among teachers and among learners, highly standardised organisational and physical units – may serve heuristically but in reality is far too simplistic. Schools cover a very wide range of approaches to learning. Thus, the focus on different models and arrangements for learning is not the same as looking for alternatives to schools.

In addition to the three cases described in this section, Annex A of this publication includes a detailed summary of four Mexican cases studied during the exploratory phase of the project.

These four elements – a) principles derived from learning sciences; b) different learning models and approaches; c) the examples from alternative schooling; and d) concrete innovative cases – highlight some of the elements which enter into the reform equation in OECD countries. In order to prepare learners with the cognitive, meta-cognitive and emotional tools and skills they need for the years to come, education needs to be learner-focused, fostering collaborative dynamics and creative and deep thinking, where intrinsic motivation is encouraged while recognising diverse knowledge sources and forms of assessment. What is the challenge in making this happen? Some chapters in this volume address this question.

1.4. Is reform for far-reaching change possible?

While many developing countries are still fighting to attain universal basic and secondary education, industrialised societies have concentrated their reform efforts and resources in increasing quality, efficiency and accountability. Accurate evaluation mechanisms have been developed at national and international levels to measure this progress. However, many of these efforts are reinforcing an existing education paradigm that does not necessarily meet the demands of the knowledge society of the 21st Century, for the reasons outlined at the beginning of this chapter.

Tom Bentley (Chapter 9) maintains that with few exceptions, the basic approach to reform across OECD countries revolves around the same governance paradigm and the on-going dominance of public bureaucracies. For him, the aim of the reform strategy has been to ensure that each school has an appropriately focused strategy for improving its own performance all within a single system of governance and accountability. In his view, however, this has not resulted in the replacement of the traditional bureaucratic model of schooling and therefore in the creation of appropriate settings to acquire the competences and knowledge that were discussed at the beginning of this chapter.

Aguerrondo (2008) similarly argues that different innovations and even alternative schooling arrangements that resist the "homogenising school model" have long existed. However none of them has resulted in a radical change in the education system as a whole. In recent decades, the emphasis of reform has focused increasingly on the macro level, addressing issues related to management and administration. The debates have been around issues such as centralisation vs. decentralisation; the development or improvement of national evaluation systems; the accreditation of institutions and teachers, etc. In her view, these efforts have not been informed by a new organisational vision that might result in the reinvention of the learning and teaching dynamics and a new form of negotiation and interaction among the different actors across the education systems. Why are education systems so resistant to fundamental change?

Flexibility as resilience

It is traditional to characterise the bureaucracy of which schooling is part as rigid, rule-based, and internally focused. One explanation for the entrenchment of dominant models of schooling may thus be that it is simply impossible to overturn due to vested interests and centuries-old habits. But, as Bentley argues, even where these interests are weak or have been swept away, for example through industrial relations reform or the introduction of market competition, the model has not changed radically. Successful private schools rarely stray from the organisational form or the regulatory methods found in state sectors. Across countries and cultures, the received definition of a "successful school" has become remarkably similar, increasingly influenced by both the international research movement on school improvement and the internationalisation of performance indicators and measurement (including through the OECD).

Bentley launches another potential response: perhaps the resilience of education systems lies in their peculiar flexibility. Rather than the formal, rational objectives and accountabilities of institutional systems, much recent thinking about the nature of social and economic behaviour has focused on the evolution of complex adaptive systems. Human behaviour is adaptive in that it continuously adjusts to changing environments and new experience, even without conscious decision-making. The bureaucratic model allows its members – schools, administrators, teachers and so on – to participate in a process of continuous adaptation to changing student identities, changing socio-economic conditions, and changing policy requirements. It does this through an ordered, incremental process of adjustment, refinement, and organisational learning. The bureaucratic model is not impervious to change because it is inflexible, but because it offers a particular kind of flexibility: it makes continuous adaptation manageable within its own organisational parameters. The system is implicitly geared towards maintaining the integrity of *its own* design.

But, as Bentley argues, this system is not necessarily designed to optimise learning outcomes for all of its participants. These organisational structures are functional in the sense of making ordered learning possible by creating predictability and the responsibilities needed to operate at large scale. But they produce boundaries which limit the possibilities of learning, because they limit the scope of inquiry, interaction and information flow in teaching and learning activities. Furthermore, they limit the transfer of innovation because they maintain relatively fragmented organisational units, largely insulated from the pressures of competition and market-type incentives. Schooling also tends to be insulated from innovation because of the perceived risks of responding directly to the voices and demands of younger generations without losing the socialising role that society wants education to play. It results in a combination of stability and incremental change which allows the traditional model of schooling and bureaucratic school systems to adapt continuously to all kinds of external change.

From education-focused to learning and innovation-driven reform

In the face of the resilience of the bureaucratic system underpinning schooling, the lesson Bentley draws is that, rather than seeking to subvert or bypass the adaptive capacity of existing systems, new reform strategies for improvement need to harness them. They must connect with the relentless, open-ended pursuit of better learning outcomes, rather than the implicit preservation of their own core values and underlying structure while widening entrenched patterns of inequality. Thus a deeper, more ambitious shift is required – a new view of innovation and its relationship to system design, and a refreshed sense of the global context.

Aguerrondo similarly argues that the knowledge era demands that change – economic, social and educational – is no longer considered as disruption of the established order but as the basis of new innovation (2008, Chapter 8). In her view, a new paradigm of learning and teaching presupposes: re-thinking first the organisation of and around "the didactic triangle" (or the interaction among teachers/educators, learners and knowledge) with the aim of creating authentic learning environments; second, the process and dynamics of the systemic education change and management that will be coherent with this aim. The latter is, in her view, just as important to consider even if its effects are less direct to teaching and learning themselves as the distribution of political, administrative and financial responsibilities in education between the state, private sector and civil society and the transition process itself are critical. Learning how to manage the process of change in terms of generalised public policies is as important as being able to re-conceptualise the didactic triangle. Fierro-Evans (Chapter 7) supports this argument and reminds us that innovation could be seen as managerial process that looks to respond to practical needs or problems. A critical review of current education and learning practices will be of main importance in order to build legitimacy and support for change.

In sum, the authors of this publication argue for a new vision of the reform of education, in which knowledge is seen as part of a creative and evolving process; where learning principles are the driving aims; and where innovation is, at the same time, the main trigger and the systemic output. The analysis argues for priority to be given to an agenda of research and policy issues now and in the future:

- Strengthening the evidence-based policies on learning and innovation while encouraging research-based innovations in order to open promising fields and practices in education.

- Disseminating and applying the findings from the learning sciences on learning and teaching, including through providing accessible outputs for policy makers, education leaders, educators, students and families.

- Systematising the information gathering, evaluation and support of innovations and creative practices in the field.

- Understanding more profoundly the nature of learning and the dynamics of innovation with the focus on their encouragement and sustainability, even bureaucratisation, rather than just gathering examples of innovative practice.

This agenda defines the current agenda of work on innovative learning environments within OECD's Centre for Educational Research and Innovation (CERI).

References

Aguerrondo, I. (2008), "Revisar el modelo: un desafío para lograr la inclusión", PROSPECTS IBE Inclusión.

Bereiter, C. (2002), "Design Research for Sustained Innovation", *Cognitive Studies: Bulletin of the Japanese Cognitive Science Society*, Vol. 9, No. 3, pp. 321-327.

Collins, A., D. Joseph and K. Bielaczyc (2004), "Design Research: Theoretical and Methodological Issues", *The Journal of the Learning Sciences*, Vol. 13, pp. 15-42.

Drucker, P.F. (1993), *Post-capitalist Society*, HarperBusiness, New York.

Elmore, R. (1990), "La reestructuración de las escuelas, la siguiente generación de la reforma educative", Fondo de Cultura Económica, México.

Florida, R. (2002), *The Rise of the Creative Class and How it's Transforming Work, Life, Community and Everyday Life*, Basic Books, New York.

Greeno, J.G. (2006), "Learning in Activity", in R.K. Sawyer (ed.), *Cambridge Handbook of the Learning Sciences*, Cambridge University Press, New York, pp. 79-96.

Jarvela, S. (2006), "Personalised Learning? New Insights into Fostering Learning Capacity", *Personalising Education*, OECD Publishing, Paris.

Leadbeater, C. (2006), "The Future of Public Services: Personalised Learning", *Personalising Education*, OECD Publishing, Paris.

OECD (2000a), *Knowledge Management in the Learning Society*, OECD Publishing, Paris.

OECD (2000b), *Measuring Student Knowledge and Skills: The PISA 2000 Assessment of Reading, Mathematical and Scientific Literacy*, OECD Publishing, Paris.

OECD (2001b), *Knowledge and Skills for Life: First Results from PISA 2000*, OECD Publishing, Paris.

OECD (2002), *Understanding the Brain: Towards a New Learning Science*, OECD Publishing, Paris.

OECD (2003a), *Networks of Innovation: Towards New Models for Managing Schools and Systems*, OECD Publishing, Paris.

OECD (2003b), *The PISA 2003 Assessment Framework: Mathematics, Reading, Science and Problem Solving Knowledge and Skills*, OECD Publishing, Paris.

OECD (2003c), *Learners for Life: Student Approaches to Learning: Results from PISA 2000*, OECD Publishing, Paris.

OECD (2004a), *Innovation in the Knowledge Economy: Implications for Education and Learning*, OECD Publishing, Paris.

OECD (2004b), *Learning for Tomorrow's World: First Results from PISA 2003*, OECD Publishing, Paris.

OECD (2005a), *Formative Assessment: Improving Learning in Secondary Classrooms*, OECD Publishing, Paris.

OECD (2005b), *Education Policy Analysis – 2004 Edition*, OECD Publishing, Paris.

OECD (2005c), *Problem Solving for Tomorrow's World: First Measures of Cross-Curricular Competencies from PISA 2003*, OECD Publishing, Paris.

OECD (2006a), *Think Scenarios, Rethink Education*, OECD Publishing, Paris.

OECD (2006b), *Personalising Education*, OECD Publishing, Paris.

OECD (2007a), *Understanding the Brain: The Birth of a Learning Science*, OECD Publishing, Paris.

OECD (2007b), *Assessing Scientific, Reading and Mathematical Literacy: A Framework for PISA 2006*, OECD Publishing, Paris.

"Recommendation of the European Parliament and of the Council of 18 December 2006 on key competences for lifelong learning", (2006/962/EC), Official Journal of the European Union *http://eur-lex.europa.eu/LexUriServ/site/en/oj/2006/l_394/l_39420061230en00100 018.pdf*

Sawyer, R.K. (ed.) (2006), *Cambridge Handbook of the Learning Sciences*, Cambridge University Press, New York.

Websites

DeSeCo (The Definition and Selection of Key Competences):
www.oecd.org/document/17/0,3343,en_2649_39263238_2669073_1_1_1_1,00.htm

OECD project on Innovative Learning Environments:
www.oecd.org/edu/learningenvironments

OECD Innovation Strategy for Education: *www.oecd.org/edu/innovation*

OECD project on New Millennium Learners: *www.oecd.org/edu/nml*

PIAAC: *www.oecd.org/edu/piaac*

PISA brochure: *www.oecd.org/dataoecd/51/27/37474503.pdf*

The MET: *www.themetschool.org*

The Laboratory School: *www.uni-bielefeld.de/LS*

Notschool.net: *www.notschool.net*

Chapter 2
Optimising Learning
Implications of Learning Sciences Research
by
R. Keith Sawyer[1]

This chapter introduces the field of learning sciences, and outlines some of its key findings in recent years. It explains that while the standard model of schooling was designed to prepare students for the industrial age, the global shift to the knowledge economy will require the rethinking of schooling in order to accommodate evolving needs. Several key findings of learning sciences research and how they align with the needs of the knowledge economy are explained.

2.1. Introduction

Learning sciences is an interdisciplinary field that studies teaching and learning. Learning scientists study learning in a variety of settings – not only the more formal learning of school classrooms, but also the more informal learning that takes place at home, on the job, and among peers. The goal of the learning sciences is to better understand the cognitive and social processes that result in the most effective learning, and to use this knowledge to redesign classrooms and other learning environments so that people learn more deeply and more effectively. The sciences of learning include cognitive science, educational psychology, computer science, anthropology, sociology, information sciences, neurosciences, education, design studies, instructional design, and other fields. In the late 1980s,

---

[1] Associate Professor of education, psychology, and business at Washington University, St. Louis. He is an expert in creativity research and learning sciences. Author of *Group Genius: the Creative Power of Collaboration* (2007) and editor of the *Cambridge Handbook of the Learning Sciences* (2006).

researchers in these fields who were studying learning realised that they needed to develop new scientific approaches that went beyond what their own discipline could offer, and to collaborate with other disciplines. Learning sciences was born in 1991, when the first international conference was held, and the *Journal of the Learning Sciences* was first published. This new science is called *the learning sciences* because it is an interdisciplinary science; the collaboration among these disciplines has resulted in new ideas, new methodologies, and new ways of thinking about learning. The first comprehensive overview of the field was published in 2006: *The Cambridge Handbook of the Learning Sciences* (Sawyer, 2006b).

Learning sciences researchers are working to design more effective learning environments – including school classrooms, and also informal settings such as science centres or after-school clubs, on-line distance learning, and computer-based tutoring software. These classroom environments combine new curricular materials, new collaborative activities, support for teachers, and innovative educational software. Learning sciences research suggests several alternative models of learning, particularly those that involve deep links between formal schooling and the many other learning institutions available to students – libraries, science centres and history museums, after school clubs, on-line activities that can be accessed from home, and even collaborations between students and working professionals. In this report, I draw on learning sciences findings to identify a set of principles that should guide the development of different models of learning.

2.2. The standard model of schooling

By the 20th Century, all major industrialised countries offered formal schooling to all of their children. These many educational systems took different paths, but eventually converged on essentially the same model of schooling. When this model emerged in the 19th and 20th centuries, scientists did not know very much about how people learn. Even by the 1920s, when schools started to become the large bureaucratic institutions that we know today, there still was no sustained study of how people learn. As a result, this model of schooling was based on common-sense assumptions that had never been tested scientifically:

- Knowledge is a collection of *facts* about the world and *procedures* for how to solve problems. Facts are statements like "The earth is tilted on its axis by 23.45 degrees" and procedures are step-by-step instructions like how to do multi-digit addition by carrying to the next column.

- The goal of schooling is to get these facts and procedures into the student's head. People are considered to be educated when they possess a large collection of these facts and procedures.

- Teachers know these facts and procedures, and their job is to transmit them to students.

- Simpler facts and procedures should be learned first, followed by progressively more complex facts and procedures. The definitions of "simplicity" and "complexity" and the proper sequencing of material were determined either by teachers, by textbook authors, or by asking expert adults like mathematicians, scientists, or historians – not by studying how children actually learn.

- The way to determine the success of schooling is to test students to see how many of these facts and procedures they have acquired.

Because this traditional vision of schooling has been taken for granted for so long, it has not been explicitly named until recently. Within the OECD/CERI programme "Innovative Learning Environments" project, this traditional model is referred to as *the standard model*. Learning scientists often refer to the traditional model as *instructionism*, a term coined by Seymour Papert (1993), because it assumes that the core activity of the classroom is instruction by the teacher. Other education researchers have called this a *transmission and acquisition* model of schooling (*e.g.* Rogoff, 1990), because it emphasises that a knowledgeable teacher transmits knowledge, and a learner then acquires that knowledge.

Standard model schools effectively prepared students for the industrialised economy of the early 20th Century; schools based on this model have been effective at transmitting a standard body of facts and procedures to students. The goals of standard model schools were to ensure standardization – all students were to memorise and master the same core curriculum – and this model has been reasonably effective at accomplishing these goals. Standard model schools were structured, scheduled, and regimented in a fashion that was explicitly designed by analogy with the industrial-age factory (Callahan, 1962), and this structural alignment facilitated the ease of transition from school student to factory worker.

2.3. The shift to the innovation economy

In recent decades, many OECD member countries have experienced a rapid transformation from an industrial to a knowledge economy (Bell, 1976; Drucker, 1993). The knowledge economy is based on "the production and distribution of knowledge and information, rather than the production and distribution of things" (Drucker, 1993, p. 182). In the knowledge economy, knowledge workers are "symbolic analysts" (Reich, 1991) who manipulate symbols rather than machines, and who create conceptual artefacts rather than physical objects (Bereiter, 2002; Drucker, 1993). Several economists have begun to argue that in today's economy, knowledge is an intrinsic part of the economic system – a third factor, added to the traditional two of labour and capital (Florida, 2002; Romer, 1990).

These analysts emphasise the importance of creativity, innovation, and ingenuity in the knowledge economy; some scholars now refer to today's economy as a *creative economy* (Florida, 2002; Howkins, 2001). Florida argued that "we now have an economy powered by human creativity" (2002, pp. 5-6) and that human creativity is "the defining feature of economic life" (p. 21). Florida represents an economic school of thought known as New Growth Theory, which argues that creativity and idea generation are central to today's economy (Cortright, 2001).

By the 1990s, educators had begun to realise that if the economy was no longer an industrial-age factory economy, then our schools were designed for a quickly vanishing world (Bereiter, 2002; Hargreaves, 2003; Sawyer, 2006c). This consensus led major governmental and international bodies to commission reports summarising learning sciences research; these reports include the United States National Research Council's *How People Learn* (Bransford, Brown and Cocking, 2000), the OECD's *Innovation in the Knowledge Economy: Implications for Education and Learning* (2004), and a study of 28 countries conducted by the International Society for Technology in Education, called *Technology, Innovation, and Educational Change: A Global Perspective* (Kozma, 2003).

In the standard model of schooling, the role of educational research is to help schools more effectively transmit facts and procedures to students. But when learning scientists first went into classrooms in the 1970s and 1980s, they discovered that schools were not teaching the deep knowledge that underlies knowledge work. By the 1980s, cognitive scientists had discovered that children retain material better, and are able to generalise it to a broader range of contexts, when they learn deep knowledge rather than surface knowledge, and when they learn how to use that knowledge in real-world social and practical settings. In the late 1980s, these learning scientists began to argue that standard model schools were not aligned with the knowledge economy.

Many of today's schools are not teaching the deep knowledge that underlies innovative activity. But it is not just a matter of asking teachers to teach different curriculum, because the structural configurations of the standard model make it very hard to create learning environments that result in deeper understanding. One of the central underlying themes of the learning sciences is that students learn deeper knowledge when they engage in activities that are similar to the everyday activities of professionals who work in a discipline. This focus on authentic practice is based on a new conception of the expert knowledge that underlies knowledge work in today's economy. In the 1980s and 1990s, scientists began to study science itself, and they began to discover that newcomers become members of a discipline by learning how to participate in all of the practices that are central to professional life in that discipline. Increasingly, cutting-edge work in the sciences is done at the boundaries of disciplines; for this reason, students need to learn the underlying models, mechanisms, and practices that apply across many scientific disciplines, rather than learning in the disconnected and isolated six-week units that are found in many standard model science classrooms – moving from studying the solar system to studying photosynthesis to studying force and motion, without ever learning about connections among these units.

Studies of knowledge workers show that they almost always apply their expertise in complex social settings, with a wide array of technologically advanced tools along with old-fashioned pencil, paper, chalk, and blackboards. These observations have led learning sciences researchers to a *situated* view of knowledge (Greeno, 2006). "Situated" means that knowledge is not just a static mental structure inside the learner's head; instead, knowing is a process that involves the person, the tools and other people in the environment, and the activities in which that knowledge is being applied. This perspective moves beyond a transmission and acquisition conception of learning that is implicit in the standard model; in addition to acquiring content, what happens during learning is that patterns of participation in collaborative activity change over time (Rogoff, 1990, 1998).

In the knowledge economy, memorisation of facts and procedures is not enough for success. Educated graduates need a deep conceptual understanding of complex concepts, and the ability to work with them creatively to generate new ideas, new theories, new products, and new knowledge. They need to be able to critically evaluate what they read, to be able to express themselves clearly both verbally and in writing, and to be able to understand scientific and mathematical thinking. They need to learn integrated and usable knowledge, rather than the sets of compartmentalised and decontextualised facts emphasised by instructionism. They need to be able to take responsibility for their own continuing, lifelong learning. These abilities are important to the economy, to the continued success of participatory democracy, and to living a fulfilling, meaningful life. The standard model of schooling is particularly ill-suited to the education of creative professionals who can develop new knowledge and continually further their own understanding.

2.4. Key learning sciences findings

In the three decades that learning sciences research has been under way, several key findings have emerged. These findings align with the needs of the knowledge economy, as identified above.

The importance of deeper conceptual understanding

Scientific studies of knowledge workers demonstrate that expert knowledge includes the facts and procedures that the standard model is designed to transmit to learners. However, these studies also demonstrate that acquiring those facts and procedures is not sufficient to prepare a person to perform as a knowledge worker. Factual and procedural knowledge is only useful when a person knows which situations to apply it in, and exactly how to modify it for each new situation. The standard model of schooling results in a kind of learning which is very difficult to use outside of the classroom. When students gain a deeper conceptual understanding, they learn facts and procedures in a much more useful and profound way that transfers to real-world settings. This deeper conceptual understanding has several components, as described in the following sections.

The cognitive bases of expertise

One of the most surprising discoveries of cognitive science in the 1970s was that everyday behaviour was harder to represent computationally than expert behaviour. Some of the most successful artificial intelligence (AI) programmes simulated expert performance in knowledge-intensive domains like medicine, manufacturing, telecommunications, and finance (Liebowitz, 1998). As a result of these efforts, cognitive science developed a sophisticated understanding of the cognitive bases of expertise. Everyday common-sense behaviour remains beyond the abilities of AI computer programmes, even as expert performance in many knowledge-intensive domains like medicine has been successfully simulated.

A large body of cognitive science research shows that expertise is based on:

- A large and complex set of representational structures.

- A large set of procedures and plans.

- The ability to improvisationally apply and adapt those plans to each situation's unique demands.

- The ability to reflect on one's own cognitive processes while they are occurring.

Problem solving

Cognitive scientists have spent several decades attempting to identify the cognitive bases of problem solving. One of the most persistent theories about problem solving is that it depends on a person having a mental representation of a *problem space* (Newell and Simon, 1972) which contains *beliefs* and *mental representations* – of concepts, specific actions, and the external world. Problem solving is then conceived of as searching through the problem space until the desired *goal state* is reached. Because knowledge work typically requires problem solving, many learning sciences approaches to learning are based on this research. For example, Koedinger and Corbett's cognitive tutors (2006) assume that *production rules* are used to move through the problem space, and Kolodner's *case-based reasoning* (2006) assumes that case lookup and matching algorithms are used.

Thinking

Educators often talk about the importance of higher-order thinking skills, but educational programmes that emphasise thinking skills are often not based on scientific research. Instead, they are based on one or another intuitively-based taxonomy of thinking skills, with almost no scientific justification of why this specific set of skills should be taught in schools (Kuhn, 1990, p. 2). Beginning in the 1980s and 1990s, cognitive psychologists began to study informal reasoning (Voss, Perkins and Segal, 1991) – the good and bad reasoning that people engage in everyday, when faced with real-life problems that do not have simple solutions. They also began to study everyday decision making, discovering a wide range of common thinking errors that most people make (Kahneman, Slovic and Tversky, 1982). Also during this time, developmental psychologists began to identify a range of good and bad thinking strategies and how these strategies develop over the lifespan. They extended Piaget's original insight, showing how children's thinking differs from that of adults – information that is absolutely critical to education based on the learning sciences (*e.g.* Dunbar and Klahr, 1989).

Focusing on learning in addition to teaching

Before Jean Piaget, most people held to the common-sense belief that children have less knowledge than adults. Piaget argued a radically different theory: although children certainly possess less knowledge than adults, what's even more important to learning is that children's minds contain different knowledge structures than are in adults' minds. In other words, children differ not only in the quantity of knowledge they possess; their knowledge is *qualitatively* different.

By the 1980s, researchers had confirmed this fundamental claim that children think differently from adults. Educational researchers had discovered, for example, that children do not get math problems wrong only because they did not study hard enough or because they forgot what they read in the textbook – they often got the problems wrong because their minds were thinking about the math problems in a different way than educators expected, and math education was not designed to correct these misconceptions. Learning scientists began to identify the cognitive characteristics of children's "naïve math" and "naïve physics", and began to accumulate an important body of knowledge about the typical misconceptions that people have about these content areas (diSessa, 2006; Linn, 2006). This body of research allows designers of learning environments to connect learning to students' prior knowledge and misconceptions.

Constructivism explains why students often do not learn deeply by listening to a teacher, or reading from a textbook. Learning sciences research is revealing the deeper underlying bases of how knowledge construction works. To design effective learning environments, one needs a very good understanding of what children know when they come to the classroom. This requires sophisticated research into children's cognitive development, and the learning sciences draw heavily on psychological studies of cognitive development (*e.g.* Siegler, 1998).

Building on prior knowledge

One of the most important discoveries guiding learning sciences research is that learning always takes place against a backdrop of existing knowledge. Students do not enter the classroom as empty vessels, waiting to be filled; they enter the classroom with half-formed ideas and misconceptions about how the world works – sometimes called "naïve" physics, math, or biology. Many cognitive developmentalists have studied children's theories about the world, and how children's understanding of the world develops through the preschool and early school years. The basic knowledge about cognitive development that has resulted from this research is absolutely critical to reforming schooling so that it is based on the basic sciences of learning.

Standard model schools were developed under the behaviourist assumption that children enter school with empty minds, and the role of school is to fill up those minds with knowledge. Standard model curricula were designed before the learning sciences discovered how children think and what knowledge structures they bring to the classroom.

Reflection

The learning sciences have discovered that when learners externalise and articulate their developing knowledge, they learn more effectively (Bransford, Brown and Cocking, 2000). This is more complex than it might sound, because it is not the case that learners first learn something, and then express it. Instead, the best learning takes place when learners articulate their unformed and still developing understanding, and continue to articulate it throughout the process of learning. Articulating and learning go hand in hand, in a mutually reinforcing feedback loop. In many cases, learners do not actually learn something until they start to articulate it – in other words, while thinking out loud, they learn more rapidly and deeply than studying quietly.

One of the reasons that articulation is so helpful to learning is that it makes possible *reflection* or *metacognition* – thinking about the process of learning and thinking about knowledge. Learning scientists have repeatedly demonstrated the importance of reflection in learning for deeper understanding. Many learning sciences classrooms are designed to foster reflection, and most of them foster reflection by providing students with tools that make it easier for them to articulate their developing understandings. Once students have articulated their developing understandings, learning environments should support them in reflecting on what they have just articulated. One of the most central topics in learning sciences research is how to support students in educationally beneficial reflection.

Scaffolding learning

One of the most important topics of learning sciences research is how to support students in this ongoing process of articulation and reflection, and which forms of articulation and reflection are the most beneficial to learning. The learning sciences have discovered that articulation is more effective if it is *scaffolded* – channelled so that certain kinds of knowledge are articulated, and in a certain form that is most likely to result in useful reflection. Students need help in articulating their understandings; they do not yet know how to think about thinking, and they do not yet know how to talk about thinking.

Scaffolding is the help given to a learner that is tailored to that learner's needs in achieving his or her goals of the moment. The best scaffolding provides this help in a way that contributes to learning. For example, telling someone how to do something, or doing it for them, may help them accomplish their immediate goal; but it is not good scaffolding because the child does not actively participate in constructing that knowledge. In contrast, effective scaffolding provides prompts and hints that help learners to figure it out on their own. Effective learning environments scaffold students' active construction of knowledge in ways similar to the way that scaffolding supports the construction of a building. When construction workers need to reach higher, additional scaffolding is added, and when the building is complete, the scaffolding can be removed. In effective learning environments, scaffolding is gradually added, modified, and removed according to the needs of the learner, and eventually the scaffolding fades away entirely.

2.5. Design principles from the learning sciences

Research emerging from the learning sciences is still too premature to specify a single, well articulated alternative model of schooling. However, learning sciences findings imply several principles that can be used to guide the development of new models of schooling that are more closely aligned with the innovation economy.

Customised learning

In the standard model, everyone learns the same thing at the same time. Many parallel structures and processes of these schools align to enforce standardisation. However learning sciences findings suggest that each student learns best when they are placed in a learning environment that is sensitive to their pre-existing cognitive structures; and learning sciences research has shown that different learners enter the classroom with different structures. Learning sciences research suggests that more effective learning will occur if each learner receives a customised learning experience.

Educational software gives us the opportunity to provide a customised learning experience to each student to a degree not possible when one teacher is responsible for six classrooms of 25 students each. Well-designed software could sense each learner's unique learning style and developmental level, and tailor the presentation of material appropriately (see Koedinger and Corbett, 2006 for an example). Some students could take longer to master a subject, while others would be faster, because the computer can provide information to each student at his or her own pace. And each student could learn each subject at different rates; for example, learning what we think of today as "5th grade" reading and "3rd grade" math at the same time. In age-graded classrooms this would be impossible, but in alternative models of schooling there may be no educational need to age-grade classrooms, no need to hold back the more advanced children or to leave behind those who need more help, and no reason for a child to learn all subjects at the same rate. Of course, age-graded classrooms also serve to socialise children, providing opportunities to make friends, to form peer groups, and to participate in team sports. If learning and schooling were no longer age-graded, other institutions would have to emerge to provide these opportunities.

Diverse knowledge sources

The standard model is based on a transmission-and-acquisition approach, where the teacher is assumed to possess all of the knowledge, and classroom activities are designed to facilitate the teacher-to-student transfer of knowledge. In the constructivist and project-based learning suggested by learning sciences research, students gain expertise from a variety of sources – from the Internet, at the library, or through email exchange with a working professional – and the teacher will no longer be the only source of expertise in the classroom. Learners will acquire knowledge from diverse sources; of course, expert support from the teacher can facilitate these learning processes, but the teacher's involvement will not be one of transmitting knowledge.

Distributed knowledge

In knowledge intensive occupations, people act intelligently by making frequent use of books, papers, and technology. Knowledge work occurs in teams and organisations, so that several times every hour, a person is interacting with others. But in today's schools, there is a belief that a student only knows something when that student can do it on his or her own, without any use of outside resources. There is a mismatch between today's school culture and the situated knowledge required in the knowledge society.

At the same time, learning sciences research is showing that collaborating student groups can accelerate learning (Sawyer, 2006a). Here is a case where learning sciences research supports increased classroom collaboration, and the innovation economy, as well, demands graduates who are highly skilled at creating together in groups (Sawyer, 2007).

Curriculum

Standard model schools typically have highly regimented and articulated curricula. A central question guiding education research must always be: What should be taught in second grade math, or in sixth grade social studies? In the United States in the 1950s and 1960s, practicing scientists became heavily involved in the development of school science curricula (Rudolph, 2002). These new curricula were an improvement on what previously existed. However, learning scientists have discovered that what seems more simple to an adult professional is not necessarily more simple to a learner, and that the most effective sequencing of activities is not always a sequence from what experts consider to be more simple to more complex. Children arrive at school with naïve theories and misconceptions; and during the school years, children pass through a series of cognitive developmental stages. Even these 1960s textbooks and curricula, developed in collaboration with expert scientists, were designed before learning scientists began to map out the educational relevance of cognitive development. In the next ten to twenty years, new curricula for K-12 education will emerge that are based in the learning sciences.

Related to the issue of curriculum is the sensitive topic of coverage – how much material, and how many topics, should students learn about at each age? In the standard model, the debate about curriculum is almost exclusively a debate about topic coverage – what should be included at each grade, and how much. But this focus on breadth is misguided. According to the Trends in International Mathematics and Science Study (TIMSS), which compares student achievement in math and science in 50 countries every four years, United States science and math curricula contain much more content than other countries as a result of their survey approaches to material – but rather than strengthening students' abilities, this survey approach weakens United States achievement relative to other countries (Schmidt and McKnight, 1997). In a typical United States classroom, each topic is taught as its own distinct unit – and the new knowledge is often forgotten as soon as the students turn to the next topic. Studies of the TIMSS data show that children in nations that pursue a more focused, coherent, and deep strategy do substantially better on the mathematics assessment than do children in the United States (Schmidt and McKnight, 1997). This is consistent with the learning sciences finding that students learn better when they learn deep knowledge that allows them to think and to solve problems with the content that they are learning.

The role of the teacher

In a knowledge economy school, teachers should also be knowledge workers, with equivalent skills to other knowledge workers such as lawyers, doctors, engineers, managers, and consultants. They should deeply understand the theoretical principles and the latest knowledge about how children learn. They should be deeply familiar with the authentic practices of professional scientists, historians, mathematics, or literary critics. They will have to receive salaries comparable to other knowledge workers, or else the profession will have difficulty attracting new teachers with the potential to teach for deep knowledge. To align with the innovation economy, teachers will require more autonomy, more creativity, and more content knowledge.

These teachers should be highly trained professionals, comfortable with technology, with a deep pedagogical understanding of the subject matter, able to respond in an improvised manner to the uniquely emerging flow of each classroom (Sawyer, 2004). To foster collaborative and authentic learning, they will lead teams of students – much like a manager of a business or the master in a workshop – rather than controlling students autocratically, as the factory bosses of old.

Assessment

In the knowledge economy, today's assessments have two critical flaws, both due to the fact that today's assessments were designed for the standard model of schooling. First, whereas the schools of the future will increasingly result in customised learning, today's assessments require that every student learn the same thing at the same time. The standards movement and the resulting high-stakes testing are increasing standardisation, at the same time that learning sciences and technology are making it possible for individual students to have customised learning experiences. Customisation combined with diverse knowledge sources enable students to learn different things. Schools will still need to measure learning for accountability purposes, but we do not yet know how to reconcile accountability with customised learning.

Second, today's standardised tests assess relatively superficial knowledge and do not assess the deep knowledge required by the knowledge society. Standardised tests, almost by their very nature, evaluate decontextualised and compartmentalised knowledge. For example, mathematics tests do not assess model-based reasoning (Lehrer and Schauble, 2006); science tests do not assess whether pre-existing misconceptions have indeed been left behind (diSessa, 2006; Linn, 2006) nor do they assess problem-solving or inquiry skills (Krajcik and Blumenfeld, 2006). As long as schools are evaluated on how well their students do on such tests, it will be difficult for them to leave the standard model behind.

One of the key issues facing the learning sciences is how to design new kinds of assessment that correspond to the deep knowledge required in today's knowledge society (Carver, 2006; Means, 2006). Several learning sciences researchers are developing new assessments that focus on deeper conceptual understanding.

2.6. The learning sciences and alternative models of learning

Following the above discussion, a set of key findings has emerged from learning sciences research:

- The importance of learning deeper conceptual understanding, rather than superficial facts and procedures.

- The importance of learning connected and coherent knowledge, rather than knowledge compartmentalised into distinct subjects and courses.

- The importance of learning authentic knowledge in its context of use, rather than decontextualised classroom exercises.

- The importance of learning in collaboration, rather than in isolation.

These key findings imply that the most effective learning environments will have the following characteristics:

- *Customised learning.* Each child receives a customised learning experience.

- *Availability of diverse knowledge sources.* Learners can acquire knowledge whenever they need it from a variety of sources: books, web sites, and experts around the globe.

- *Collaborative group learning.* Students learn together as they work collaboratively on authentic, inquiry-oriented projects.

- *Assessment for deeper understanding.* Tests should evaluate the students' deeper conceptual understanding, the extent to which their knowledge is integrated, coherent, and contextualised.

To date, the standard model of schooling does not align with these characteristics. Learning is standardised; knowledge sources are limited to the teacher and the textbook; most learning occurs by a solitary learner; and assessment typically measures the memorisation of superficial facts and procedural knowledge. Some of these characteristics can be implemented within the standard model; for example, existing classrooms could introduce collaborative learning tasks (as many schools are doing today). But some of these characteristics will be extremely difficult to implement within the standard model; for example, the notion of customised learning is inconsistent with the high degree of standardisation associated with the standard model school.

The work of the OECD's Centre for Educational Research and Innovation (CERI) on innovative learning environments needs to explore whether or not there are other models of learning that align more naturally with these learning sciences characteristics. A natural place to start the exploration is to study non-school locations where learning occurs – whether called self-directed learning or informal learning. Many non-school learning environments have existed through history and continue to exist alongside formal schooling. One example that has been widely studied is apprenticeship (Collins, 2006; Rogoff, 1990) – where a young adult who aspires to learn a trade works closely with an older expert. In some disciplines, such as medicine, apprenticeship is a core feature of the learning experience; in medical school, students spend two years in classrooms and then two years in the hospital, working alongside senior physicians. Apprenticeship is a core component of education in craft trades such as carpentry and electrical wiring. A second example of non-school learning that has been widely studied is the huge amount of knowledge that young children acquire, at home, in the years before they begin formal schooling – they learn their first language, and a wide range of physical and social skills.

Many learning scientists are experimenting with new models of learning that blend some features of formal schools with some features of these non-school learning environments. Institutions where self-directed learning is common have been of particular interest; these include museums and public libraries. In recent years, the managers of these institutions have been expanding their educational offerings. Science centres have already taken the lead in this area, developing inquiry-based curricula and conducting teacher professional development, but art and history museums may soon follow suit. Over time, these institutions could evolve into full-fledged learning resource centres, and some segments of the school day might be better spent in these institutions, rather than in traditional schools.

The creative economy is also a learning society, one in which all workers must continue to acquire new knowledge throughout their lives. It is no longer possible to imagine that education ends by a certain age, after which learning is no longer necessary. As a result of these broader economic changes, the boundary between formal schooling and continuing education could begin to break down. The milestones of a high school and a college diploma could gradually decrease in importance, as the nature of learning in school begins to look more and more like on-the-job apprenticeship and adult distance education. Many types of knowledge – for example, the trade knowledge that is today acquired through apprenticeship – are better learned in workplace environments; this kind of learning will be radically transformed by the availability of anywhere, anytime learning, as new employees take their laptops or handhelds on the job with them, with software specially designed to provide apprenticeship support in the workplace. Professional schools could be radically affected; new forms of *portable just-in-time* learning could increasingly put their campus-based educational models at risk.

The Internet provides an opportunity for a new kind of learning environment: a sophisticated form of distance learning, where the learners and the teachers may all be in different physical locations, communicating via the network. As of 2005, twenty-two of the United States had established on-line virtual schools; during the 2003-04 school year, the Florida Virtual School became the state's 73rd school district, and now receives per-student funding from the state just like any other district. In the 2004-05 school year, 21 000 students enrolled in at least one of its courses (Borja, 2005). When each student is working at their own computer, there is no longer a compelling social reason to group students by age; students could easily be grouped according to their current level of understanding, allowing the customised learning implicated by the learning sciences.

2.7. Conclusion

The standard model of schooling emerged during the industrial age, and it has been effective at generating the kinds of graduates needed by the industrial economy. However, the broad global shift to an innovation economy has revealed some weaknesses with the standard model. The learning sciences offer us a set of research findings that allow us to begin to create new models of learning. Those societies that can effectively develop learning environments that are in accordance with learning sciences principles will be the leaders in the 21st Century (OECD, 2000, 2004).

We are at an exciting time in the study of learning. Researchers have been working since the 1970s, developing the basic sciences of learning – beginning in psychology, cognitive science, sociology, and other disciplinary traditions, and in the 1980s and 1990s, increasingly working closely with educators and in schools. Researchers have just begun to explore what models of schooling might emerge in response to the new research emerging from the learning sciences, and to the computer technology that makes these new learning environments possible. As these scholars continue to work together in a spirit of interdisciplinary collaboration, the end result will be an increasingly detailed understanding of how people learn. Existing schools should redesign themselves with a foundation in the learning sciences, and should work closely with non-school learning environments – libraries, museums, after-school clubs, on-line virtual schools, and the home – to develop a new model of learning for the future. As our scientific understanding of the processes of learning is increasingly refined, the final step to transform schools must be taken by our whole society: parents and teachers, and the administrators, policy makers, and politicians whom we entrust with our schools.

References

Bell, D. (1973), *The Coming of the Post-industrial Society: A Venture in Social Forecasting*, Basic Books, New York.

Bereiter, C. (2002), *Education and Mind in the Knowledge Age*, Mahwah, NJ: Erlbaum.

Borja, R.J. (2005, May 5), "Cyber Schools Status", *Education Week*, Vol. 24, pp. 22-23.

Bransford, J.D., A.L Brown and R.R. Cocking (eds.) (2000), *How People Learn: Brain, Mind, Experience, and School*, National Academy Press, Washington, DC.

Callahan, R.E. (1962), *Education and the Cult of Efficiency: A Study of the Social Forces that have Shaped the Administration of the Public Schools*, University of Chicago Press, Chicago.

Carver, S.M. (2006), "Assessing for Deep Understanding", in R.K. Sawyer (ed.), *The Cambridge Handbook of the Learning Sciences*, Cambridge University Press, New York, pp. 205-221.

Collins, A. (2006), "Cognitive Apprenticeship", in R.K. Sawyer (ed.), *Cambridge Handbook of the Learning Sciences*, Cambridge University Press, New York, pp. 47-60.

Cortright, J. (2001), *New Growth Theory, Technology and Learning: A Practitioner's Guide* (Reviews of Economic Development Literature and Practice No. 4), U.S. Economic Development Administration, Washington, DC.

diSessa, A.A. (2006), "A History of Conceptual Change Research", in R.K. Sawyer (ed.), *The Cambridge Handbook of the Learning Sciences*, Cambridge University Press, New York, pp. 265-281.

Drucker, P.F. (1993), *Post-capitalist Society*, HarperBusiness, New York.

Dunbar, K. and D. Klahr (1989), "Developmental Differences in Scientific Discovery Strategies", in D. Klahr and K. Kotovsky (eds.), *Complex*

Information Processing: The Impact of Herbert A. Simon, Mahwah, NJ: Erlbaum, pp. 109-143.

Florida, R. (2002), *The Rise of the Creative Class and How it's Transforming Work, Life, Community and Everyday Life*, Basic Books, New York.

Greeno, J.G. (2006), "Learning in Activity", in R.K. Sawyer (ed.), *Cambridge Handbook of the Learning Sciences*, Cambridge University Press, New York, pp. 79-96.

Hargreaves, A. (2003), *Teaching in the Knowledge Society: Education in the Age of Insecurity*, Teacher's College Press, New York.

Howkins, J. (2001), *The Creative Economy: How People Make Money from Ideas*, The Penguin Press, London.

Kahneman, D., P. Slovic and A. Tversky (eds.) (1982), *Judgment under Uncertainty: Heuristics and Biases*, Cambridge, New York.

Koedinger, K.R. and A.T. Corbett (2006), "Cognitive Tutors: Technology Bringing Learning Sciences to the Classroom", in R.K. Sawyer (ed.), *Cambridge Handbook of the Learning Sciences*, Cambridge University Press, New York, pp. 61-77.

Kolodner, J.L. (2006), "Case-based Reasoning", in R.K. Sawyer (ed.), *The Cambridge Handbook of the Learning Sciences*, Cambridge University Press, New York, pp. 225-242.

Kozma, R.B. (ed.) (2003), *Technology, Innovation, and Educational Change: A Global Perspective*, International Society for Technology in Education, Eugene, OR.

Krajcik, J.S. and P. Blumenfeld (2006), "Project Based Learning", in R.K. Sawyer (ed.), *Cambridge Handbook of the Learning Sciences*, Cambridge University Press, New York, pp. 317-333.

Kuhn, D. (1990), "Introduction", in D. Kuhn (ed.), *Developmental Perspectives on Teaching and Learning Thinking Skills*, Karger, Basel, pp. 1-8.

Lehrer, R. and L. Schauble (2006), "Cultivating Model-based Reasoning in Science Education", in R.K. Sawyer (ed.), *Cambridge Handbook of the Learning Sciences*, Cambridge University Press, New York, pp. 371-387.

Liebowitz, J. (ed.) (1998), *The Handbook of Applied Expert Systems*, CRC Press, Boca Raton, FL.

Linn, M.C. (2006), "The Knowledge Integration Perspective on Learning and Instruction", in R.K. Sawyer (ed.), *The Cambridge Handbook of the Learning Sciences*, Cambridge University Press, New York, pp. 243-264.

Means, B. (2006), "Prospects for Transforming Schools with Technology-supported Assessment", in R.K. Sawyer (ed.), *The Cambridge Handbook of the Learning Sciences*, Cambridge University Press, New York, pp. 505-519.

Newell, A. and H.A. Simon (1972), *Human Problem Solving*, Prentice-Hall, Englewood Cliffs, NJ.

OECD (2000), *Knowledge Management in the Learning Society*, OECD Publishing, Paris.

OECD (2004), *Innovation in the Knowledge Economy: Implications for Education and Learning*, OECD Publishing, Paris.

Papert, S. (1980), *Mindstorms: Children, Computers, and Powerful Ideas*, Basic Books, New York.

Papert, S. (1993), *The Children's Machine: Rethinking School in the Age of the Computer*, Basic Books, New York.

Reich, R.B. (1991), *The Work of Nations: Capitalism in the 21st Century*, A.A. Knopf, New York.

Rogoff, B. (1990), *Apprenticeship in Thinking: Cognitive Development in Social Context*, Oxford University Press, New York.

Rogoff, B. (1998), "Cognition as a Collaborative Process", in D. Kuhn and R.S. Siegler (eds.), *Handbook of Child Psychology, 5th Edition, Vol. 2: Cognition, Perception, and Language*, Wiley, New York, pp. 679-744.

Romer, P.M. (1990), "Endogenous Technological Change", *Journal of Political Economy*, Vol. 98, No. 5, pp. 71-102.

Rudolph, J.L. (2002), *Scientists in the Classroom: The Cold War Reconstruction of American Science Education*, Palgrave, New York.

Sawyer, R.K. (2004), "Creative Teaching: Collaborative Discussion as Disciplined Improvisation", *Educational Researcher*, Vol. 33, No. 2, pp. 12-20.

Sawyer, R.K. (2006a), "Analyzing Collaborative Discourse", in R.K. Sawyer (ed.), *Cambridge Handbook of the Learning Sciences*, Cambridge University Press, New York, pp. 187-204.

Sawyer, R.K. (ed.) (2006b), *Cambridge Handbook of the Learning Sciences*, Cambridge University Press, New York.

Sawyer, R.K. (2006c), "Educating for Innovation", *The International Journal of Thinking Skills and Creativity*, Vol. 1, No.1, pp. 41-48.

Sawyer, R.K. (2007), *Group Genius: The Creative Power of Collaboration*, Basic Books, New York.

Schank, R.C. (2006), "Epilogue: The Fundamental Issue in the Learning Sciences", in R.K. Sawyer (ed.), *The Cambridge Handbook of the Learning Sciences*, Cambridge University Press, New York, pp. 587-592.

Schmidt, W.A. and C.C. McKnight (1997), *A Splintered Vision: An Investigation of U.S. Science and Mathematics Education*, Kluwer Academic, Dordrecht, the Netherlands.

Siegler, R.S. (1998), *Children's Thinking* (third edition), Prentice-Hall, Upper Saddle River, NJ.

Stallard, C.K. and J.S. Cocker (2001), *The Promise of Technology in Schools: The Next 20 Years*, Scarecrow Press, Lanham, MD.

Voss, J.F., D.N. Perkins and J.W. Segal (eds.) (1991), *Informal Reasoning and Education*, Mahwah, NJ: Erlbaum.

Chapter 3
Toward Research-based Innovation
by
Carl Bereiter and Marlene Scardamalia[1]

This chapter focuses on defining and exploring the area of research-based innovation in education. The authors provide an overview of several new approaches of research-based innovation in the learning sciences, and propose five dimensions of comparing other educational approaches to their own approach of Knowledge Building.

In education, as in any applied field, three kinds of research are relevant. There is basic research, aimed at understanding the phenomenon or problem of interest. There is decision-oriented research, aimed at identifying "best practice" and guiding policy decisions. Then there is research-based innovation, which is the engine of progress in an applied field. The first two kinds of research have long been recognised in education, but the third is only beginning to gain recognition. During the 1960s, the US National Academy of Education commissioned a report on the role of research in the improvement of education. The report, by two leading education researchers (Cronbach and Suppes, 1969), recognised only the first two kinds of research, which they labelled "conclusion-oriented" and "decision-oriented". This chapter focuses on the neglected third kind, research-based innovation.

In everyday usage, "innovation" may mean simply *adopting* some practice reputed to be innovative. The relevant research in that case is "decision-oriented" research – research bearing on the decision to adopt. "Research-based innovation", however, is research aimed at creating innovations. In basic research, the ultimate criterion for judging an idea is its explanatory power. In "decision-oriented" research it is the consequences of applying the idea. In research-based innovation the criterion is fruitfulness.

---

[1] Institute for Knowledge Innovation and Technology, University of Toronto.

Does the idea have potential? Is it worth developing further? This marks a significant departure from "evidence-based" or "best" practice. The current demand for "evidence-based" methods, if applied in the late 19th Century, would surely have resulted in abandonment of automobile development in favour of refinements of more proven technologies. The first automobiles were poor competitors with the horse-drawn vehicle. Nevertheless, engineers and entrepreneurs pressed onward with development of the "horseless carriage" or "gas buggy" because they saw potential in it that the horse-drawn carriage lacked. "Decision-oriented" research may be a good basis for choosing whether to adopt a certain approach, but it is not a basis for determining which approaches are improvable and which are dead ends and for generating findings that will engender new finding – and so on in the ascending arc that we have come to expect of science and technology. "Design research" is a term applied to research whose aim is creation and progressive improvement of innovations (Bereiter, 2002; Collins, Joseph, and Bielaczyc, 2004). In the applied sciences and engineering the term is superfluous because virtually all the research is design research – research that feeds back into further design decisions. However this remains a novelty in education.

Of course, there are innovations in education, but neither the profession nor the public at large looks to research to produce them. Instead they are expected to come from imaginative practitioners and from outside sources, such as technology companies. The situation is comparable to that which characterised medicine during much of the 19th Century. Scientific medicine at that time was not sufficiently developed to produce new and more effective treatments. Instead, innovations came from nonscientific practitioners ("quacks" as the scientists called them) and were justified by nonscientific theories that appealed to magnetism, electricity, and other popular phenomena. We may call these medical folk theories, for they resembled and sometimes actually drew upon ancient prescientific theories about energy flows, the nature of disease, and the action of medicines. Their counterparts in education today – what we may correspondingly call educational folk theories – are theories that appeal in nonscientific ways to brain growth and cognitive styles and that entertain unsupported notions about the nature of skills, abilities, and learning (for instance, that reading is as natural a process as speaking and that there exist an array of thinking skills improvable through practice and applicable wherever needed).

Educational folk theories thrived during the 20th Century for the same reason that medical folk theories flourished during the 19th: scientific research was not yet in a position to address or even to clarify the problems faced by practitioners. The learning sciences (Sawyer, 2006), which are customarily dated from 1991, represent an attempt to remedy this condition.

Drawing on basic research in overlapping disciplines and also on information and social technologies, the learning sciences have been dedicated to going beyond "decision-oriented" and "conclusion-oriented" research to research that actually generates innovations.

Research-based innovation, whether it is developing a treatment for HIV infection or a method for improving reading comprehension, depends crucially on understanding the nature of the problem. Educational folk theory and the learning sciences bring fundamentally different perspectives to problem definition. Educational folk theory is overwhelmingly concerned with individual differences, perhaps reflecting the fact that in the lives of teachers the failing child is a source of continual concern. From this standpoint, the fundamental question is "Why do some students have so much trouble learning?". This approach tends to take the "successful" student as the standard and to treat educational improvement as a matter of bringing less successful students up to the level of the more successful. (The same logic is seen in efforts to bring national test scores up to the level of higher-scoring nations.) This has two unfortunate consequences. It leads to neglecting those areas in which failure is the norm rather than the exception. In different societies, near-universal failure may be found in attaining fluency in a foreign language, in attaining a functional mastery of rational numbers or algebra, or in acquiring a useful knowledge of history or geography. Failure to overcome certain scientific misconceptions appears to be common in all societies. Educational folk theory may recognise this as a fact, but not as a problem requiring perhaps radical change in teaching. The other unfortunate consequence is that the question, "Why do some students have so much trouble learning?" obliterates the question, "Why is this concept or subject difficult to learn?". This question is key to problem understanding in the learning sciences. It is a question that educational theories of the past were generally unable to answer.

Research-based innovation in the learning sciences has given rise to a number of promising new approaches,[2] including Fostering Communities of Learners (Brown and Campione, 1996), Problem-based Learning (Evensen and Hmelo, 2000), Learning Science by Design (Holbrook and Kolodner, 2000), Constructionism (Kafai, 2006), Knowledge Building (Scardamalia and Bereiter, 2006), the Web-based Inquiry Science Environment (Linn, Davis, and Bell, 2004), Cognitive Tutors (Koedinger, 2006), Central Conceptual Structures (Case and Okamoto, 1996), and certain refined versions of Project-based Learning (Lee and Songer, 2003). A common view seems to be that these are merely procedural variations on

---

[2] All the educational models and approaches to learning referred to in this chapter are briefly introduced in the Annex 3.A.1.

constructivist or social-constructivist learning, which has its roots in the work of Dewey, Vygotsky, and Piaget. This may be true at a gross level of description, and the belief is encouraged by the tendency of innovators to compare their approach to a stereotypic traditional approach (lecture, recitation, and seatwork) rather than comparing it to nearer neighbours. We have argued that there are important – indeed, fundamental – differences within the broad family of social-constructivist approaches, and that these need to be examined if education is to progress (Bereiter and Scardamalia, 2003; 2006).

3.1. Dimensions of difference

Five dimensions of educational practice represent variations that are of particular value in distinguishing among recent research-based innovations. In summary, these are:

1. Amount of direction.

2. Emphasis on ideas versus activities.

3. Individual versus community emphasis.

4. Extent to which ideas are dealt with in "design mode" versus "belief mode".

5. Extent of accommodation to external constraints – such as official and market requirements and educational folk beliefs.

There are, of course, other important dimensions of difference in educational practice, including ones having to do with the arts, personal identity, and social values. However, the above dimensions capture a large part of the variation that has been the object of research in the learning sciences. In what follows we will elaborate on these. None of them is as simple as the image of a five-dimensional Cartesian space would suggest. So what we are proposing is not a scoring rubric for classroom practices but rather a framework for considering some of the deeper implications of these observable variations.

Before proceeding with the five dimensions, however, it is necessary to take note of one educational approach that lies outside this dimensional space. It is alluded to in a remark that has been attributed to several different pundits, explaining large initial gains from standard-raising reforms and the difficulty of achieving continuing gains: *When you move from no teaching to some teaching, you get a big jump in performance; after that it gets much harder.* So let us call it the "no teaching" alternative. Elsewhere we have referred to it as the "Teacher A" model (Bereiter and Scardamalia, 1987).

("Teacher B" represents a high level of directed learning, "Teacher C" a high investment in helping students take agency for cognitive goals.) The hallmark of the "no teaching" classroom is the extensive use of worksheets and other forms of seatwork (or computer work) that keep students occupied but require hardly any active involvement of the teacher in the students' learning. No one, of course, defends the "no teaching" alternative, but it exists and it is important not to confuse it with direct instruction or with students having responsibility for their own learning. It is, in fact, a condition in which no one takes responsibility for learning. The teacher takes responsibility for managing routine activities that may generate some expected learning, but when they fail there is no recourse except additional seatwork.

Amount of direction: from instruction to epistemic agency

Throughout the past century, battle lines have been drawn along this dimension, with much stereotyping and some demonizing on both sides. According to the Macmillan English Dictionary, "The basic idea of instructivism is that teaching is just a matter of giving facts to students. Instructivist classes work in transmission mode. This means that the flow of information is one way, from the teacher to students. The students are simply passive receivers of knowledge" (*www.macmillandictionary.com/glossaries/instructivism.htm*). *This definition is a travesty.* Coming from a supposedly objective source, it demonstrates how a century of often acrimonious debate has virtually killed rational discourse about pedagogy. It used to be that the opposite pole from extreme directedness in learning was laissez-faire. Now, however, inasmuch as there are no actual examples of laissez-faire education (that we know of) and no credible advocates, this pole is of little interest. In current learning science the opposite pole from extreme directedness is *student agency*. It is very far from laissez-faire: As hard as some teachers may work at inculcating knowledge and skills, others may work equally hard at enabling and motivating students to assume responsibility for the attainment of cognitive goals. And exercising a high level of agency in dealing with knowledge is at least as hard work for students as mastering the content and tasks set out by a demanding teacher.

The current state of scientific discussion about directedness in learning is well represented in an article titled "Why Minimal Guidance During Instruction Does Not Work: An Analysis of the Failure of Constructivist, Discovery, Problem-Based, Experiential, and Inquiry-Based Teaching" (Kirschner, Sweller and Clark, 2006). The authors take at face value the finding that in most large-scale comparative studies higher achievement scores are obtained by those provided the most direct instruction. However, they go on to offer a scientific explanation of why this is the case (whereas most commentators either reject the evidence or simply take the evidence as indicating an undeniable truth). Their explanation is that the more "constructivist" approaches impose an excessive burden on students' working memory capacity. Working memory load has proved to be a powerful concept for explaining why some things are harder to learn than others and why some instructional sequences are more effective than others – something traditional instructional psychology, including its behaviourist versions, has been unable to do (Case and Bereiter, 1984). How does the concept apply in the present case?

Working memory load depends on the number of things that must be attended to at the same time. If things can be attended to serially, there is in principle no limit to what we can handle. (The pilots of a space shuttle had a list of 162 items to be checked before lift-off, but the working memory load was probably less than you would experience on driving into a busy and confusing traffic circle.) It is, therefore, difficult to state categorically that self-directed inquiry imposes a greater working memory load than learning from instruction. However, well-engineered instruction will attempt to reduce load by introducing complications one at a time, whereas the independent learner is more at the mercy of the source material. The skilful lecturer will not actually simplify the material to be learned but will meter out the complexity through a series of steps, whereas the textbook is liable to swamp the learners by dumping all the complexity on them at once.

An alternative to having the teacher manage working memory load for the students is collaborative inquiry, in which students work together to understand something – be it a text, a theory, a set of data, or an observed phenomenon. This is what we mean by "epistemic agency". The management of working memory load is much less orderly in this case, but can nevertheless be quite efficient. We all depend on it. The hours teenagers spend on their telephones are often devoted to working out an understanding of a shared experience. New insights are added and integrated one at a time, with the emergent result being an understanding that could not have been achieved by the lone inquirer, even if all the contributed insights were made available. Any discussion of the news of the day will have this same characteristic of incremental complexity. As a way of achieving understanding of academic subject matter, it is a fair contest between epistemic agency and carefully engineered instruction. However, it must be recognised that many classrooms have neither. The kind of sustained inquiry and dialogue that could generate understanding through the students' own efforts is not given sufficient time and encouragement and the teacher is often not sufficiently master of the subject matter to lead the students step-by-step to understanding. We then have something intermediate on the instruction-to-epistemic agency dimension, where there is a mixture of not quite adequate instruction and not quite realised collaborative inquiry. "Self-directed learning", "cooperative learning", "self-regulated learning" and "guided discovery" are terms applicable to this intermediate range of activity types.

Among the more plausible arguments in defence of increasing student agency are claims that it develops a variety of personal qualities of value outside the classroom – independent learning, planning, and reasoning; research skills; collaboration skills; and so on through the catalogue of what have been called "higher-order skills" and, more recently, "21st Century skills". Such claims are popular in both the education and the business literature. Although there is some supportive evidence, the whole idea of learnable mental traits that will generalise to an indefinitely large range of situations is doubtful on both theoretical and empirical grounds. The most that can be said is that skills, knowledge, and habits acquired in one situation may make it easier to learn related skills, knowledge, and habits in new – but not too radically different – situations (Bransford and Schwartz, 1999). That is not a trivial benefit, but it is a far cry from the common claims that such-and-such activity "teaches" critical thinking, creativity, collaboration, or whatever. It is probably safe to discard all such claims as groundless, and to question the value of any learning activity that has no apparent justification other than to foster such "higher-order" attainments.

A different perspective on the instruction-agency issue is provided by asking, "What kind of culture is this educational process socialising students into?". Enculturation has been central to educational development since ancient times, but it has faded from contemporary discourse in education, perhaps because of its association with the passing on of a static tradition. With the prospect of a major cultural shift, however – signalled by such terms as "Knowledge Age" – socialisation to cultural norms takes on a new and important meaning. We have argued that the job of schools ought to be to socialise students into a knowledge-creating civilisation (Bereiter and Scardamalia, 2006). This entails turning over to students a large measure of epistemic agency, although that cannot be sufficient. There are elevated knowledge and skill demands. Beyond that, it entails a certain way of treating ideas – the second dimension of educational practice, to which we now turn.

Emphasis on ideas versus activities

The "big ideas" at the heart of various disciplines are the object of much research in the learning sciences and in the branches of curriculum research concerned with particular disciplines. No one disputes the importance of the big ideas, but work with them may occupy a very small part of the school curriculum. This dimension is orthogonal to the first, in that ideas may receive much or little emphasis under conditions of either high teacher-directedness or high student agency. Among approaches claimed to be "constructivist", the low end of emphasis on ideas usually takes the form of "hands-on" activities that, although possibly connected to big ideas from the viewpoint of the teacher, have no such connection in the minds of the students. In "instructivist" approaches, the low end is usually, as it has been for generations, emphasis on recallable facts.

The identification of pervasive and enduring misconceptions has been one of the main achievements of learning research in the past quarter-century. Although there has been much dispute about what to call them and how to explain them, the overall import has been clear: students are coming out of the education system having failed to grasp many of the most fundamental ideas they were supposedly taught. (An important side issue relevant to educational evaluation is, why did it take cleverly designed cognitive research to discover this? Why was it not apparent to teachers and why was it not being demonstrated by standard achievement tests?) "Learning with understanding" has been a slogan of progressive education movements throughout the past century, yet the evidence indicates that most school learning is "learning without understanding".

What to do about this unfortunate situation has been addressed in several ways. One way has been through improving standardised tests so they do measure understanding. Progress has been made, but it runs up against a serious obstacle: tests of understanding must generally work by posing problems requiring application of intended concepts, but such problems can be failed for a number of reasons besides lack of understanding. In fact, tests of understanding begin to look suspiciously like tests of verbal or quantitative intelligence, and so they invite all the charges of bias that have been levelled against such tests. (E.L. Thorndike made this point 70 years ago.)

Another way, pursued by many of the most inventive learning scientists, has been through the design of simulations, simulation-based games, and "intelligent toys" intended to make difficult concepts easier to learn. The concepts of dynamic systems theory, for instance, which constitute a set of broadly significant "big ideas", have proved very difficult to learn and almost impossible without simulations that allow students to experiment with how various dynamic systems work. But earlier work using simulations of arithmetic operations made it clear that engagement is not enough: Work or play with a simulation, game, or toy has to be embedded in a serious effort to understand.

How to motivate sustained effort to understand is the formidable problem that must be solved to make "learning with understanding" more than an empty slogan. The traditional answer is to get better-educated teachers, who have a deep understanding of their subject and can present it lucidly and in ways that grip the imagination. The alternative answers are probably all conditioned at least partly by the assumption that the traditional solution is beyond reach. To take its place, there are romantic beliefs that children's natural curiosity will be enough to motivate pursuit of understanding. There are also hard-nosed beliefs of the "make them think" variety, generally relying on the posing of problems and challenging questions. The "community" approaches discussed in the next section, at their best, make collaborative pursuit of understanding central to what it means to be a member of the community, thus taking advantage of normal motivations to "belong". The fundamental difficulty in promoting learning with understanding was stated bluntly by biologist E.O. Wilson: "Natural selection built the brain to survive in the world and only incidentally to understand it at a depth greater than is necessary to survive." The pursuit of ever-deepening understanding just does not come naturally.

Over and above the grasping of particular important ideas is the matter of what may be called "knowledge literacy" – understanding the nature of knowledge and how it is produced, how progress in science and other disciplines is achieved. Research indicates that teachers as well as students tend to be lacking in this type of literacy. Carey and Smith (1993) identified 3 levels of understanding the nature of science. At the first level, science consists of the unproblematic accumulation of facts. At the second level, the tentative nature of empirical knowledge and evidence is recognised. That is as far as most school treatments of scientific epistemology go, but Carey and Smith recognised a third level, at which the role of ideas and theory development are recognised. This is the level at which theories cease to be regarded as candidate truths and are regarded as improvable objects that serve to explain and generate the further discovery of facts. Evidence of level 3 understanding has been virtually nonexistent at the school level. On one hand this results in the trivialising of "learning by discovery". It becomes merely identifying which variables account for an observed result rather than explaining the process that produces the result. On the other hand, it leads to undervaluing students' own efforts to theorise. When we present educators with striking examples of theory-building by students, someone invariably asks how we prevent students from arriving at wrong theories. An appropriate but not welcomed response is, "How do scientists ensure that they do not arrive at wrong theories?". The answer, of course, is that they do not. The history of science is full of wrong theories (some of which are similar to the ones students produce), and scientists can be sure that what they produce now will eventually be found to have shortcomings. Fruitfulness rather than approximation to an unattainable truth is the primary criterion for judging today's ideas. What makes science progressive is sustained and well-tooled effort at idea improvement (something notably lacking in many other areas of human activity). Initiating students into this process and trusting that progress will result is perhaps the most important single thing schools could do to prepare students for the Knowledge Age.

Individual versus community emphasis

This is a dimension along which the learning sciences themselves have undergone a shift. Through the 1970s, the emphasis was mainly on individual knowledge and cognitive strategies. The 1980s were transitional, and by the 1990s most of the researchers who had originally focused on individual learning and cognition had moved to a focus on communities of learners (Brown and Campione, 1990), communities of practice (Lave and Wenger, 1991) or knowledge building communities (Scardamalia and Bereiter, 1994).

In business, it is widely recognised that the growing emphasis on collaboration is thwarted by rewards and promotions being tied to individual accomplishment. The same is true in schools. We have seen some (there are large cultural differences here) where students withhold their ideas from collaborative activities because they fear other students will gain credit for them. Parents, naturally, tend to take the individualistic view, because it is their child's future, not the success of the class as a temporary community that they care about. It is, however, quite possible to evaluate students on both their individual attainments and on their contribution to and understanding of collective knowledge advancement (Lee, Chan and van Aalst, 2006).

The shift from an individual to a community focus in the learning sciences has been attributed to the influence of Vygotsky and his theory that "Every function in the child's cultural development appears twice: first, on the social level, and later, on the individual level". However, in many cases Vygotsky may have served mainly as a way of justifying a change that was taking place for other reasons – much as, at an earlier time, Piaget was used to justify child-centred education. A strong impetus for the shift was recognition that, although teaching cognitive strategies often yielded good short-term results, classroom conditions provided little incentive for students to exert the extra effort that the taught strategies required, and they soon regressed to the efficient but educationally unproductive strategies they had been using before. The sustaining force for change, however, was growing recognition of the importance of dialogue in the educational process.

The treatment of dialogue can be indexed at five levels:

1. Recitation. This is the traditional form of oral interaction between teacher and students and is still common. It basically consists of a continuing oral examination conducted by the teacher. A recitation consists of a series of what are called "IRE" units: teacher Initiates, student Responds, teacher Evaluates – after which a new and possibly unrelated IRE unit is started.

2. Teacher-mediated dialogue. This preserves the IRE format but there is some logic and constructive purpose to the sequence of units. It may take the form of Socratic questioning or a relatively free discussion, which, however, has the teacher as the hub, calling on students to speak.

3. Teacher-managed argument or debate. Here the teacher is on the sideline, no longer the hub through which all discourse passes. Instead, an established form – such as a debate, or a presentation followed by discussion – provides the structure of the discourse.

4. Independent small group discussion. As pioneered in Great Britain, this approach divides the class into small groups that carry on their own informal discussions, usually on set topics, with the teacher as monitor. Reciprocal Teaching, which has gained much attention among learning scientists, is a transitional form intended to progress from level 2 to 3 to 4. It starts with teacher-managed dialogue centred on a text being read. The students carry out specific actions: question-asking, predicting, summarising, and asking for clarification (Palincsar and Brown, 1984). Gradually students are to be weaned away from teacher direction and eventually from the activity structure itself, moving toward informal discussions of the kinds adults carry out.

5. Authentic problem-solving discourse. Whereas class discussions may simply be about some topic, authentic problem-solving discourse has a goal toward which it is intended to progress – usually toward explaining something, but possibly toward planning or designing something. "Authentic" here means that students actually care about a problem and do not see it as merely an exercise. "Knowledge-building discourse" is discourse of this kind that has as its object the production and improvement of public knowledge (Scardamalia and Bereiter, 2006). Accordingly, it represents the kind of discourse observed in mature knowledge-creating teams (Dunbar, 1997).

Level 3 is about the highest one to be observed in most schools. Levels 4 and 5 require that teachers learn new skills and be willing to risk some loss of control. Ann Brown, one of the developers of Reciprocal Teaching, lamented that teachers remained fixated at the initial ritualistic stage (thus, according to the present scheme, failing to progress beyond level 2).

A firm traditional practice in modern elementary schools is to devote the first days or weeks of a term to building community, after which educational objectives are to be added. There is certainly value in quickly establishing norms of classroom conduct, but a heavy initial investment in community building seems misdirected. It often creates expectations that must subsequently be overcome in order to get on with educational work. Better to start with establishing the highest level of discourse that is feasible (and our experience in various kinds of schools indicates that level 5 is attainable even at the youngest ages). Once there is sustained and meaningful discourse, you inevitably have a community, and if the discourse is oriented toward cognitive goals you have a learning- or knowledge-building community that enlists students' natural motives to belong and to conform in the service of educational goals.

"Design mode" versus "belief mode"

This dimension of difference is not really a continuum. Instead, it consists of two states or modes of activity, with the possibility of considerable switching back and forth.

> *When in belief mode, we are concerned with what we and other people believe or ought to believe. Our response to ideas in this mode is to agree or disagree, to present arguments and evidence for or against, to express and try to resolve doubts. When in design mode, we are concerned with the usefulness, adequacy, improvability, and developmental potential of ideas. (Bereiter and Scardamalia, 2003)*

Since ancient times and on to contemporary "thinking curricula", the treatment of ideas in formal education has been almost exclusively in belief mode, yet knowledge creation in all its many forms is carried out primarily in design mode.

Educational folk theory is disposed to equate belief mode with dogmatic instruction, but that misses the whole point of the distinction. It is not a good-bad distinction and it leaves entirely open the manner in which belief and design issues are dealt with. Instead, the two modes are distinguished by the kinds of questions that are asked. Good questions to ask in belief mode are:

- What does this statement mean?

- Is it true?

- What is the evidence?

- What are the arguments for and against?

Important questions to ask in design mode are:

- What is this idea good for?

- What does it do and fail to do?

- Does it have a future?

- How could it be improved?

We do not suggest that "design mode" should replace "belief mode" in schools. Both are important. Virtually everything that we call an "issue" demands consideration in belief mode, and every educational programme addresses issues in some way, whether it be dogmatically or through a free consideration of alternatives. Yet one can go all the way through an education system and never encounter design mode questions applied to academic subject matter. Knowledge creation depends on moving back and forth between belief and design questions in ways that maintain progress in idea improvement. In a design context, issues of truth or belief are generally addressed as issues of information quality. This is a very practical way of dealing with issues of belief, which could be used to good effect in many educational contexts. Dealing with belief issues in terms of information quality allows consideration both of degree of certainty and of the consequences of being wrong. How much does it matter whether statement *P* is true? Sometimes it matters a lot and sometimes it matters little. But in belief mode the question seldom arises.

Accommodation to external constraints

Naturally, practitioners of research-based innovation want to see their innovations put into practice. How much compromise this will require is an important but vexing question. Compromises almost always involve some sacrifice of effectiveness, clarity, and integrity. For instance, most serious educational designers are in favour of longer units of study that permit greater depth, but in the interest of acceptability, some have accommodated to the demand for brief units in which all the materials are provided and everything is laid out in specified steps. A general playing down of differences is often helpful in gaining acceptance. Some learning researchers will declare, for instance, that their innovative approach is actually what good teachers already do – thus attaching it to the popular notion of "best practice". Most learning scientists recognise that transfer of intellectual skills is extremely problematic, yet to gain acceptance they may make unsupportable claims of "teaching" creativity, critical thinking, collaborativeness, "scientific method", and other generic competencies.

A more general issue of accommodation is the extent to which scientific language should be translated into language more accessible to practitioners. This is generally regarded as a good thing, and there is a whole profession of science writing devoted to it. Yet in education it has serious risks. This is because educational folk theory is not merely a less informed version of theory from the learning sciences. It is a parallel world of theorising that has its own concepts and issues, influenced by, but also largely insulated from, the world of scientific theorising. Efforts by educational journalists to do the translation are almost total failures, because the journalists are themselves steeped in folk theory and thus tend to see theoretical terms from the learning sciences as mere jargon standing for the more familiar folk ideas. In research-based innovation, principles – often called "design principles" – are important for conveying the thinking behind an innovation and for ensuring that further developments, such as improvisations by practitioners, remain consistent with the basic intent. In educational folk theory, however, principles are more in the nature of sermon themes – statements such as "Every child is different" or "It isn't the technology, it is how you use it"; statements with which no one can disagree but which do not set bounds on practice.

It may seem that we are being too harsh toward educational folk theory. We must emphasise that criticising educational folk theory is not the same as criticising educational practice. Just as there are effective traditional medical practices based on groundless theories (acupuncture is a notable example) there can be effective evolved educational practices with dubious theoretical backing. Problems arise, however, when the goal is to improve on accepted practices. Folk theories then typically act as barriers to progress, and progress is what is at issue in this discussion. If you want to improve acupuncture, you are going to need something other than a diagram of imaginary energy flows in the body. If you want to improve students' thinking you are going to need something other than a catalogue of "higher-order skills".[3]

3.2. Comparing learning models and approaches

Most current theoretical models of learning, like those of times past, have little practical application. There are two major exceptions: John Anderson's ACT-R theory (1993), which underlies the development of

---

[3] Of interest here are efforts by the American Federation of Teachers to challenge folk theory and to replace its beliefs by scientifically grounded ones. See the regular column titled "Ask the Cognitive Scientist", by Daniel T. Willingham, appearing in the AFT journal, *American Educator* – online at *http://www.aft.org/pubs-reports/american_educator/subject.htm*

"Cognitive Tutors" (Koedinger, 2006), and Robbie Case's theory of Central Conceptual Structures (Case and Okamoto, 1996). Both of these have undergone decades of development, backed by strong research programmes, and they have been the basis for innovative and demonstrably effective instructional designs. Yet we would guess that most new teachers and administrators graduate without ever hearing of them. The most-cited authors in the *Cambridge Handbook of the Learning Sciences* (Sawyer, 2006) are people who have developed innovative approaches to learning that are grounded in social and cognitive theories of learning and thinking. So "approaches to learning" might be a better label than "models of learning". However this alternative has problems, too. Everything that goes on in education represents an "approach" in some fashion. An effort to dimensionalise and categorise the full range of existing approaches would require categories of such breadth that truly original approaches to learning (such as those of Anderson and Case) would be lost in the multitude and what is distinctive about them would be missed. We are mindful of Robert Ebel's remark that education is not a natural phenomenon (like respiration, for instance):

It is not governed by any natural laws. It is not in need of research to find out how it works. It is in need of creative invention to make *it work better. (In Farley, 1982, p. 18)*

(Ebel's remark came a decade before "design research" appeared on the scene, but it is clear this is what he was advocating.)

Comparing educational approaches on the basis of administrative structures and regulations and on the basis of observable activities can be of value from the standpoint of what was referred to earlier as "decision-oriented" research. However, to be of value in advancing research-based innovation, comparisons must be at a deeper level. A host of difficulties complicate such comparisons. One must be careful in accepting designers' statements about the theoretical origins of their approaches. Sometimes these "origins" are introduced after the fact to lend academic respectability to their inventions. Teachers' subjective reports of cognitive effects on students are unfortunately unreliable. (Every thinking skills programme is effective by the standard of user reports, even though hardly any are effective by more objective measures.) There are some novel educational models that have undergone extensive development and testing and have produced impressive learning results which are largely ignored by the academic community because they lack theoretical credentials. Two of these are Direct Instruction (Adams and Engelmann, 1996) and HOTS (Higher-Order Thinking Skills – Pogrow, 2005). Although rare, there are also some commercially produced programmes that have involved established researchers that have undergone similar development and testing, yet are similarly ignored by the academic community (cf. Henderson, 2006). Finally, every well-developed model or approach involves a good deal of rational analysis that goes beyond scientific theory. Some approaches rely primarily on rational analysis (Direct Instruction and HOTS are examples). These are often mistakenly labelled "behaviourist". Close adherence to a theory is usually more a reflection of dogmatism than of theoretical sophistication.

Observation-based comparison is also complicated by the fact that adopting a certain model or approach does not necessarily mean applying it to the exclusion of others, and a mixed approach is not necessarily eclectic. For instance, one may distinguish certain educational goals as finalistic or "once-and-for-all", meaning that they are to be mastered in a finite time and that instruction may then pass on to other goals. Examples are basic word recognition skills in reading and mastery of addition and multiplication facts. Other goals are developmental in that instruction and intentional learning have continual relevance throughout the formative years. It is neither inconsistent nor eclectic to adopt one approach for finalistic goals and another for developmental goals. (On the other hand, it does not follow that one must adopt different models for different kinds of goals; the issue should remain open because you never know when someone will come up with a unified approach that successfully handles goals that previously called for different approaches.)

In this chapter we have proposed 5 dimensions of comparison that have proved informative in our own efforts to compare the approach we developed: Knowledge Building (Scardamalia and Bereiter, 2006), to its near neighbours (as described briefly in the Annex 3.A.1). They are mainly useful, therefore, in drawing distinctions among approaches that could all be labelled "constructivist" or "social-constructivist". This is justifiable on grounds that most current research-based innovation falls into this category. However there is a whole other family of educational approaches referred to broadly as "instructivist" and often associated with "Instructional Design Theory" (Reigeluth, 1999). Much current work by researchers in this area involves repositories of "learning objects", Learning Management Systems, and course-authoring systems. To ignore variations among instructivist approaches would be as much an error as treating all constructivist approaches as mere procedural variations. However, the important dimensions of variation would naturally be different from the ones proposed here; see, for instance, Edmonds, Branch and Mukherjee (1994).

In the long run, however, scaling on 5 dimensions or 20 or even 100 may fail to identify the differences most important for the future of educational design. That will require more systemic analysis, something more like high-grade literary criticism than like biological taxonomy. By that we mean analysis that does not impose an external framework but locates a particular design within a space constituted by analysis of its near neighbours, this space in turn being constituted by analysis of the tradition of which it is a part, and so on, thus progressing "toward making the whole… intelligible" (Frye, 1957, p. 9).

There is a whole stratum of research in education that takes "effect size" as coin of the realm. Effect size, the standardised mean difference between outcomes of one approach and another, provides a basis for deciding among available alternatives. However it does not point a direction for future progress. Often effect size compares approaches that share significant weaknesses – mathematics programmes that all fail to give students a grasp of rational numbers, science programmes that leave major misconceptions untouched, reading programmes that produce significant differences in test scores but leave the majority of students unprepared for complex learning from texts. Future-oriented educators need to be able to look beyond such comparisons in order to identify approaches that offer promise of making qualitative leaps beyond current outcomes. They need to identify approaches that are not only worth adopting but that are worth working to develop in new directions. In fruitful scientific and technological research, each major advance opens up novel possibilities for future advances. (Consider present-day uses of computers, hardly any of which were foreseen by the computer scientists of 60 years ago.) It is our hope that the CERI work on innovative learning environments will be able to bring the concept of fruitfulness to the forefront and thus enlist researchers, practitioners, and policy makers alike in the enterprise that has received so little notice in education: *research-based innovation.*

Annex 3.A.1.
Educational Models and Approaches to Learning

Central conceptual structures (Case and Okamoto, 1996)

http://facultysenate.stanford.edu/memorial_resolutions/Case_Robbie_SenD5478.pdf

Case theorised that a limited number of conceptual structures lie at the heart of human intellectual competencies, and that mastering these structures is essential for educational attainment. Through experimental research by Case and his students, conceptual structures were identified for number sense (in essence a mental number line), proportional reasoning, causality, story production, and even musical composition. These structures were taught through a combination of instruction and games of graduated complexity, and in each case the results significantly exceeded those of conventional instruction.

Cognitive tutors (Anderson, 1993; Koedinger, 2006)

ACT-R is a theory for simulating and understanding human cognition, which was developed by J.R. Anderson. It demonstrates how intelligent behaviour can result from a system of rules that function automatically, without the need for a higher-level system (a homunculus) to regulate their use. A series of computer-based tutors were developed and refined to apply this rule-based approach to the teaching of various subjects. As the tutors were revised to address problems of motivation, understanding, and sociality, the overall approach has become progressively more "metacognitive" and "social-constructivist" in character.

Constructionism (Kafai, 2006)

"Constructionism" is a concept introduced by Seymour Papert, advancing the idea that learning is best achieved by going beyond the internal, largely unconscious construction of knowledge (as theorised by Piaget) to the external and inventive construction of knowledge-embodying artifacts. As implemented by a number of researchers and inventors at MIT, constructionism has focused on engaging learners in work with programmable toys and virtual objects, making students designers of games and simulations rather than mere "users" of such products.

Direct instruction (Adams and Engelmann, 1996)

http://nifdi.org/

"Direct instruction" is based on the idea that clear instruction, eliminating misinterpretations, can improve and accelerate learning. Accordingly, the emphasis is on well-developed and carefully planned lessons designed around small learning increments and clearly defined and prescribed teaching procedures. Continually refined over its 40-year-history to improve effectiveness, it has shown strong results in reading and mathematics, but has been continuously controversial because of its highly prescriptive character.

Fostering communities of learners (FCL) (Brown and Campione, 1996)

Although FCL is frequently identified with a number of distinctive "activity structures", these are subservient to an innovative pedagogy based on an integration of the roles of students-as-learners and students-as-teachers. Within a broad topic area, such as ecology, different groups of students acquire expertise in different subtopics, produce instructional materials, and then teach what they have learned to the other students. Cross-age tutoring is also an important part of this teaching-learning approach. "Benchmark" lessons introduce a more conventional element, in which the students learn from a classroom teacher or a guest expert. The somewhat ritualistic activity structures are designed to facilitate students' self-regulated movement between roles.

HOTS (Higher Order Thinking Skills) (Pogrow, 2005)

www.hots.org/index.html

"HOTS" is a general thinking skills programme for low ability and learning disabled children in grades 4-8. The programme combines software with a sophisticated curriculum and Socratic dialogue in small group settings. The dialogues are designed to enhance the following cognitive processes involved in learning: (a) metacognition, (b) inference from context, (c) decontextualisation and (d) information synthesis. HOTS has been shown to produce accelerated gains in reading and mathematics.

Knowledge Building (Scardamalia and Bereiter, 2006)

Knowledge Building, which is synonymous with "knowledge creation", aims to restructure education around the goals and processes that generate new knowledge in research and innovation-intensive organisations. Accordingly, the main emphasis is on a community dynamic that supports "epistemic invention" – students taking responsibility for identifying knowledge problems, producing their own tentative solutions (theories), and improving them through empirical research, constructive use of authoritative sources, and knowledge-building dialogue. Among constructivist approaches, it is distinctive in the centrality given to students' own ideas.

Learning science by design (Holbrook and Kolodner, 2000)

Holbrook and Kolodner (2000, p. 221) describe this approach as follows:

Science learning is achieved through addressing a major design challenge (such as building a self-powered car that can go a certain distance over a certain terrain).... To address a challenge, class members develop designs, build prototypes, gather performance data and use other resources to provide justification for refining their designs, and they iteratively investigate, redesign, test, and analyse the results of their ideas. They articulate their understanding of science concepts, first in terms of the concrete artifact which they have designed, then in transfer to similar artifacts or situations, and finally to abstract principles of science.

Problem-based learning (Evensen and Hmelo, 2000)

Originating in medical education, problem-based learning engages students with problems similar to those they will encounter in practice (for instance, a case description on the basis of which a diagnosis must be made and therapeutic action prescribed). Under tutorial guidance, the students work in groups to identify and obtain needed information, discuss proposed solutions, and arrive at consensus. Problem-based learning has gained acceptance in other kinds of professional education. When applied to general education, however, it has tended to drift toward project-based learning, described below.

Project-based learning

The term "project-based learning" is often loosely applied to all sorts of independent student work. As defined by Marx *et al.* (1997, p. 341), however, authentic project-based learning "focuses on student-designed inquiry that is organised by investigations to answer driving questions, includes collaboration among learners and others, the use of new technology, and the creation of authentic artefacts that represent student understanding". The "driving questions" are preferably ones of social importance (such as environmental issues) and the project work is typically engineered with dedicated software, instrumentation, and data representation formats.

Web-based inquiry science environment (WISE) (Linn, Davis, and Bell, 2004)

WISE belongs to the family of project-based/problem-based learning approaches, but is distinctive in its emphasis on evidence-based argumentation as a means of advancing and integrating students' knowledge. The WISE research group – centred at the University of California, Berkeley, but with a number of affiliates – has produced complete science units addressing frequently mandated topics and scaled to fit within the severe time constraints common in school curricula.

References

Adams, G.L. and S. Engelmann (1996), *Research on Direct Instruction: 25 Years beyond DISTAR*, Educational Achievement Systems, Seattle.

Anderson, J.R. (1993), "Problem Solving and Learning", *American Psychologist*, Vol. 48, pp. 35-44.

Bereiter, C. (2002), "Design Research for Sustained Innovation," *Cognitive Studies: Bulletin of the Japanese Cognitive Science Society*, Vol. 9, No. 3, pp. 321-327.

Bereiter, C. and M. Scardamalia (1987), "An Attainable Version of High Literacy: Approaches to Teaching Higher-order Skills in Reading and Writing", *Curriculum Inquiry*, Vol. 17, No. 1, pp. 9-30.

Bereiter, C. and M. Scardamalia (2003), "Learning to Work Creatively with Knowledge", in E.D. Corte, L. Verschaffel, N. Entwistle and J.V. Merriënboer (eds.), *Powerful Learning Environments: Unravelling Basic Components and Dimensions*, Elsevier Science, Oxford, pp. 73-78.

Bereiter, C. and M. Scardamalia (2006), "Education for the Knowledge Age: Design-centered Models of Teaching and Instruction", in P.A. Alexander and P.H. Winne (eds.), *Handbook of Educational Psychology*, Lawrence Erlbaum Associates, Mahwah, NJ, pp. 695-711.

Bransford, J. and D. Schwartz (1999), "Rethinking Transfer: A Simple Proposal with Multiple Implications", *Review of Research in Education*, Vol. 25.

Brown, A.L. and J.C. Campione (1990), "Communities of Learning and Thinking, or A Context by Any Other Name", *Contributions to Human Development*, Vol. 21, pp. 108-126.

Brown, A. and J. Campione (1996), "Psychological Theory and the Design of Innovative Learning Environments: On Procedures, Principles, and Systems", in L. Schauble and R. Glaser (eds.), *Innovations in Learning: New Environments for Education*, Lawrence Erlbaum Associates, Mahwah, NJ, pp. 289-325.

Carey, S. and C. Smith (1993), "On Understanding the Nature of Scientific Knowledge", *Educational Psychologist*, Vol. 28, pp. 235-251.

Case, R. and C. Bereiter (1984), "From Behaviourism to Cognitive Behaviourism to Cognitive Development: Steps in the Evolution of Instructional Design", *Instructional Science*, Vol. 13, pp. 141-158.

Case, R. and Y. Okamoto (1996), "The Role of Central Conceptual Structures in the Development of Children's Thought", *Monographs of the Society for Research in Child Development*, Vol. 61, No. 2, serial No. 246.

Collins, A., D. Joseph and K. Bielaczyc (2004), "Design Research: Theoretical and Methodological Issues", *The Journal of the Learning Sciences*, Vol. 13, pp. 15-42.

Cronbach, L.J, and P. Suppes (ed.) (1969), *Research for Tomorrow's Schools: Disciplined Inquiry for Education*, Macmillan, New York.

Dunbar, K. (1997), "How Scientists Think: Online Creativity and Conceptual Change in Science", in T.B. Ward, S.M. Smith and S. Vaid (eds.), *Conceptual Structures and Processes: Emergence, Discovery and Change,* American Psychological Association, Washington, DC, pp. 461-493.

Edmonds, G.S., R.C. Branch and P. Mukherjee (1994), "A Conceptual Framework for Comparing Instructional Design Models", *Journal of Educational Technology Research and Development*, Vol. 42, No. 4.

Evensen, D.H. and C.E. Hmelo (eds.) (2000), *Problem-Based Learning: A Research Perspective on Learning Interactions*, Erlbaum, Mahwah, NJ.

Farley, F.H. (1982), "The Future of Educational Research", *Educational Researcher*, Vol. 1, No. 8, pp. 11-19.

Frye, N. (1957), *Anatomy of Criticism: Four Essays,* Princeton University Press, Princeton, NJ.

Henderson, H. (2006), *Let's Kill Dick and Jane: How the Open Court Publishing Company Fought the Culture of American Education,* St. Augustine's Press, South Bend, IN.

Holbrook, J. and J.L. Kolodner (2000), "Scaffolding the Development of an Inquiry-based (science) Classroom", in B. Fishman and S. O'Connor-Divelbiss (eds.), *Fourth International Conference of the Learning Sciences,* Lawrence Erlbaum Associates, Mahwah, NJ, pp. 221-227.

Kafai, J. (2006), "Constructionism", in R.K. Sawyer (ed.), *The Cambridge Handbook of the Learning Sciences*, Cambridge University Press, Cambridge, UK.

Kirschner, P.A., J. Sweller and R.E. Clark (2006), "Why Minimally Guided Instruction Does not Work: An analysis of the Failure of Constructivist, Discovery, Problem-based, Experiential, and Inquiry-Based Teaching", *Educational Psychologist*, Vol. 41, No. 2, pp.75-86.

Koedinger, K. (2006), "Cognitive Tutors: Technology Bringing Learning Sciences to the Classroom", in R.K. Sawyer (ed.), *The Cambridge Handbook of the Learning Sciences*, Cambridge University Press, Cambridge, United Kingdom, pp. 61-77.

Lave, J. and E. Wenger (1991), *Situated Learning: Legitimate Peripheral Participation*, Cambridge University Press, Cambridge, England.

Lee, E.Y.C., C.K.K. Chan and J. van Aalst (2006), "Students Assessing their Own Knowledge Building", *International Journal of Computer-Supported Collaborative Learning,* Vol. 1, pp. 277-307.

Lee, H.-S. and N.B. Songer (2003), "Making Authentic Science Accessible to Students", *International Journal of Science Education,* Vol. 25, No. 8, pp. 923-948.

Linn, M.C., E.A. Davis and P. Bell (eds.) (2004), *Internet Environments for Science Education*, Lawrence Erlbaum Associates, Mahwah, NJ.

Marx, R.W., P.C. Blumenfeld, J.S. Krajcik and E. Soloway (1997), "Enacting Project-based Science", *Elementary School Journal*, Vol. 97, pp. 341-358.

Palincsar, A.S. and A.L. Brown (1984), "Reciprocal Teaching of Comprehension-fostering and Comprehension-monitoring Activities", *Cognition and Instruction,* Vol. 1, pp. 117-175.

Pogrow, S. (2005), "HOTS Revisited: A Thinking Development Approach to Reducing the Learning Gap After Grade 3", *Phi Delta Kappan*, Vol. 87, No. 1, pp. 64-75, available, June 2007, at *http://www.pdkintl.org/kappan/k_v87/k0509pog.htm*

Reigeluth, C.M. (ed.) (1999), "What is Instructional-design Theory and How is it Changing?", *Instructional-design Theories and Models*, Vol. II, Lawrence Erlbaum Associates, New Jersey, pp. 5-29.

Sawyer, R.K. (ed.) (2006), *The Cambridge Handbook of the Learning Sciences*, Cambridge University Press, Cambridge, United Kingdom.

Scardamalia, M. and C. Bereiter (1994), "Computer Support for Knowledge-building Communities", *Journal of the Learning Sciences*, Vol. 3, pp. 265-283.

Scardamalia, M. and C. Bereiter (2006), "Knowledge Building: Theory, Pedagogy and Technology", in R.K. Sawyer (ed.), *The Cambridge Handbook of the Learning Sciences*, Cambridge University Press, Cambridge, United Kingdom, pp. 97-117.

Chapter 4
The Contribution of Alternative Education
by
Anne Sliwka[1]

This chapter introduces the concept of alternative education in its various different forms and approaches. The author explores the context, history and development of several alternative forms of education utilised worldwide. In addition she explores the notions of the culture of learning for each, including the conception of the learner, realisation of the learning environment, role of teachers, curricula and culture of assessment. The chapter also calls for a reassessment of alternative models of education in light of what the learning sciences reveal on cognitive and social processes which result in effective learning.

4.1. Alternative education: a fragmented landscape

Lacking a precise meaning, the term "alternative education" describes different approaches to teaching and learning other than state-provided mainstream education, usually in the form of public or private schools with a special, often innovative curriculum and a flexible programme of study which is based to a large extent on the individual student's interests and needs (Raywid, 1988; Koetzsch, 1997; Aron, 2003; Carnie 2003). Although in its broadest sense, the term "alternative education" covers all educational activities that fall outside the traditional school system (including special programmes for school dropouts and gifted students, home schooling, etc.) this paper focuses on models of schooling that have paved the way for alternatives to mainstream school systems provided by the State.

---

[1] Anne Sliwka, Ph.D., is Professor of Education at the University of Trier in Germany. Her research focuses on school development, teacher education and education for democratic citizenship.

Across the world, we find a broad range of alternative forms of education rooted in different philosophies. Thus, the landscape of alternative education is highly fragmented, which makes it difficult to quantify the number of students in alternative schools and programmes. Large, global networks of alternative schools based on particular educational concepts such as Montessori and Waldorf/Steiner pedagogy coexist with some new movements in alternative schooling as well as individual alternative schools. In addition, several OECD school systems have created legislation that makes room for and funds alternative schools and education programmes within public school systems (Rofes and Stulberg, 2004).

Historically, alternative models of education have coexisted with the public education system ever since its inception in the first half of the 19th Century (Raywid, 1999). Attempts by the state to provide a common, culturally unifying education for all children have provoked the response of educators, parents and students who have declined to participate in these systems. Their reasons are manifold, and the forms of schooling (and non-schooling) they designed are equally diverse. "The history of alternative education is a colourful story of social reformers and individualists, religious believers and romantics" (Miller, 2007). In the United States, for example, Horace Mann's pioneering efforts to centralise public schooling were opposed from the start by religious leaders and other critics who perceived education to be a personal, family and community endeavour, not a political programme to be mandated by the State. Many critics of the public school system referred to Jean-Jacques Rousseau's *Émile*, published in 1762, in which he argued that education should follow the child's innate growth rather than the demands of society. Throughout the 19th Century, education reformers in several countries accused their state school systems of disciplining young people for the sake of political and social uniformity and the success of an emerging industrial society. Bronson Alcott, for example, started the Temple School in Boston as early as 1834 because he rejected the rote memorisation and recitation predominant at early American schools.

The first decades of the 20th Century saw the advent of several alternative education movements that proved to be influential even today. With her influential book *The Century of the Child* (1909), the Swedish educator Ellen Key was among the first of several advocates of child-centred education. The German education reformers Hermann Lietz, Paul Geheeb and Kurt Hahn founded reformist rural boarding schools ("*Landerziehungsheime*") that were meant to provide children with a holistic education secluded from the negative effects of industrial urban life. In 1907, the Italian paediatrician Maria Montessori opened the first *Casa de Bambini*, a house of elementary education based on her own observations in child development. The first Waldorf school was founded by Austrian philosopher Rudolf Steiner in 1919. Because of official criticism of his innovative teaching methods, French educator, Célestin Freinet in 1935 resigned from his job as public school teacher to start his own school in Vence. In North America, John Dewey, Francis Parker and others formed a powerful progressive education movement based on the belief that education should primarily serve the needs of children and focus on understanding, action and experience rather than rote knowledge and memorisation.

During the 1960s and 1970s, alternative education grew into a widespread social movement. Writers like Ivan Illich, A.S. Neill and Hartmut von Hentig in Europe, John Holt, Jonathan Kozol and Herbert Kohl in the United States and Paulo Freire in Brazil questioned the values and methods of public schooling. The period between 1967 and 1972 in particular saw profound criticism of public education, resulting in student demonstrations and teacher strikes in many countries. As a result, the first magnet schools were introduced in the US public school system. By the 1990s, the transformation of the industrial to a knowledge economy had stimulated a debate about the future of the standard model of schooling (Bransford, Brown and Cocking, 2000; Bereiter, 2002; Hargreaves, 2003). In recent years, several OECD school systems have made provisions for the greater autonomy of state schools and some countries have made it possible for parents and innovative educators to receive public funding for the foundation of schools with special profiles, such as Charter schools in the United States and Alberta, Canada, Foundation schools in England or Designated Character schools in New Zealand. With the beginning of the 21st Century, many teaching practices developed in alternative schools, such as student-centred and independent learning, project-based and cooperative learning, as well as authentic assessment seem to have gone mainstream by influencing the culture of public education.

4.2. Global networks of alternative schools

Montessori schools (Lillard, 1996; Kahn, Dubble and Pendleton, 1999; Seldin and Epstein, 2003) pursue an educational philosophy and methodology, characterised by a special set of didactic materials, multi-age classrooms, student-chosen work in longer time blocks, a collaborative environment with student mentors, absence of testing and grades, and individual and small group instruction in academic and social skills. The programme name is not copyrighted and many mainstream schools across the world have now adopted parts of the Montessori methodology. Most schools entirely built on the Montessori methodology and philosophy are, however, organised in international and national networks such as the International Montessori Council or the American Montessori Society.

Waldorf schools (Petrash, 2002; Clouder and Rawson, 2003; Masters, 2005) also known as Steiner schools, are based on the educational ideas of the philosopher Rudolf Steiner. Waldorf education is currently practiced in kindergartens and schools in 60 countries and is thus, together with Montessori education, the predominant form of alternative education around the globe. Waldorf education aims at developing children and adolescents into free, moral and integrated individuals through integrating practical, artistic and intellectual approaches into the teaching of all subjects.

Round Square Schools (Tacy, 2006), of which there are currently about 50 on all five continents, are based on concepts of experiential educational developed by Kurt Hahn, who believed that schools prepare students for life by experiencing it in authentic learning situations as generated by work projects, community services, leadership training, international exchanges and different forms of outdoor exploration and adventure. All Round Square Schools emphasise learning through doing with the aim of developing every student academically, physically, culturally and spiritually, through a process of self-confrontation and self-formation within the supportive environment of a school community.

Free or democratic schools (Lamb, 1995; Gribble, 1998) are organised around the principles of autonomy and democracy. The oldest democratic school, Summerhill, a boarding school in Southern England, was founded in 1921 by the Scottish teacher A.S. Neill. Sudbury Valley School, radically democratic school in Massachusetts/USA, has served as a model for many subsequent democratic schools. Today, about 100 schools around the world describe themselves as "free" or "democratic" schools. Since 1993, free schools have formed a loose network. While official rules about the organisational principles of democratic or free schools would contradict the schools' independent spirit, they share many common characteristics: decisions about the school are taken by a self-governing school body, in which each student and each teacher has one vote in a majority voting system.

Escuelas Nuevas are alternative schools based on the idea of improved rural and urban basic education for children from low-income families. Started in 1987, there are now more than 20 000 *Escuelas Nuevas* in Colombia as well as in 14 other Latin American countries, the Philippines and Uganda – schools that have proven to be effective according to the World Bank and UNESCO, among others. The schools' pedagogy emphasises respect for the rights of children and is based on innovative educational projects involving a range of educational materials that encourage collaborative, participatory and personalised teaching methods. Schools are organised as community schools, involving the wider community as well as students' families who are invited to play an active role in school activities and their child's learning.

In addition to the alternative schools that are part of broader networks, there are numerous individual alternative schools across the world. The following examples show the variety of pedagogical approaches realised at these schools:

- Brockwood Park School, founded by the Indian philosopher and educator Jiddu Krishnamurti in 1969, has a strong ethical base and focuses on both academic excellence as well as spiritual development through exploring the balance between freedom and responsibility, meditation freeing from self-centred action and inner conflict as well as appreciation and conservation of nature.

- The American educational reformer Helen Pankhurst developed the Dalton Laboratory Plan (1922), which enables students to work independently on the basis of a contract, within the public school system. Today Dalton schools exist in Australia, the United States, Japan, Russia, Central Europe, England, Germany and the Netherlands.

- Schools modelled on the pedagogy of French educator Célestin Freinet (Acker, 2007) see the child's interest and natural curiosity as a starting point for learning and attempt to use real experiences of children as authentic opportunities for learning. Children are encouraged to learn by cooperatively making products or providing services. In Freinet schools, students are familiarised with democratic self-government to take responsibility for themselves and for their community. Today, Freinet schools exist mostly in France, Belgium and Germany, often as alternative schools within the public school system.

- Peter Petersen's Jenaplan-Schule (Hansen-Schaberg and Schonig, 1997), founded as a progressive education project in 1927, is based on three core ideas: autonomous student work, living and learning in a community, and students and parent participation in school life. Learning takes place in mixed-age-groups. A typical school day consists of a 100-minute block, in which students work on an interdisciplinary project, autonomous student work on self-chosen projects as well as ritualised times of deliberation, play and celebration. Today, schools modelled on the original Jenaplan exist in Germany and the Netherlands but do not form an organised network.

While most alternative education models described so far are rooted in the progressivist education movement of the 20th Century, two recently founded alternative schools, the Swiss Institut Beatenberg and the Canadian PROTIC, serve as examples of 21st Century models of alternative education, based on constructivist theories of learning:

- Institut Beatenberg focuses on the organisation of student self-efficacy and meta-cognition, thus laying a foundation for lifelong learning. Students learn alone or in small groups on self-designed learning projects coached by their teachers. They evaluate their work aided by rubrics and document learning processes and results in portfolios. "Intensive training sessions" and "special learning days" offer structured opportunities for skill development and knowledge acquisition in small-group-settings.

- PROTIC, an alternative school within a state school in Quebec City, Canada, was founded in response to parent demand for modern, constructivist forms of learning. It organises the development of social, cognitive and meta-cognitive competences through ICT-supported interdisciplinary learning projects. In small groups, students solve interdisciplinary problems by means of active research, investigation and experimentation, complementary group work and the presentation of results. Self and peer evaluation using rubrics and portfolios serve to develop meta-cognitive skills seen as a prerequisite for lifelong learning.

4.3. Understanding the culture of learning in alternative forms of education

The conception of the learner

Even if all alternative models of education perceive and organise learning as an active process based on the needs and interests of individual students, their conception of the learner differs to some extent:

- Montessori pedagogy views children as competent beings capable of self-directed learning who learn in a distinctly different way from adults. Whereas learning for adults is often a deliberate and planned process requiring intention and discipline, their "absorbent mind" lets infants and children learn naturally through interaction with their environment. In their development, children go through different sensitive periods, during which they are particularly open to learning specific skills. According to Montessori pedagogy, learning is stimulated best through the provision of a prepared environment enriched by didactic materials inviting exploration. For much of the time during the school day, students in Montessori schools are encouraged to select work that captures their interest and attention. Through active learning children acquire basic concepts in various knowledge domains. Repetition of activities is considered an integral part of the learning process, and children are allowed to repeat activities as often as they wish. If a child expresses boredom because of the repetition, the child is considered to be ready for new didactic material on the next level of learning. While there is a specific sequence of activities, there is no prescribed timetable, so that children can move through all activities at their own pace.

- Waldorf/Steiner pedagogy is based on seven-year developmental stages with particular perceptions of the learner: During early childhood, children's learning is seen as predominantly sensory-based, experiential and imitative, so that learning through doing is considered most effective. From age 7 to 14, learning is seen to be naturally imaginative, so Waldorf schools focus on developing children's emotional life and artistic expression. The gradual evolution of the capacity for abstract and conceptual thinking and moral judgement during adolescence (age 15 to 21) requires learning through intellectual understanding in integrated and partially self-initiated learning projects and active social responsibility through community service.

- Students in Round Square Schools benefit primarily from a variety of experiences that challenge them to confront and learn about their own person in a transformational way. Experiences are intentionally designed to instil moral values and to develop a range of attitudes and skills. Through confronting uncertain outcomes and acceptable risks during adventure-like outdoor activities in groups, adolescents develop tenacity, self-knowledge, physical fitness and the ability to go beyond self-imposed limitations. In heterogeneous groups, they best understand the benefits of different strengths, ideas and perspectives for mutual problem solving. Social and environmental community services instil in students a sense of responsibility and compassion for their community and the wider world and develop their capacity for leadership.

Primarily fostering an intrinsic motivation to learn, different types of alternative schools provide a considerable range of freedom to their students within reasonable limits of appropriate behaviour. Montessori schools encourage students to move about freely in their classrooms. Dalton, Freinet, Jenaplan, Steiner and other alternative schools encourage active learning in partially or fully self-directed activities. Students are encouraged to select their own work and to continue work on chosen projects over spans of hours, days, weeks and, sometimes, months.

The most radical vision of the student as a self-responsible and intrinsically motivated individual exists in democratic or free schools. In

Sands school, for example, a second-generation English democratic school, founded in 1987, children are encouraged to take responsibility for their own learning. Sands has timetabled lessons like traditional schools, but leaves it open to children to decide which courses they choose to attend. Before choosing a subject, students are encouraged to sit with their academic tutors to find out about the course. When a student commits to a subject, he or she is then expected to attend all of its lessons. If students choose not to study a subject, leaving them with a gap in their personal timetable, they are encouraged to find a constructive activity to fill that time.

The Beach School in Toronto, Ontario is based on the idea that self-initiated learning produces the most meaningful and lasting results for students. Students decide how they would like to spend their time at the school. Teachers serve as role models and resources. Every day, students determine their own activities, set goals and develop schedules and evaluate progress in order to acquire skills such as self-motivation, self-evaluation, goal-setting, creativity, time-management, persistence and leadership. The school's philosophy is that learning how to learn is more important than learning a specific skill at a certain age. By giving students the freedom to explore various aspects of their culture and environment at will, students are expected to realise that they need basic skills such as reading, writing and mathematics to fulfil their own goals in life. Providing resources for students to learn those basics at their own pace is seen as the most effective way to tap intrinsic motivation and to motivate students to challenge themselves.

Like Tamariki School, a free school in Christchurch, New Zealand, many alternative schools try to make sure that children always work at their individual level of competence. The focus of teaching strategies is to acknowledge and support what children do well, and to use these strengths in areas of weakness. It is the teachers' responsibility to ensure that any lesson is appropriate to the child requesting it, that the child's individual needs are taken into account and to assist the child to identify their next steps in learning.

The learning environment

The traditional set-up of classrooms with desks arranged in rows, an exposed teacher's desk and a board in the front of the room has been deliberately discontinued by all alternative schools. Their learning environments are set up to put the learner centre stage, to provide a wide array of learning resources and to facilitate individual as well as collaborative learning. As alternative models of education tend to emphasise the interrelation between effective learning and the learner's emotional well-being, they often pay special attention to the aesthetic side of learning environments. Waldorf school architecture often takes up organic shapes and forms, such as rounded walls. As Waldorf attempts to educate the whole human being, "head, heart and hands", through an integrated curriculum emphasising imagination, the set-up of Waldorf classrooms reflects the broad range of creative and artistic approaches to learning through colour and form (using paint, clay, wood and metal), drama, bodily movement, singing and dance. The systematic display of students' work is a core feature of many alternative learning environments.

Maria Montessori claimed that the design of schools was to transcend functionality to create spaces matching children's needs (DeJesus, 2000). Thus, in Montessori pedagogy learning takes place in classrooms which are "bright, warm, and inviting, filled with plants, animals, art, music, and books" (Montessori Way, p. 247), both comfortable and allowing a maximum amount of independence. Children learn through active discovery of their environment, in which didactic materials are presented in a stimulating and challenging way. Montessori classrooms are organised into several curriculum areas, each of which is made up of one or more shelf units, cabinets and display tables with a wide variety of materials on open display, ready for use as students select them. As children are seen as learning through discovery, learning materials are self-contained and self-correcting as much as possible. Many of the didactic materials are specific in design, conforming to exact dimensions, and each activity is designed to focus on a single skill, concept or exercise. Other materials are often constructed by teachers themselves and tend to be made of natural materials. In addition, most classrooms include a library as well as ways for the children to interact with the natural world, usually through a classroom pet or a small garden.

Whereas Waldorf education objects to the use of computers in learning environments up to grade eight, modern Montessori classrooms, even on the elementary level, often include ICT learning opportunities. In Montessori schools, students will typically be found scattered around the classroom, working alone or with one or two others. Montessori schools work with mixed-age groups, with each classroom including an approximately three-year age range. This system is seen to enhance flexibility in learning pace and to create a non-competitive atmosphere of mutual learning and support allowing children to teach others by sharing what they have learned.

As students at alternative schools are given considerable freedom to choose learning activities they desire, or feel the need, to do, alternative education often uses the community as a deliberate extension to the classroom, and students use various in-school and community resources including people, natural resources and cultural institutions to enrich their own learning.

The role of teachers

As can be seen from the various pathways in teacher education for alternative schools, there is no uniform definition of "the teacher" in alternative education. Given the range of different conceptions of learning and teaching in alternative schools, it is easier to describe what a teacher in alternative education is not: As all models of alternative education are learner-focused, teachers are never seen as mere agents of curriculum delivery. With varying degrees of intervention, the teacher role ranges from being a coach on the side that students can draw on (but do not have to) to a provider, organiser and manager of customised learning in experiential learning environments.

The least interventionist teacher's role can be found in democratic or free schools. At Summerhill, for example, teachers teach classes at scheduled times but students get to decide whether they attend the classes. The Swiss Institut Beatenberg defines teachers as "personal coaches" who, in one-to-one sessions, help individual children understand their own learning and motivation and set aims for themselves.

Tamariki School in Christchurch, New Zealand has developed explicit guidelines that reflect the demanding role of teachers in free/democratic schools: children's learning is to be under their own control to a large extent. It is the teacher's responsibility to work at the balance between support and intrusion and to know when not to interfere with a child's activity. Any teacher-initiated activities are to be introduced in a non-invasive way, *e.g.* by having materials available when children are ready for a lesson. Teachers are to recognise and follow up the child's interests and needs and, when appropriate, to assist the child in articulating these. Children are free to choose what teacher to work with so that teachers need to be able to recognise when a child may wish to work with a different teacher. To resolve conflicts, teachers have to use an elaborate system of requests and meetings, in which a teacher has the same rights as a child. Play is regarded as children's *work*, and it is thus the teacher's responsibility to provide an environment in which activities may be carried through to their natural conclusion and not be interrupted arbitrarily by adult demands. If they request them, children alone or in groups receive lessons in language and maths, for which teachers have to be available and prepared. Special programmes are, however, offered for those children who are not showing any literacy or numeracy skills by the age 7 1/2.

The Waldorf-Steiner pedagogy with its strong focus on students' emotional and ethical development emphasises longer-term student-teacher relationships that allow teachers to respond better to each child's emotional and developmental needs. The so-called "class teacher" often teaches the same group of children for up to eight years. The schools' holistic approach of curriculum delivery requires that teachers integrate teaching methods and materials in creative ways based on their own judgement. A class teacher is responsible for a two-hour "main lesson" every morning and usually for one or two lessons later in the day. During the main lesson, the teacher tries to integrate several of the core academic subjects with imaginative and creative activities such as painting, music and drama.

The role of teachers in Montessori schools is more indirect: one of their main tasks is to prepare a stimulating learning environment consisting of self-contained and self-correcting learning materials adequate for the developmental stage particular children are in. Whereas materials for younger children can often be bought ready-made, Montessori teachers at higher grade levels spend considerable time creating learning materials fitting the particular needs of a diversified curriculum and growing student capacities.

Several alternative schools have abandoned the one teacher per classroom tradition. In most Montessori classrooms there is a lead teacher supported by a second teacher or an assistant. Teachers will normally be working with one or two children at a time, advising and observing students working individually or in small self-selected groups. At many alternative schools, teachers spend more time mentoring and facilitating the learning process of individuals or small groups than directly giving lessons. In a school based on the concept of customised learning for individual children, teachers require significant diagnostic skills as they have to present individual students with new challenging material based on the competence level they have achieved.

Many alternative schools make room for experiential education in larger projects. At Round Square and Outward Bound schools, this is the predominant pedagogic approach. Experiential education is a methodology in which teachers purposefully engage with learners in hands-on experiences and focused reflection in order to increase knowledge, develop skills and clarify values. Teachers arrange challenging experiences, in which learners are able to take initiative, make decisions and are accountable for results. It is the teacher's task to pose problems and support learners during the process of learning though doing and experience, insuring their physical and emotional safety. A key teacher competence lies in recognising authentic learning opportunities. As the possibility to learn from natural consequences, mistakes and successes are seen as main benefits attributed to authentic experience and problem solving, teachers need to be able to deal with ambiguity, uncertainty, risk and failure in a professional manner.

Curricula and the content of learning

Most alternative schools enjoy considerable freedom in the design of their curricula. The older the students, however, that they teach, the more schools tend to align core content of their teaching with central exams and state requirements. A noticeable commonality between most alternative schools is their attempt to teach an integrated curriculum that does not strictly separate traditional subject areas but rather emphasises the interconnections between the disciplines. The Montessori curriculum follows an integrated thematic approach, tying together separate disciplines into studies of the physical universe, the world of nature and the human experience. In the prepared learning environment typical of Montessori schools, children proceed at their own pace from concrete objects and tactile experiences to abstract thinking, writing, reading, science and mathematics. Each activity leads to a new level of learning. The core purpose of the hands-on math materials, for example, is to make abstract concepts clear and concrete, to lay the foundation for cognitive development and to prepare for the gradual transition to abstract thinking. In language development, didactic material foster lexicon development, communication skills, writing and reading readiness. Science, as an integral part of the Montessori curriculum, teaches gathering information, thinking and structured problem solving. Music and the Arts offer children ways to express themselves, their feelings, experiences and ideas.

The curriculum at Waldorf schools is organised as an ascending spiral: a long lesson starts off each day, focusing on one subject for a block of several weeks. Each subject is introduced in a particular grade and is subsequently taught in a block of several weeks on a slightly higher level each year. All students participate in all basic subjects regardless of their talent or interest because Waldorf education commits to the idea that every human being needs a broad basic understanding of the world. In addition, older students in Waldorf schools pursue special projects and can choose from a range of electives. The Waldorf curriculum is built on the concepts of vertical and horizontal education. The ascending spiral of the curriculum offers a vertical integration of subject knowledge from year to year. Horizontal integration is achieved through integrating cognitive learning with the arts and practical skills at every stage. Children are to experience that everybody can strive for a unity of knowledge and experience. The long main lesson allows teachers to develop a wide variety of activities around the subject taught. After the day's lesson, which includes a review of earlier learning, students record what they learned in their notebooks. Following a break, teachers present shorter lessons with a less project-based and more instructional character. Foreign languages are taught starting in first grade, typically later in the morning. Afternoons are devoted to lessons in which the children are active in the arts and crafts.

Dalton schools try to individualise learning as much as possible within a defined but flexible curriculum. In all subject areas, learning takes place on a one-to-one basis, in small groups or as part of whole class activities. Whenever possible, children are encouraged to become active and independent learners, writing their own little books, undertaking independent research projects in social studies and science, conducting community service projects, painting a mural or performing in a dance project.

In free schools such as Summerhill or Sands, both teachers and students are curriculum resources. Teachers often contribute more than just the subject area they are experts in. They are required to act as learning coaches, helping students to learn whatever they are interested in. Just like in mainstream schools, students at Summerhill have a timetable, but classes and projects are non-compulsory. At the beginning of term all students receive blank timetables on which they devise their individual lesson plans. Children below the age of 12 have their own teachers and classrooms with multi-activity spaces. Teachers provide a timetable for the week and organise activities in response to the children's needs and wishes. Older students sign up at the beginning of term for a wide variety of subjects and projects. The idea is to allow the students to make informed choices within the context of a structured day. All Summerhill teachers have considerable freedom concerning teaching methods and objectives, but are assisted by curriculum advisors who discuss teaching aims, methods and practices. Senior teachers are expected to be able to teach their subjects at the level of the national exams for 16-year-olds. Although Summerhill offers more or less the same formal subjects as most traditional schools, students and teachers offer a variety of projects and activities that can be selected within the timetable ranging from "airplane construction" to "making a radio play".

At Institut Beatenberg in Switzerland, the curriculum is passed on through elaborate rubrics that define competence levels in various subject areas. With the help of their "learning coach", students are encouraged to identify the level they are on and to set specific and measurable goals for themselves on how to achieve the next level. At the beginning of every week, students write down these goals in a weekly learning plan and with the help of their learning coaches formulate specific activities to work on alone or in small groups. In addition to these self-directed learning activities, teacher-led intensive trainings and special learning days help scaffold the development of skills and the acquisition of knowledge.

The function and culture of assessment

Alternative schools share the conviction that children and adolescents learn most effectively when they are interested in and motivated for a topic or a project. For obvious reasons, this core paradigm of alternative education shapes the form, function and culture of assessment in alternative schools. This orientation towards fostering intrinsic rather than extrinsic motivation influences the design of learning environments and the devolution of freedom, choice and responsibility to students. All alternative schools focus on the individual child and his or her specific talents, interests, learning style and learning speed. Social comparison between children is discouraged and for that reason, traditional forms of testing and summative assessments are objected to, given the social benchmarking they invite. Summerhill, for example, does not send reports to parents unless both children and parents actively ask for feedback.

Alternative schools tend to focus on individual and criterion-referenced forms of assessment, such as learning reports, learning logs and portfolios, in which students document and reflect their own learning. In Waldorf pedagogy, for example, standardised testing is considered problematic, especially in the elementary years, because it is believed that such testing does not measure valuable attributes of children such as curiosity and initiative, creativity and imagination, good will and ethical reflection. The Montessori method also discourages traditional measurements of achievement such as grades and tests as potentially damaging to a child's self-concept. By reason of their critical perspective on traditional summative assessment, alternative schools have devoted considerable thought and creativity to developing, testing and improving alternative forms of assessment suitable to their overall philosophy. Many of the so-called "authentic forms" of assessment that are used in mainstream education today originated in alternative schools. Alternative schools have developed elaborate forms of feedback and qualitative analysis of students' performances, which tend to be provided either as lists or rubrics of skills, activities and critical points or as narratives of an individual student's achievements, strengths and developmental needs, with emphasis on providing the student and his or her parents with detailed information on the improvement of those developmental needs.

Tamariki School in New Zealand has made it a principle that "mistakes are regarded as important learning information" and has developed corresponding guidelines for teachers on the school's culture of formative assessment. At Tamariki School, Institut Beatenberg and most other alternative schools children are encouraged to compare their work and skills with their own previous achievements and their own goals. Teachers are responsible to ensure that assessment processes are non-invasive and do not provoke anxiety. At Tamariki School, teachers have to ask a child's permission before retaining samples of their work. It is the teacher's responsibility to relate the child's learning to the national achievement objectives and to identify causes of difficulty. The overall principle underlying the culture of assessment at most alternative schools is to support the individual child on the basis of a "credit" not a "debit" model.

4.4. Alternative education in light of recent research in the learning sciences

The emergence of the learning sciences allows for a critical reassessment of learning environments in light of what we know about the cognitive and social processes that result in effective learning. The criticism of the standard model of schooling expressed over the past two centuries seems to have gained new support in light of recent findings in the learning sciences. On the one hand, they confirm the shortcomings of the traditional transmission and acquisition model of schooling; on the other hand, they provide empirical support for core features of many alternative schools: their instructional methodology focusing on experience and reflection, their integrated curriculum and their focus on independent and customised learning combined with formative assessment.

There is sound evidence now showing that the "deep conceptual understanding of complex concepts, and the ability to work with them creatively to generate new ideas, new theories, new products, and new knowledge" (Sawyer, Chapter 2) is best achieved in complex social settings enabling processes that involve learners, tools and other people in the environment in activities in which knowledge is being applied. As Sawyer underlines it, traditional structures of schooling "make it very hard to create learning environments that result in deeper understanding". These findings provide backing for the experiential, project-, problem-based and collaborative learning that many alternative schools have been focusing on. In constructivist learning environments, students gain expertise from a variety of sources beyond the teacher (Greeno, 2006). There is also evidence that the knowledge society's need for more integrated and usable knowledge is best met by more integrated and deep (rather than broad) curricula, as used by many alternative schools.

Another area in which the emerging sciences of learning seem to confirm the assumptions underlying alternative schools is their strong focus on the individual learner. It is now clear from cognitive research that learning always takes place against a backdrop of existing knowledge, which differs from learner to learner. Whereas many traditional schools still practice a "one size fits all" model, according to which every student of a certain age is supposed to learn the same thing at the same time, most alternative schools provide their students with a more customised learning experience, often mixing students of different ages in the same classroom. Findings from the learning sciences reconfirm the potential effectiveness of individualised forms of learning as long as the learning settings are sensitive to the learners' pre-existing cognitive structures. More independent, negotiated forms of learning, as practised in alternative schools, also seem to prepare for the knowledge society's requirement of intrinsically motivated individuals able to take responsibility for their own continuing, lifelong learning. Finally, alternative schools seem to be able to contribute to some extent to the quest for more effective forms of assessment testing profound rather than superficial knowledge on the one hand and facilitating further learning through formative feedback on the other.

Given the range of features at alternative schools that seem to make sense from a learning sciences perspective, could alternative schools thus serve as models for a broader renewal of mainstream education in the knowledge society? To a certain extent, it seems, alternative schools have already played that role in recent years, because so many of the instructional strategies and assessment techniques they developed have impacted learning and teaching in public school systems across the world.

Nonetheless, it needs to be said that so much depends on the professionalism of individual teachers, be it in mainstream or alternative education. To assess the effectiveness of any alternative pedagogical approach, it would thus be necessary to take a closer look at teacher professionalism and the measurable effects of learning.

Deep understanding (Carver, 2006) develops when learning is integrated with reflection or meta-cognition. Most effective learning takes place when teachers help students to achieve their learning goals and to articulate their developing understanding through scaffolding, which "is gradually added, modified, and removed according to the needs of the learner" (Collins, 2006; Sawyer, Chapter 2). Effective learning requires a high level of teacher professionalism in the design of learning environments and experiences and the scaffolding of individual students' learning. To foster effective learning, teachers, at alternative and mainstream schools alike, need the ability to facilitate learning in individual, small group and class settings.

Wherever educational alternatives combine customised learning with collaborative group learning in authentic, inquiry-oriented projects, provide their students with access to diverse knowledge sources and assess them for deeper understanding and further learning, alternative schools seem to be ahead of mainstream education and can serve as meaningful models for the renewal of mainstream education across the globe.

References

Acker, V. (2007), *The French Educator Celestin Freinet (1896-1966): An Inquiry into How his Ideas Shaped Education*, Lexington Books, Lanham, MD.

Aron, L.Y. (2003), *Towards a Typology of Alternative Education Programs: a Compilation of Elements from the Literature*, The Urban Institute, Washington, DC.

Ayers, W. (2003), *On the Side of the Child: Summerhill Revisited*, Teachers College Press, New York.

Bereiter, C. (2002), *Education and Mind in the Knowledge Age*, Erlbaum, Mahwah, NJ.

Bransford, J.D., A.L. Brown and R.R. Cocking (eds.) (2000), *How People Learn: Brain, Mind, Experience, and School*, National Academy Press, Washington, DC.

Carnie, F. (2003), *Alternatives in Education – A Guide*, Routledge Falmer, London.

Carver, S.M. (2006), "Assessing for Deep Understanding" in R.K. Sawyer (ed.), *The Cambridge Handbook of the Learning Sciences*, Cambridge University Press, New York, pp. 205-221.

Clouder, C. and M. Rawson (2003), *Waldorf Education: Rudolf Steiner's Ideas in Practice*, Floris, Edinburgh.

Collins, A. (2006), "Cognitive Apprenticeship", in R.K. Sawyer (ed.), *Cambridge Handbook of the Learning Sciences*, Cambridge New York, pp. 47-60.

Cremin, L. (1978), "The Free School Movement", in T. Deal and R. Nolan (eds.), *Alternative Schools: Ideologies, Realities, Guidelines*, Nelson Hall, Chicago, pp. 204-282.

Deal, T. (1978), "Overview", in T. Deal and R. Nolan (eds.), *Alternative Schools: Ideologies, Realities, Guidelines*, Nelson Hall, Chicago, pp. 1-63.

DeJesus, R. (2000), *Design Guidelines for Montessori Schools. Milwaukee*, Univ. of Wisconsin-Milwaukee, Center for Architecture/Urban Planning Research.

Dewey, J. (1916), *Democracy and Education; an Introduction to the Philosophy of Education*, Macmillan, New York.

Flavin, M. (1996), *Kurt Hahn's Schools and Legacy: To Discover You Can Be More and Do More Than You Believed*, Middle Atlantic Press, Wilmington, Delaware.

Freire, P. (2000), *Pedagogy of the Oppressed*, Continuum, London.

Greeno, J.G. (2006), "Learning in Activity", in R.K. Sawyer (ed.), *Cambridge Handbook of the Learning Sciences*, Cambridge, New York, pp. 79-96.

Gribble, D. (1998), *Real Education – Varieties of Freedom*, Libertarian Education, Bristol.

Hansen-Schaberg, I. and B. Schonig (1997), Basiswissen Pädagogik, Reformpädagogische Schulkonzepte, Bd.3, Jenaplan-Pädagogik, Schneider Verlag, Hohengehren.

Hargreaves, A. (2003), *Teaching in the Knowledge Society: Education in the Age of Insecurity*, Teacher's College Press, New York.

Harms, W. and I. De Pencier (1996), *Experiencing Education: 100 Years of Learning at the University of Chicago Laboratory Schools*, University of Chicago Laboratory Schools, Chicago.

Hayes, W. (2006), *The Progressive Education Movement: Is it Still a Factor in Today's' Schools?*, Rowman and Littlefield, New York.

Hentig, H. (2006), *Die Schule neu denken*, Beltz, Weinheim.

Holt, J. (1995), *How Children Fail*, Perseus, New York.

Illich, I. (1996), *Deschooling Society*, Marion Boyers, London.

Kahn, D., S. Dubble and D.R. Pendleton (1999), *The Whole-School Montessori Handbook*, NAMTA, Cleveland, OH.

Kellmayer, J. (1995), *How to Establish an Alternative School*, Corwin Press, Thousand Oaks, California.

Koetzsch, R. (1997), *The Parents' Guide to Alternative Education*, Shambala, Boston.

Kohl, H. (1998), *The Discipline of Hope*, Simon and Schuster, New York.

Kohn, A. (1999), *The Schools Children Deserve*, Houghton Mifflin, New York.

Kozol, J. (1972), *Free Schools*, Houghton Mifflin, Boston.

Krajcik, J.S. and P. Blumenfeld (2006), "Project Based Learning", in R.K. Sawyer (ed.), *Cambridge Handbook of the Learning Sciences*, Cambridge University Press, New York, pp. 317-333.

Lamb, A. (ed.) (1995), *A.S. Neill: Summerhill School – A New View of Childhood*, St.Martin's Griffin, New York.

Lillard, P.P. (1996), *Montessori Today: A Comprehensive Approach to Education from Birth to Adulthood*, Schocken, New York.

Linn, M.C. (2006), "The Knowledge Integration Perspective on Learning and Instruction", in R.K. Sawyer (ed.), *The Cambridge Handbook of the Learning Sciences*, Cambridge University Press, New York, pp. 243-264.

Masters, B. (2005), *Adventures in Steiner Education: An Introduction to the Waldorf Approach*, Rudolf Steiner Press, Forest Row/United Kingdom.

Miller, R. (2007), *A Brief History of Alternative Education*, www.educationrevolution.org/history

Mintz, J., R. Solomon and S. Solomon (1994), *The Handbook of Alternative Education*, MacMillan, London.

Montessori, M. (1912/2002), *The Montessori Method*, Dover Publications, New York.

Montessori, M. (1949/1995), *The Absorbent Mind*, Henry Holt & Co, New York.

Parkhurst, H. (1922), *Education on the Dalton Plan*, E.P. Dutton & Co, New York.

Petrash, J. (2002), *Understanding Waldorf Education: Teaching from the Inside Out*, Gryphon House, Bletsville, MD.

Popp, S. (1995), Der Daltonplan in Theorie und Praxis, Bad Heilbrunn, Julius Klinkhardt.

Raywid, M.A. (1988), "Alternative Schools: What Makes Them Alternative?", *The Education Digest*, Vol. 54, No. 3, pp. 11-12.

Raywid, M.A. (1994), *Alternative Schools: The State of the Art. Educational Leadership*, September, pp. 26-31.

Raywid, M.A. (1999), "History and Issues of Alternative Schools", *The Education Digest*, May, pp. 47-51.

Rofes, E. and L.M. Stulberg (eds.) (2004), *The Emancipatory Promise of Charter Schools*, State University of New York Press, Albany.

Rogoff, B. (1998), "Cognition as a Collaborative Process", in D. Kuhn and R.S. Siegler (eds.), *Handbook of Child Psychology, 5th edition, Vol. 2: Cognition, Perception, and Language*, Wiley, New York, pp. 679-744.

Röhner, R. and H. Wenke (2002), Dalton-onderwijs, een blijvende inspiratie, Arko, Nieuwegein.

Sawyer, R.K. (ed.) (2006b), *Cambridge Handbook of the Learning Sciences*, Cambridge University Press, New York.

Seldin T. and P. Epstein (2003), *The Montessori Way: An Education for Life*, The Montessori Foundation.

Tacy, P. (2006), *Ideals at Work: Education for World Stewardship in the Round Square Schools*, Deerfield Academy Press, Deerfield, MA.

Websites

Brockwood Park School: *www.brockwood.org.uk*

Dalton schools: *www.daltoninternational.org*

Democratic schools: *www.Educationrevolution.org*

Escuelas Nuevas: *www.volvamos.org/*

Freinet schools: *www.freinet.org*

Institut Beatenberg, Switzerland: *www.institut-beatenberg.ch*

Jenaplan-Schule/Germany: *www.jenaplan-schule-jena.de/*

Landerziehungsheime: *www.leh-internate.de*

Montessori schools, the Montessori Foundation: *www.montessori.org*

PROTIC/Canada: *www.protic.net*

Round Square Schools: *www.roundsquare.org*

Sands School: *www.sands-school.co.uk*

Sudbury Valley School/USA: *www.sudval.org*

Summerhill School: *www.summerhillschool.co.uk*

Tamariki School/New Zealand: *www.tamariki.school.nz/*

The Beach School, Canada: *www.thebeachschool.org*

Waldorf schools: Association of Waldorf Schools in North America: *www.awsna.org* and European Council of Steiner-Waldorf Education: *www.ecswe.org*

Chapter 5
Situated Pedagogies, Curricular Justice and Democratic Teaching
by
Mar Rodríguez-Romero[1]

This chapter explores new forms of teaching and learning – pedagogical alternatives which are committed to challenging unquestioned school traditions. The notion that the transformation of traditional grade school pedagogy can enlarge the possibilities of personal, community and social development is explored.

Advances in knowledge in western cultures have largely ignored the existing knowledge from everyday practices that "unknown" actors deploy in order to improve their ways of life, work and education. This kind of rationality, which Boaventura de Sousa Santos (2003) calls "indolent", has encouraged the systematic waste of experience. Considerable problems and awareness of the exhaustion of the frames of reference that have habitually been used until now for leading humanity towards better levels of dignity, mean we cannot allow ourselves to waste the wealth of knowledge which is hidden in anonymous initiatives.

These "local innovations" are essential in order to discover new forms of teaching and learning, which guide us in the difficult renovation of pedagogical orientations that have shaped the school as we have known it until now. As David Hamilton (1996) warns us, the idea of the school as a lasting institution is tied up with the Cartesian and Newtonian ideas on the

---

[1] Associate Professor and researcher of educational change and curriculum studies at the University of A Coruña. She is author of the books *El asesoramiento en educación* (Consultation in Education) and *Las metamorfosis del cambio educativo* (Metamorphoses of Educational Change).

maintenance and perpetuity of the order of things. These proposals have been responsible for the naturalisation of social institutions and the perception of them as being atemporal, ahistorical and perennial. Nevertheless, the grade school is a specific response of western societies to the issue of cultural transmission to younger generations, corresponding to a specific historical period in these societies. During this time the state acquired a predominant role in the planning and provision of social services – including education – and forms of organisation deriving from manufacturing production were introduced into educational institutions. Mass schooling has come about through institutionalisation of the grade school.[2]

This pedagogical option has allowed the education of a considerable number of students using a reduced teaching staff and has also allowed students to obtain educational qualifications through a progression of stages, after overcoming the previously fixed learning requirements for the population in the care of the state. This standard treatment of a great number of subjects explains the success of this educational modality as applied to different social groups and cultural contexts, seeking the socialisation of men and women in accordance with the universal rules of reason and the postulates of modernity. This is exactly the response needed with regard to the wider process of collectivisation of welfare activities such as care of the sick, education of the ignorant and help in times of need (Swaan, 1992) which has been the foundation of the welfare state.

In order specifically to avoid the naturalisation of grade school, I have read the four experiences discussed in the OECD International Conference on Models of Learning[3] from a problematising perspective. I have identified traditionally accepted pedagogical suppositions and have questioned them in order to explore and imagine alternatives to them (Brookfield, 1987 in Smyth, 2000), which may be called utopian if taken out of context, but

---

[2] The appearance and diffusion of the new model of school organisation is related to certain circumstances, such as: implantation of the mutual method – simultaneous or mixed – which has been very useful for inculcating habits of discipline and order; grouping of children with a similar average level of knowledge in different spaces with a single teacher, as a result of the need for classification and selection; the establishment of a general study plan, subdivided by disciplines, academic years, courses and grades; the parallel configuration of sections, grades or courses along with the exams necessary to pass from one to the other; the repetitions and failure or success of the students. See Keith Sawyer's Chapter 2 as well as A. Viñao Frago (1990), *Innovación pedagógica y racionalidad científica: la escuela graduada pública en España (1889-1936)*, Akal, Madrid.

[3] The OECD-Mexico International Conference: "Emerging Models of Learning and Innovation" was held on June 14-16, 2006 in Merida Yucatan, Mexico.

which nevertheless are feasible, as shown by their development at local level and in the experiences related in the case studies. They are experiences that speak of the utopian realism of marginalised people and social groups who, despite all adversities, try to construct local alternatives in order to make a dignified and decent life possible here and now (de Sousa Santos, 2003).[4] The case studies offer us examples of practical alternatives in education that are related to three pedagogical orientations with great potential: **situated pedagogies, curricular justice** and **democratic teaching and learning**. Lastly, the courage shown by educators participating in the case studies requires reflection on the type of educational professional needed to kick-start authentic learning processes that increase the dignity of students and their capacity for more complete self-development, however adverse the starting conditions may be.

5.1. Situated pedagogies and situated learning

The sphere of local action, clearly seen in two of the case studies carried out by the Friendship Centre (Case 1) and in BICAP (Case 4) is consistent with **situated pedagogies**. All educational practices are situated in the sense that they are rooted in the dense particularities of specific situations and respond to specific legacies of privilege and repression brought in by teachers and students (Miller, 1996). Recognising this particularity, situated pedagogies form a proposal to focus on education and learning in a contextualised manner – exactly the opposite of what is sought by grade schools.[5] They allow interventions in the multiple facets of exclusion according to the specific forms that discrimination adopts for each group and in each educational context. As can be seen in the case studies, the presence of different types of exclusion complicates pedagogical intervention, given that each form of domination makes use of the others and each of them are mutually reinforcing in very complex ways (Harding, 1996). For example, if we take as a reference the study of the intersection

---

[4] For example, the investigation carried out by Boaventura de Sousa Santos, "The reinvention of social emancipation" that tracks down the base initiatives in various countries related to alternative globalisation, has shown the rich social experience that occurs regarding alternative actions and which nevertheless is wasted, allowing the idea of the impossibility of alternatives to neoliberal globalisation to remain intact. The project may be consulted at *www.ces.uc.pt/emancipa*

[5] Recently it has shown signs of its potential in change initiatives applied to indigenous education in remote and rural areas in Australia, in which situated pedagogy is a decisive conceptual reference because it characterises education starting from its social, historical and spatial localisation (McConaghy, 2002).

between race, gender and class exclusions at local school level, we can state that they will produce interruptions, discontinuities, increases and decreases in the original effects that any of these dynamics might produce (McCarthy, 1993).[6] Contextualised actions are required to put the appropriate strategies into practice and to overcome the specific forms adopted by inequality in each educational setting.

Situated pedagogies make use of local commitment. This type of commitment has an emancipatory focus because it works against exclusion with a strategic and diversified orientation, in order to take advantage of the potential of grassroots educational experiences. If teaching itself obliges one to develop idiosyncratic processes, then the recognition of the impossibility of having a totalising and generalised vision of the good things in education makes it even more necessary to work with local commitment. This kind of commitment is the best suited to respond to the multiple identities of people and social groups, as well as to the diversity of demands made according to the idea of teaching and learning that they sustain. Local commitment permits adaptation to each context and provides a strategic vision according to the specific demands and potential of the different groups (especially vulnerable groups). It can also be revised in order to combine – in a critical way – with the evolution of the needs and new understanding that result from the mutual deliberation and legitimisation processes it seeks to set in motion. Given that it is a mode of emancipatory commitment, it has a clear political dimension – as Jennifer Gore (1996) reminds us – because it allows us to deal with alternative visions of education and of society constructed at local level. It is precisely this quality that is appropriate for promoting the experimentation of alternatives in the field of community, as in the case studies for the Friendship Centre (Case 1) and BICAP (Case 4).

Situated pedagogy can maximise the emergence of experimental initiatives based on feasible expectations that respond to real possibilities and abilities. This is because they work with contextual expectations and their main interest lies in channelling the viability of the alternatives, without undervaluing any reflection on them. However, one needs the commitment of the state and autonomous and local governments, which should ensure the necessary conditions for carrying out experimentation with guarantees. This protection will only be available to those teaching initiatives that are united in the safeguarding of certain democratic virtues such as respect for minority rights and the freedom of subjects, the

---

[6] As Cameron McCarthy (1993) has shown, the dynamic relations of race, social class and gender have contradictory effects at everyday level of school practices, producing an asynchronous context in which the three dynamics constantly shape – and are shaped by – the others.

promotion of equality in relation to cultural opportunities and economic goods, as well as respect for social differences and the development of relations of care and support. How then does one envision teaching and learning within the framework of situated pedagogies? Cognitive studies using socio-cultural focuses are revitalising already-known teaching strategies that are being renewed with the aid of situated learning and situated teaching.

Situated learning and **situated teaching** find support in **situated knowledge**.[7] This perspective conceptualises knowledge as being partial and localised as well as forming part of and being produced by the activity, context and culture in which it is generated (Díaz Barriga, 2003). From a situated perspective, knowledge and identity are recreated through interaction and participation in culturally significant activities. Situated teaching seeks to promote authentic – *i.e.* significant – educational practices in relation to a particular culture and community. The authenticity of an educational practice may be defined according to the cultural relevance it possesses for students and by the type and level of social activity it produces (Derry, Levin and Schnauble, 1995 in Díaz Barriga, 2003). Authentic practices are also committed to high-level cognitive processes and to civic and democratic learning.[8]

It is no coincidence that the concept of situated teaching and learning revitalises the legacy of two great thinkers like Lev Vygotsky (1995 and 2000) and John Dewey (2004). Both incorporate indices of modernity in their theories; for example, one sees affinities in the communitarian dimension of their approaches and both could be considered pragmatic theorists in their conception of teaching and learning as being "something conditional and contingent". According to Vygotsky, who constitutes an essential reference of all socio-cultural learning theory (Popkewitz, 1998 in Daniels, 2003, p. 21), members of a culture appropriate it through interaction with the most experienced members. Therefore the negotiation of

---

[7] Different intellectual fields are theorising about situated epistemology, including Donna Hathaway in the field of Poststructuralist Feminism (1996), and Harry Daniels in the field of pedagogy and psychology (2003).

[8] As can be seen in the project "Schooling Reform and Social Justice in Queensland" (McConaghy, 2002), dimensions considered important include the intellectual quality relating to high-level thought, deep knowledge and understanding; second, they mention the relevance of understanding which refers to the integration of knowledge and its relation to the real world, including its application in problem solving; third, they include the existence of a supportive atmosphere in the classroom; and fourth, the recognition of differences with respect to the presence of culturally different sets of knowledge, inclusion, group identity and citizenship.

meaning and the shared construction of knowledge are key elements and learning revolves around reciprocal action in social contexts. For Dewey and his theory of learning through experience, education is authentic if it is produced through experience, which accompanies reflection, along with the desire to know more about one's learning and about democratic and humanitarian values. Learning through experience works with real situations and valuable experiences in order to generate positive changes in people and to have an impact by reinforcing the bond between the community and the school.

Frida Díaz Barriga (2003) presents a selection of didactic strategies that are used in situated teaching and which characteristically allow the student to confront real-life phenomena in a direct or simulated way. The intention is to allow the application and transfer of knowledge in a significant way, to manage social situations through contributing to the development of the community, as well as to relate thought and action and develop reflexive abilities when dealing with social problems and ethical questions. Her list of didactic strategies includes: resolving real problems, case analysis, the Project Method, practices in real settings, learning based on service to the community – which interestingly, coincides with BICAP (Case 4) – cooperative teamwork, situated demonstrations and simulations and learning mediated by the new information and communication technologies.[9] Some of these are "pedagogical classics", such as the Project Method; others represent the signs of identity of the initiatives of democratic learning, such as teamwork, or are associated with the development of complex learning processes, as in the case of problem solving. As the author recognises, the conceptual framework of situated cognition is renewing the possibilities for the application of all of them (Díaz Barriga, 2003). In this group we could undoubtedly include María Montessori's pedagogical orientation as adapted by the Friendship Centre and the method of teaching used in Case 4 (BICAP) which is contextualised and rooted in the community. All of these also clearly challenge the uniform methods of the grade school.

In the framework of situated pedagogies, teaching is sensitive to cultural difference meaning that the cultural and linguistic base of students from silenced social groups is relevant for teaching staff. Since the pedagogy which prevails against cultural difference is based on structural separation or seeks total assimilation, education should engage in the profound transformation of ideologies, because educational decisions which repress or give value to cultural differences are a product of social beliefs, as well as of the power relations between groups struggling to establish spaces of social

---

[9] See monographic issues "Aprendizaje-servicio", *Cuadernos de Pedagogía,* p. 357, 2006, y "Proyectos de Trabajo", *Cuadernos de Pedagogía,* p. 332, 2004.

influence. This requires a comprehensive alternative framework, one which allows us to overcome obsolete views of literacy. This key is provided by socio-cultural focuses, especially the **liberational literacy** proposed by James Gee (2005).

From this theoretical position, one interprets cultural difference as a matter related to the diversity of cultural models of social groups and to the conflicts that students find when models originating in their home culture clash with those of the majority culture and the culture of the school. Socio-cultural groups realise their meaningful differences – that is to say, their options and conjectures – according to certain beliefs and values that form part of a special type of theory that James Gee calls **cultural models**. These are popular models or schemes that contain shared – generally unconscious – suppositions or principal myths about the world. Cultural models are representations of the simplified worlds in which typical events are developed. They are related to determined metaphors, or turns of phrase and thought that capture the key ways of thinking of a group or society. They have come to seem invisible, natural and common-sensical, although for other cultures and in other eras they have been considered inappropriate and exotic. As they make our thoughts and perceptions routine, they facilitate our understanding of the world, but in contrast they prevent us from seeing other forms of thinking which might co-exist with our own. Cultural models are learned through acculturation, by having experiences in a culture, by exercising the language and interaction in the natural and meaningful contexts in which typical events are put into practice.

How can we focus them so that they are productive from the educational point of view? One could try to make conflicts between cultural models forming part of the teaching process and allow teaching staff to draw the relevant aspects of the cultural models to the attention of students, both in the home culture and in many other identities, as well as in the majority and school culture. The teacher could point out the relevant details, focusing attention on prominent aspects of experiences so that a network of cultural models begins to form, one to which the students should have access. Working with culturally relevant material should "centre the student's attention" on the conflicts produced between the cultural models of different socio-cultural groups, examining the contents, ways of using them and the values and perspectives that they entail. The goal is that students should transcend both the cultural models of their home culture and that of the majority and school cultures (Gee, 2005). The school, which gives relevance to students' culture, constructs what Sonia Nieto (1998) calls a **third space**: a space for social change where various cultures, discourses and sets of knowledge are accessible to all the participants. As James Gee (2005) states, people who control various contending discourses implant the seeds of change, especially if – through learning and taking advantage of the conflict – one can establish critiques between discourses in such a way that a metalevel understanding of various discourses can be constructed. This is the ultimate aim of liberational literacy.

The acceptance of these kinds of transformation on the part of the school and educational community requires a certain impetus. Inequality is strongly rooted in social institutions; in education this is a terrain often unwilling to change due to the pressure of local elite groups to maintain the traditional academic curriculum, along with the social selection that the school favours. It is necessary to drive a process of negotiation that shows the tolerance thresholds of the community with respect to the increase in educational equality policies. Precisely within those margins, Jennifer Oakes *et al.* (1998) localise a **mediation zone** in which it may be possible to reach agreements about defining alternatives for organising the curriculum and teaching. The mediation zone will be limited to a greater or lesser extent according to the restrictions imposed by regulations and political pressure, which interact on the local, regional, national and global levels in order to delimit it. In order for change to be significant – in terms of increasing equality – it is essential to have influence in the local sphere, by widening the mediation zone through the administrative regulations that drive transformation. From this, social groups controlling the school, which furthermore benefit from its present organisation, will find it difficult to emerge, as can be seen in Case 3 for internal migrant children (Intelligent Classroom) who are dependent on the companies that employ the families.

Educational equality policies should renegotiate the terms of mediation with the forces external to educational institutions – for example companies – and cause an intentional modification in the influence that these forces exert in social groups, families and subjects, in order to impede the persistence of inequality. That is to say, reforms leading to fairness require specific strategies of implementation and adoption, because they require the deliberate participation of the powerful classes.

Pedagogies that seek fairness collaborate with de-tracking efforts, because they try to dismantle the mechanisms of streaming, selection and confinement of students in particular segments of education, such as school choice, standardised evaluation and the introduction of educational itineraries or merit-based grouping.[10] In an increasingly explicit way, the school is presented as a sort of machine for classifying and distributing

---

[10] These tactics are multiplying everywhere in the educational system through the practices of exclusion that support the reforms promoted by discursive communities of excellence and restructuring. See Rodríguez Romero (2003).

students along educational paths that imply differences in curricula and channelling students into unequal professional futures. This organisation in circuits directing the educational course of students is committed to the reproduction of inequalities of race, social class, gender, etc., from one generation to another. It also helps erode the idea of a comprehensive school and all the initiatives that fight to shape the schools as incipient democratic communities.

The tactics of external pressure, that are habitually not well thought of by schools and teaching staff, should be accompanied by changes in teaching strategies that are more compatible with the pursuit of fairness. Educators need to develop a committed attitude towards deconstructing the ideologies that implicitly legitimise inequality as well as to develop practices in line with this, which should not remain merely as good intentions. The perspective of liberational literacy is coherent with an educational practice in pursuit of equality, because the cultural models and their discourses differ according to social class and the fact that students coming from disadvantaged social classes suffer conflicts similar to those pointed out in the case of cultural difference. Liberational literacy shares the same sociological focus as situated learning and situated teaching, which is the didactic option most coherent with situated pedagogies.

Situated teaching and learning offer a conceptual framework and some didactic strategies that are suitable for challenging prearranged and meritocratic visions of educability in everyday classroom practice. Because they place students in settings that are meaningful for them, they are confronted with tasks that are relevant from the point of view of their own culture and accordingly they prioritise social interaction. Providing students with the best learning opportunities offers teachers, families and other members of the community well-founded evidence to help them understand and accept that all human beings have talents and abilities that can be reflected in their education.

5.2. Curricular justice

The reflection on social justice occupies a special place in recent pedagogical discussion, for two fundamental reasons. In the social sphere, we are witnessing progressive social segmentation, which on a global scale is being sculpted by the forces of late capitalism (Castel, 1997) and the weak opposing response offered by nation states. This state of affairs is legitimised through discourses that naturalise and disseminate a common sense plagued by fatalism. At academic level, but also at the level of social action, the reformulation of social justice in education is being produced in order to try and break the disheartening circle of social inequality and diversify its horizon, including in its approaches visions and policies related to the recognition of difference.

The renovation of social justice in education is questioning the concepts based on the distribution of educational goods and exclusive focalisation on the inequality produced in view of social class. New, more sophisticated approaches incorporate exclusions related to gender, ethnicity, culture, geographical origin, ability and religion, etc. They also study their interrelationships in order to examine the ways in which they are mutually reinforcing and furthermore try to widen the vision of social justice by combining the distribution of educational goods with education content.[11] These new perspectives try to shape pedagogical initiatives that mitigate both types of oppression deriving from socio-economic injustices and those related to cultural injustices. This is the proposal of a pedagogical alternative known as curricular justice, defended diligently by Robert Connell (1997).

In fact all the cases studied demonstrate the efforts employed to improve learning opportunities for subjects confronted with different types of exclusion. The portrait of the schools for migrant families (Case 3) turns out to be deplorable; setting up a pedagogical initiative like the Intelligent Classroom in such an adverse environment admirable. The Support Unit: USAER 8 initiative (Case 2) with handicapped students in Mexico City is an example of the moral preoccupation of states that are aware of the need to defend the welfare of the most defenceless. Their approaches are somewhat more traditional, though this is not to de-legitimise the work of its promoters and the goodwill of the professionals involved who deny on a daily basis that the destiny of their students is fixed. The reason is that they seem to be very close to the compensatory education approach, a way of working which has not produced the improvements that were foreseen. Compensatory programmes are aimed at a minority of children who are selected according to characteristics concomitant with the object of compensating for the initial disadvantages through enrichment of the educational environment, adding elements to the pre-existing educational system. Resources are increased, methods are more specific, more time is offered to achieve learning, but despite this it does not tackle what is, for curricular justice, the main problem: namely the content and organisation of the curriculum.

Justice in education has been approached as a matter that is fundamentally associated with the distribution of services, in terms of access

---

[11] Approaching social justice these days requires simultaneous consideration of the redistribution of goods and recognition of the difference. It would only be possible to reconcile both facets of social justice by identifying the oppressions in which economic inequality and the absence of cultural respect are interwoven (Fraser, 2000).

to schooling and attainment of formal qualifications. Different pedagogical strategies have been developed to try to discover how to achieve the same quality of service (*i.e.* of a good standard) for all boys and girls from all social classes. It is clear that these questions continue to be important, but they ignore the most significant matter, namely the type of education that they offer (Connell, 1997).[12] Both the content of the traditional academic curriculum and its development have a socio-cultural basis. The curriculum acts by imposing a particular knowledge on one and all, trying to inculcate a particular manner of order and discipline via symbolic systems.[13] The images and concepts that the curriculum projects are not neutral, they carry with them socio-political categorisations and ways of thinking that are used to conceive and classify the different ways of being of each element: what a child is, what a teacher is, what learning is, etc. It usually projects a vision of a motionless culture that leads to the imposition of a particular variant of the official language, which usually belongs to the dominant, white, middle-class culture. The content and organisation of knowledge comes from scientific disciplines that make up the particular epistemological answer of the West to the understanding of the world and from the latter's use of it to achieve technical control. Furthermore, the very process of configuration of school disciplines is comparable to alchemy, producing a process of considerable transformation from knowledge production within culture to knowledge in the school culture (Popkewitz, 1994). Its final product, school knowledge, is very different, because a restructuring and formulation of the original sets of knowledge is produced in order to adapt them to the organisation of the school and its conventions (Bernstein, 1993). In this process, particular rules are applied, which select and transform the original knowledge, presenting it as logical entities that show the arbitrary and contingent selection that has been carried out as an image of logical, hierarchical and atemporal reality.

---

[12] If it has been recognised in countries like France, the United States, the United Kingdom, Canada and Australia that the relationship between the knowledge offered by the school and the existence of social inequality is a key question, we can extrapolate how it would be in countries that make slower progress in questions of social justice in education.

[13] Julia Varela and Fernando Alvarez-Uría (1991), *Arqueología de la escuela*, Madrid, La Piqueta, p. 282, remind us that Durkheim stated in *The Rules of Sociological Method* that "all education is a continuous effort to impose on a child ways of seeing, feeling and acting that he could not have arrived at spontaneously". They continue by saying "the school system is one of the historic forms that adopted this imposition, starting in the Modern Age, which has been perceived and achieved very differently, given that the school is simultaneously a sensitive filter of social origins and a marker of destinies".

The traditional curriculum is designed as the individual appropriation of parcels of abstract knowledge organised in a hierarchical manner, which is measured through *standardised competitive assessments*. Its design is the result of the technical organisation of work, of possessive individualism and of a type of abstract cognition that fosters the decontextualisation of knowledge. Both the traditional curriculum and standardised competitive assessments give priority to students who are socialised according to their literacy in the dominant majority. A curriculum that tries to cover the entire school population, like the traditional academic one, is hegemonic in the sense that it marginalises other forms of the organisation of knowledge. It is also integrated in the power structures of educational institutions and occupies all the cultural space by defining what learning should be, based on what common sense dictates to the majority of the people (Connell, 1997). The definition of common learning of the academic curriculum, its language, learning practices and competitive assessment, produces exclusions, at least in terms of gender, social class and ethnicity.

Following this logic, a **counter-hegemonic curriculum** is needed (Connell, 1997). To counteract the production of inequality, a common learning programme is necessary; one which changes the organisational base to include methods and contents which reflect the experiences and ways of thinking and acting of disadvantaged sectors and which extends both to these groups and to the dominant groups. The aim here is for the latter groups to have access to experience and knowledge that are habitually ignored and which nevertheless are key for putting into motion strategies of participation and social understanding. Given the diversity of inequalities, no single curricular project would be able to work. One would have to construct a variety of them to cover the diversity of gender, race, ethnicity, ability, religion and nationality, among others.

Nevertheless, a counter-hegemonic curriculum should obligatorily include the part of the traditional or majority curriculum that can be generalised and guarantee access to scientific methods and discoveries for all students. The integration of multicultural contents in the curriculum should combine in a transformational approach. This implies the presence of different perspectives included with the social action approach in the curriculum, leading the students to participate in, reflect on and even make decisions about important social matters related to their everyday lives, as well as to organise actions to help resolve them (Banks, 2001). This last orientation is coherent with democratic teaching and learning, a matter that will be examined in the following section.

Box 5.1. Widening the scope of assessment

These are different options for enlarging the assessment exercises:

- Including a greater diversity of learning, moral and cognitive conduct, mental states and quality of work.

- Taking into account the collective and coherent educational results; namely that they cannot be represented as an attribute of an individual (*e.g.* participation as a collective achievement of a group).

- Setting student assessment in the wider context of evaluation of the centres and programmes. The key question is: how are teaching and learning processes working for the students?

- Widening the spectrum of micro-technologies to substitute descriptive ones for standard ones (*e.g.* creating a file of the student profile, a cumulative set of work, examples and teacher observations, or accumulations of descriptive reports referring to particular learning objectives).[14]

- Diversifying the tasks that are to be evaluated, including written portfolios, cooperative work projects, presentations, personal communications and activities.

- Making explicit the relations between student assessment and the curriculum in such a way that the former serves to improve the latter.

- Making sure that the assessment criteria are well-known by the students and families; that the product of the student's intellectual effort has value which goes beyond the purpose of assessment and that information on students will be offered in order to improve their own learning process.

Standardised competitive assessments should also be replaced by **equity-based assessment** or descriptive assessment (Connell, 1997).[15] In utilising the former, the school "fabricates a new reality" that subjects the students to a series of judgments that gives new meanings to the social inequalities that would not exist were it not for the assessment (Perrenoud, 1990). The judgments of excellence cannot be reduced only to a matter of measuring performance, because they are the product of a complex type of conduct that includes fragmentation of the curriculum in disciplines and in annual grade levels, and because they form part of a negotiation between

---

[14] This is not without its problems, such as the difficulty for teachers to use and reflect on the information they have, because of their excessive charge of work and their lack of time.

[15] See CERI's recent publication *Formative Assessment. Improving Learning in Secondary Classrooms* (2005), *www.oecd.org/edu/ceri*

teaching and student bodies. The judgment of the school is not one of many points of view of the student. On the contrary, it seeks to confer on all students their "true" level of excellence, basing this on irrevocable decisions. "The power of the school organisation, evidently deriving from the political system, consists of making a child who gets the subtraction wrong, whose verb and subject do not agree, or who does not master the simple past tense, into a bad student" (Perrenoud, 1990).

Standardised competitive assessment converts failure into a chronic phenomenon. It can produce rejection of the school and breeds feelings of guilt regarding the perception of individual responsibility produced by the meritocratic ideology of the institution, in such a way that the wish to leave school as soon as possible makes itself clear in an irrevocable way. In order to renovate the evaluation, widening the scope of assessment on different levels is proposed, as shown in Box 5.1.

5.3. Democratic teaching and learning

Democracy in the school is the centre of attention for a set of initiatives that revitalise the legacy of John Dewey (1995) in order to counteract the trivialisation of democracy (see also Anne Sliwka in Chapter 4). For this, it is necessary to look for a creative complementarity with representative democracy, developing alternative forms of participative democracy. **Democracy** is the process of transforming power relations into shared authority; this takes place not only in the general public space, but also in the family, in the street and, of course, in the school. Democracy in school would be an extension of local democracy that tries to articulate procedures that stimulate deliberation in decision making about local matters.[16]

Democracy in the school is presented as an ideal requiring ongoing perseverance and as a continuously advancing programme of reform, whose principal spheres of action are the creation of democratic structures and processes within the school, along with the shaping of a curriculum that contributes democratic experiences (Apple and Beane, 1997). Among the guiding principles, we find affinities with situated pedagogy and with curricular justice, such as the preoccupation with the dignity and rights of

---

[16] Combining the vote, referenda, plebiscites, public policy councils, council conferences, discussion meetings and public debates in our cities and communities, participative municipal management; all these are forms of participation that could grow. Participative budgets deserve a special place here. See B. de Sousa Santos (2003), *Democracia y participación. El ejemplo del Presupuesto Participativo de Porto Alegre*, El Viejo Topo, Barcelona.

minorities and individuals, the use of critical reflection and analysis to evaluate ideas, problems and policies, the free circulation of ideas and concern for the welfare of others. We also find proposals that help to keep the public interest in mind and which are seen in reference to the common good and the organisation of social institutions to promote and extend democratic ways of life. A glance at the portraits of schools which accompany the thoughts of Michael Apple and James Beane on democratic education, shows that the schools whose experiences are described fit in with settings where the multiple social differences of students are reformulated, in order to reconvert the production of inequality and lack of cultural respect. In the same way, one sees the contextualisation of the principles of democratic education carried out in each classroom and by each school in order to put into practice processes of teaching and learning that capture the specific imprint of each context in combination with democratic ways of organisation and curriculum construction.

Democratic teaching and learning, in relation to situated teaching, possess specific pedagogical strategies that have many affinities with those presented earlier. Participative pedagogy is a complex form of teaching in which very different strategies are unfurled and which must be learned by teaching staff. For example, democracy implies understanding the cultures and interests of the other participants, thus the curriculum constructed from a single social position is rejected. The demand for all social groups to participate in education implies that all voices are heard and all positions are understood to be partial and positioned. Therefore it is necessary to have pedagogical orientations that transform the educational institutions via the introduction of the point of view of silenced groups in the curriculum, the diversification of knowledge and the use of co-operative learning practices (Beane, 2005).[17]

The object of democratic participation is not to reach a consensus on truth or viewpoint, but to clarify differences and agreements in order to create possible meeting points and relationships based on care and equity.

---

[17] A classic example of education for democracy can be seen in J. Goodman (1992), *Elementary Schooling for Critical Democracy*, SUNY Press, New York. In Spanish, J. Goodman (2002), *La educación democrática en la escuela*, Publicaciones M.C.E.P., Morón de la Frontera. Recent studies can be consulted in J. Goodman (2006), *Reforming School*, SUNY Press, New York, and in A.B. Fields and W. Feinberg (2001), *Education and Democratic Theory*, SUNY Press, New York.

In addition, see the monographic issues: "Grupos cooperativos", *Cuadernos de Pedagogía*, p. 345, 2005, "Vivir la democracia en la escuela", *Cuadernos de Pedagogía*, p. 336, 2004, "Proyecto Atlántida. Escuelas democráticas", *Cuadernos de Pedagogía*, p. 317, 2002 and "Comunidades de aprendizaje", *Cuadernos de Pedagogía*, p. 316, 2002.

Other essential aspects would include access to knowledge which facilitates creative thinking and social dialogue, along with flexible groups of students both for learning as well as decision making, to ensure interaction with heterogeneous interests, cultures and experiences (Darling-Hammond, 2001). Close consideration is also required in calling for participation and in the form and use proposed for it. Among other facets, the school should articulate stable and circumstantial participatory structures in order to exercise deliberative forms of examinations and decision making. The teaching staff should also make use of deliberative procedures and make participation a principle of collaborative work.

One fundamental issue is that a **democracy of knowledge** is needed. In this respect, situated teaching is a good ally, because it allows us to challenge the limited notions of educability. It diversifies the notion of intelligence in order to extend instrumental rationality (normally proper to the western and principally patriarchal civilisation), including forms of rationality associated with other cultures, as well as female and ethnic forms of rationality. It also allows one to cover each and every possible area of the development of human beings and not principally the intellectual one. Cognitive democracy is present in **multiple intelligences**, because it recognises that intelligence is related to culture and offers a multifaceted vision. Intelligence is defined as the capacity to resolve problems or create products that are valued in one or more cultural contexts (Gardner, 2001). The same level of cognitive development includes abilities and attitudes related to fields that are traditionally less valued by the school, such as interpersonal relationships, body movement, music and even the existential sphere.[18]

Democratic teaching has an unstable and utopian character; attaining it is considered to be a work in progress that will never be finished and connects with the perception of democracy as a set of values that we should enact and which should guide our life as a people (Apple and Beane, 1997). From my point of view (Rodríguez Romero, 2003) the transformative potential of democratic education is closely related to the attitude of confidence in the possibilities of improving humanity, which has recently been called for with growing insistence. Believing in people's individual and collective ability to create possibilities for resolving problems occupies a central place among democratic principles (Apple and Beane, 1997). It is related to the inclusion in the curriculum of the construction of social change made by social groups, as an incentive to promote in our students the

---

[18] The most recent initiative by Howard Gardner (2001) has extended the original list of multiple intelligences by adding naturalist intelligence, spiritual intelligence and existential intelligence.

confidence in their own capacities for social transformation. It should include formulations as explicit as the optimistic curriculum (Torres, 2001), or making activism obvious, by including power and inequality as explicit parts of the curriculum, both through experiences in the classroom or the school, or through the example of the teaching staff itself. Using public discussion helps one to think critically about the information to which students are exposed; it facilitates their performance as activists and confronts individual prejudices with the structural mechanisms of inequality. In this way, it encourages the initiation of students as social activists in favour of human rights (Cochran-Smith, 1998).[19] The case studies of the Friendship Centre (Case 1) and BICAP (Case 4) both reconstruct worthwhile examples promoting attitudes of civic collaboration and commitment, which we in the West have been trying to stimulate for many years.

Democracy in school has a clear link with community action, as has been repeatedly made clear by John Dewey (1995). For democracy to be shared in a vital and significant way, it is essential that it is reflected in the community and that it forms part of the cultural practices in which students and their families are involved. Briefly, it means constructing a community, in the sense of a dynamic and organised social fabric, which has resources to give impetus to action and change at community level (Darling-Hammond, 2001). At the same time, a wide-ranging social mutation that promotes individualisation in social affairs is being produced.[20] School choice, decentralisation, streaming and the privatisation of education all coincide in showing a consistent tendency towards the reshaping of social interchange in education in an increasingly individualistic manner. This way of articulating the relationship between the subject and the collective has ambiguous effects because it stimulates "positive" individualism but produces an individualism of the masses that is undermined by insecurity and a lack of protection (Castel, 1997). Without the protection of collective rights, the individualised negotiation of treatment in education, health or

---

[19] One would have to consider there are different Charters of Human Rights which, in contrast to those in the West, put special emphasis on the community and give less attention to individual rights, that all cultures are incomplete and problematic in their manner of imagining human dignity and that within a culture different versions of human dignity could occur, for example, in relation to ideological tendencies. On this regard see J.C. Monedero, "Presentación de frontera: la teoría crítica postmoderna de Boaventura de Sousa Santos", in B. de Sousa Santos (2005).

[20] Robert Castel (1997), tracking the metamorphosis of salaried work, detects a generalised predisposition towards the search for individualising solutions in the management of social affairs.

unemployment can lead to unequal conditions according to the person involved.

Owing to this radically meritocratic social situation, communitarianism is often seen as a characteristic of the weak, who are unable to practice individuality successfully. Nevertheless, for the most vulnerable, it makes more sense than ever to strengthen their connections. The solution is found in the construction of an **ethical community** (Bauman, 2003). This type of community is deeply rooted in the experience of solidarity and mutual commitment – as well as in the practice of constant dialogue – in order to continue constructing a shared concept of what is good among all people, however different their identities may be and the collective demand to ensure that human rights may be enjoyed by every individual. The school can contribute to creating ethical communities by making the teachers, students and the students' families aware of the innate wealth to be potential community-builders that is locked up within themselves. This would be a matter of strengthening the links that bind them. The ethical community contributes to the deployment of **productive power** – that is, the power to orientate their lives according to the desires that subjects have – because it promotes the intentional functioning of emerging networks of interaction in order to influence the transformation of the social environment. It also increases the possibility of democratic participation in the life of the community to which they belong through very different structures and social networks.

5.4. Community construction and the educational professional

In the process of community construction, an essential role is played by those intermediary social structures such as neighbours, family, voluntary associations, non-governmental organisations, by teachers' associations and by the school itself, which is situated between the private life of the people and the de-personalised institutions of public life. These structures act as a bridge, facilitating the participation of teachers in the educational policy of the local society and, by extension, in the wider social fabric. The state, through different administrations including educational structures, should encourage the appearance of these intermediary channels of participation. By ceasing to control these intermediary social structures – and, on the contrary, protecting them, supporting them and fostering them – one would achieve the responsible participation – in the problems that concern them – of the teaching staff, of the educational institutions, of the families and other social associations. This form of participation and influence is a symptom of maturity in the social and democratic life of the community. An alliance between schools and third sector organisations, as has been described in

Case 1, has a considerable effect on the learning possibilities and the quality of life of the individuals and its neighbourhood.

Finally, the four cases offer us a very productive guideline reflection on the type of educational professional required today. They show that academic preparation is far from being the key element of the training and teaching profession. The essential part is their belief in a) their own professional effectiveness in teaching different persons, however different they are; b) the capacity of social action by the people; and c) in educational terms, in the potential of all their students to learn at the highest intellectual level. As Marilyn Cochran-Smith (1998) states, it is not so much a matter of educators being capable of giving specific pedagogical treatment to students who show differences, but of actively undertaking a pedagogy to pursue better social justice with any groups of students. For this author, the teachers should be committed to social change and act as part of the social movements.[21] This is an approach coherent with the transformation of the state into an innovative social movement, as advocated by de Sousa Santos (2005). According to de Sousa Santos (2005) in contrast with the possibility of the "State as Entrepreneur", he chooses to conceive the **state as a "highly innovative social movement"**. This means establishing an innovative and close articulation between the principles of the state and of the community, under the leadership of the latter. State decentralisation is not seen as weakness but rather as a modification of its nature. It loses control of social regulation, but gains control of the **metaregulation**, namely the selection, coordination, hierarchisation and regulation of those non-state agents who acquire concessions of state power through political subcontracting.

The culture of dependence that social institutions create with their inertia is impeding the production of alternative visions of what educational institutions could be and do. In order for experimentation with educational alternatives to be feasible, it is necessary for the teachers to change their outlook. One would have to encourage teachers to "think in a different way", so that they take on the foucauldian aspiration of being freer than they feel and take on the spaces of liberty they have available to them but which they still cannot see. Then they can independently undertake the reinvention of their profession and alternative schooling, driving change in the socialising framework of the school (Rodríguez Romero, 2006).

---

[21] Political and ideological commitments are intimately associated with social change. Teachers should become aware of the impossibility of teaching without political references or without values and we should ask ourselves about the intention of education for the students. This is in no way a matter of politicising education, but rather of recognising that it is already politicised and that this political facet needs to be taken into consideration more explicitly. See Cochran-Smith (1998).

From my point of view, the teachers' principal motivation would be conversion of the schools into spaces for social experiments, so that they can organise the educational institutions starting from everyday experiences that promote solidarity and understanding. Continuing with de Sousa Santos (2005), this mission fits in perfectly with the new role reserved for the state: that of converting itself into a new social movement which spreads an alternative, solidarity-based form of sociability. What would be the state's mission regarding this teachers' will? It would need to provide the conditions necessary for alternative experimentations to be convincingly tested and would need to choose to promote utopian actions in school and community spaces.

5.5. Conclusion

School "grammar" has been maintained not so much by conscious conservatism as by lack of reflection about institutional habits and the widely extended cultural beliefs upon which the "real school" is built. Above all, naturalisation of the grade school has been favoured by the type of organisation of the educational institutions that provides a standard way of processing a great number of people and makes the grammar highly replicable (Tyack and Cuban, 1995).

Many attempted changes have been supported in the school-society interaction and have led to educational proposals that are supported by the social commitment of the school and the teachers. Some classic examples of these may be found in the Dalton Plan and the Winnetka System in the United States, Escuela Nueva in Latin-America and Africa and numerous other schooling experiences supported by pedagogues such as María Montessori or Ovien Decroly.[22] It is clear that all of these contain innovatory potential that has yet to be explored (Carbonell, 2001; Sliwka, Chapter 4). All these are committed to pedagogical strategies that challenge unquestioned traditions because they seek to establish:

- the non-grade school;

- the use of time, space, student numbers, subjects as flexible resources, the diversification of the uniformity of class periods, size and distribution of the classrooms, the breaking down of barriers between disciplines…; and

- the relationship between school, community and society.

---

[22] For a wider examination of this subject, see also J. Martínez Bonafé (1998).

We now know that the rupture of the rules of "grammar" that organise the grade school is not only possible but desirable, both in responding to the complexities of the challenges facing humanity and in taking advantage of the wisdom and social experience of all men and women. To initiate this enterprise we can count on two very interesting sources of inspiration: the revolutionary legacy of the innovative pedagogies – and their current reinterpretation – and the social experience of the local pedagogical initiatives presently being driven by the most vulnerable groups. CERI work on models of learning constitutes an opportunity to link both together and to legitimise the production of pedagogical alternatives with the imprint of utopian realism.

Novel forms of teaching and learning which transgress the pedagogical tradition of the grade school would serve to form the class of subjects that humanity needs, because they would be able to broaden the limits of personal, community and social development, questioning the static notions of educability and offering a utopian sense of human progress that is not likened to technical and economic development. This includes a bonding, ecological and momentous vision – and our individual and collective responsibility towards – the future of humanity and of life in general on our planet.

References

Apple, M.W. and J.A. Beane (1997), *Escuelas democráticas,* Morata, Madrid.

Banks, J. (2001), "Approaches to Multicultural Curriculum Reform", in J. Banks and Ch.A. McBanks (eds.), *Multicultural Education. Issues and Perspectives,* John Wiley and Jossey Bass, New York.

Bauman, Z. (2003), *Comunidad. En busca de seguridad en un mundo hostil,* Siglo XXI, Madrid.

Beane, J.A. (2005), *La integración del currículo: el diseño del núcleo de la educación democrática,* Morata, Madrid.

Beck, U. (2002), *La sociedad del riesgo global,* Siglo XXI, Madrid.

Bernstein, B. (1993), *La estructura del discurso pedagógico,* Morata, Madrid.

Carbonell, J. (2001), *La aventura de innovar el cambio en la escuela,* Morata, Madrid.

Castel, R. (1997), *Las metamorfosis de la cuestión social,* Paidós, Barcelona.

Castells, M. (1997), *La era de la información, La sociedad red,* Alianza Editorial, Madrid.

Cochran-Smith, M. (1998), "Teacher Development and Educational Reform", in A. Hargreaves *et al.* (eds.), *International Handbook of Educational Change,* Kluwer, London.

Connell, R.W. (1997), *Escuelas y justicia social,* Morata, Madrid.

Daniels, H. (2003), *Vygotsky y la pedagogía,* Paidós, Barcelona.

Darling-Hammond, L. (2001), *El derecho de aprender,* Ariel, Barcelona.

De Sousa Santos, B. (2003), *Crítica de la Razón Indolente: Contra el Desperdicio de la Experiencia,* Desclée de Brouwer, Bilbao.

De Sousa Santos, B. (2005), *El milenio huérfano, Ensayos para una nueva cultura política*, Trotta, Madrid.

Dewey, J. (1995), *Democracia y educación*, Morata, Madrid.

Dewey, J. (2004), *Experiencia y educación*, Biblioteca Nueva, Madrid.

Diáz Barriga, F. (2003), "Cognición situada y estrategias para el aprendizaje significativo", *Revista Electrónica de Investigación Educativa*, Vol. 5(2), *http://redie.ens.uabc.mx/vol5no2/contenido-arceo.html*

Fraser, N. (2000), "¿De la redistribución al reconocimiento?", *New Left Review*, pp. 126-155.

Gardner, H. (2001), *La inteligencia reformulada, Las inteligencias múltiples en el siglo XXI*, Paidós, Barcelona.

Gee, J.P. (2005), *La ideología en los discursos*, Morata, Madrid.

Goodman, J. (2000), "Democracia crítica", *Kikirikí*, Vol. 55/56, pp. 4-13.

Gore, J. (1996), *Controversias entre las pedagogías*, Morata, Madrid.

Hamilton, D. (1996), *La transformación de la educación en el tiempo*, Trillas, México.

Haraway, D. (1988), "Situated Knowledge: The Science Question in Feminism as a Site of Discourse on the Privilege of Partial Perspective", *Feminist Studies*, Vol. 14, No. 3, pp. 575-579.

Harding, S. (1996), *Ciencia y feminismo*, Morata, Madrid.

Martínez Bonafé, J. (1998), *Trabajar en la escuela. Profesorado y reformas en el umbral del siglo XXI*, Miño y Dávila, Madrid.

McCarthy, C. (1993), *Racismo y curriculum*, Morata, Madrid.

McConaghy, C. (2002), *Situated Pedagogies: Researching Quality Teaching and Learning for Rural New South Wales Schools*, position paper prepared for the ARC Linkage 2002-2004, NSWDET, Sydney. *http://fehps.une.edu.au/Education/RTEP/Situated_Pedagogies.pdf*

Miller, J.L. (1996), *Teachers, Researchers, and Situated School Reform: Circulations of Power, Theory into Practice,* Vol. 35, No. 2, pp. 86-92.

Monedero, J.C. (2005), "Presentación de frontera: la teoría crítica postmoderna de Boaventura de Sousa Santos", in B. de Sousa Santos (ed.), *El milenio huérfano. Ensayos para una nueva cultura política*, Trotta, Madrid.

Nieto, S. (1998), "Cultural Difference and Educational Change in a Sociopolitical Context", in A. Hargreaves *et al.* (eds.), *International Handbook of Educational Change*, Kluwer, London.

Oakes, J. *et al.* (1998), "Norms and Politics of Equity-minded Change: Researching the 'Zone of Mediation'", in A. Hargreaves *et al.* (eds.), *International Handbook of Educational Change*, Kluwer, London.

Perrenoud, P. (1990), *La construcción del éxito y del fracaso escolar*, Morata, Madrid.

Popkewitz, T.S. (1994), "Política, conocimiento y poder: algunas cuestiones para el estudio de las reforma educativas", *Revista de Educación*, Vol. 305, pp. 103-137.

Rodríguez Romero, M.M. (2003), *Las metamorfosis del cambio educativo*, Akal, Madrid.

Rodríguez Romero, M.M. (2006), "El asesoramiento comunitario en educación y la reinvención del profesorado", *Revista de Educación*, Vol. 339, pp. 59-75.

Torres, J. (2001), *Educación en tiempos de neoliberalismo*, Morata, Madrid.

Smyth, J. (2000), "La enseñanza y la política social: las imágenes de la enseñanza a favor del cambio democrático", in B.J. Biddle *et al.* (eds.), *La enseñanza y los profesores III. La reforma de la enseñanza en un mundo en transformación*, Paidós, Barcelona.

Swaan, A.d. (1992), *A cargo del Estado*, Pomares-Corredor, Barcelona.

Tyack, D. and L. Cuban (1995), *Tinkering toward Utopia*, Harvard University Press, Cambridge, Ma.

Vygotsky, L. (1995), *Pensamiento y lenguaje*, Paidós, Barcelona.

Vygotsky, L. (2000), *El desarrollo de los procesos psicológicos superiores*, Crítica, Barcelona.

Chapter 6
The Construction of Learning Environments
Lessons from the Mexico Exploratory Phase
by
Juan Cassassus, María de Ibarrola, Lilia Pérez-Franco,
Juana M. Sancho-Gil, Marcela Tovar-Gómez,
Margarita Zorrilla

This chapter provides an overview of the main outputs of the analysis undertaken during the exploratory phase of CERI work on innovative learning environments. Main themes are introduced, with reference to key ideas and research on innovations, which are largely gleaned from the four study cases explored in Mexico.

As explained in the foreword to this publication, the OECD Centre for Educational Research and Innovation (CERI) started in 2005 the analytical work on models of learning as part of the "Schooling for Tomorrow" project. The core of this analysis was co-ordinated with Mexico and was based on intensive consultations and discussions with different groups of experts, as well as on fieldwork. This period, from July 2005 to June 2006, was known as the *exploratory phase* and concluded with the OECD-Mexico International Conference: "Emerging Models of Learning and Innovation" held between 14-16 June 2006 in Mérida, Yucatán.

All the authors of this chapter were actively involved in the network of experts who participated in the different activities during the Mexico *exploratory phase*. The current chapter includes extracts of the main papers they prepared. It does not pretend to be a summary, but is more an introduction emphasising some of the key ideas of their analysis in order to encourage further reflection.

Juana Sancho-Gil sets the current push to innovate and reform against the historical backcloth of progressive movements during the 20th Century.

Evoking Dewey, Sarason or Cuban, she argues for more radical approaches given the disappointing results of reforms – learning outcomes are still limited and schools and teachers continue to work in highly traditional ways – and she stresses the need to search for new models or structures of learning with learners and their needs at their centre.

Juan Cassasus adopts an interactionist perspective and proposes that the driving forces of most innovations are needs and emotions. In what he calls the needs-emotions-actions dynamic, the extent of satisfaction of certain needs sets off emotional responses which in turn drive individuals or groups to react or innovate to respond to their needs.

Marcela Tovar-Gómez and Lilia Pérez-Franco use the four Mexico study cases extensively for their analyses. Tovar-Gómez argues for the creation of new learning structures that recognise the heterogeneous nature of education and its contexts, which call for more flexible instruments and for more participative and structured methods. She suggests inter alia revising the certification processes and explicitly encouraging counselling and research activities among teachers. Pérez-Franco notes that the innovations examined have survived while following different "building routes". Some started as on-the-ground responses to local needs; others were created in the system's middle tiers in response to top-down reforms, articulated by public servants who were sensitive to the needs, abilities and requests of local actors. In order to show this complexity she outlines different profiles for the actors of innovation which survive.

Borrowing some of the key concepts from Freire, Brown, Ausbel, Feuerstein and others, Margarita Zorrilla highlights and discusses urgent outstanding questions: how can recent learning science outcomes be translated into practice? How can teachers' understanding of these findings be facilitated and how can they be helped to apply them? How could teachers and other actors become real mediators between learners and the knowledge they need and want to acquire? How can a broader and more equitable concept of quality education be fostered?

In the last section, María de Ibarrola reminds the reader that innovations need to be understood as part of a historical process; in order to understand change, a careful reconstruction and restoration of multiple elements is required. Based on the Mexican experience, she concludes that recent reforms and education initiatives try to improve the education system as a whole, but up until now, this has not been achievable. Thus she encourages CERI and the OECD member countries to "make visible" those experiences that have obtained better learning outcomes from ground-level in order to facilitate the transition towards more flexible national policies and a more receptive education system.

6.1. Building appropriate education: an unachieved task
Juana M. Sancho-Gil[1]

At the beginning of the 20th Century, Dewey wrote that the school was the most conservative institution in the United States and that it was being used to impede the correct attainment of the democratic ideal. He stated, however, that the school could become the most radical of all institutions if it was used to liberate the students from the false philosophical tradition used to strengthen parasitical social and economic patterns as if they were eternal and timeless. For Dewey, the main goal of **progressive education** was to turn schools into instruments of social reform. For this reason, the job of the school had to be to ensure that all individuals had an opportunity to escape from the limitations of the social group in which they had been born and to enable them to have real contact with a broader environment. He understood that demanding all students to do preparatory studies for university was elitist; providing an *appropriate* education for each child was democratic.[2]

Dewey wanted to show that it was possible to teach important ideas through the use of projects and activities that attracted the interest of the children and released their mental energies. Eastman (1941), following Dewey's philosophy, argued that if a sufficient variety of activities was offered, there would be enough knowledge among the students and the teacher would understand the natural relationship between knowledge and the actions of interest, the children would have fun being educated and they would love going to school.

The Progressive School (in the United States) or the New School (in Europe) was based on this need to break down academically a school designed only for one type of individual and for the transmission of platonic, abstract, de-contextualised, permanent and true knowledge. The aim need was to create a school in which all the individuals could learn and develop their skills – a school that thought about the development of knowledge itself, as well as the evolution of society at large. In this pedagogical context are included the centres of interest, co-operative work, learning through inquiry, etc., developed by Decroly, Claparède and Freinet. Helen Parkhust's Dalton Plan and Carl Washburne's Winnetka Method constitute

---

[1] Professor in Educational Technology at the University of Barcelona, she is also Co-Director of the Centre for the Study of Change in Culture and Education at the Scientific Park of Barcelona (*www.cecace.org*).

[2] Although in some cases, this principle resulted in very anti-democratic and socially reproductive practices in schools.

other proposals that are aimed at innovation and improving the work of the school.

However, more than one hundred years after the appearance of the proposals for the Progressive and New School and the immeasurable number of initiatives and reforms that were made to improve education in order to make it more meaningful for the students – and in some cases for the teachers – the evidence seems disappointing. Studies such as the one carried out by Cuban (1993) show that the teachers still do much more talking than the students; teaching is usually front-facing and the use of class time is chiefly determined by the teacher. They also show that classroom furniture is usually arranged in rows and columns, with the desks and chairs facing the blackboard and the teacher's desk. However the most disturbing aspect of all is that students do not find school an *exciting* place for learning.

On the other hand, the **predictable failure of reforms** (Sarason, 1990) is still related, among many other factors, to the impossible practice of creating and maintaining productive learning conditions for students in the long term if there are none for the teaching staff. Finally, for Bransford *et al.* (1999) the new developments in the science of learning suggest that the degree to which educational environments are focused on the community is also important for learning. Along these lines, the rules are particularly important so that people can learn from each other in order constantly to try and improve.

In the organisation of learning and pedagogy, the four cases as a whole were faced with a fair number of strategies for encouraging learning. These are represented below as a continuum (Figure 6.1) of the more conventional strategies: front-facing teaching, the setting of exercises, use of text books, assessment by exam, etc., through to those presented as more alternative strategies such as re-evaluation of student knowledge, encouraging autonomy, student responsibility, collaborative learning, inquiry-based learning (research projects), individualised learning and continuous development using different resources.

Figure 6.1. **Conventional-alternative learning continuum**

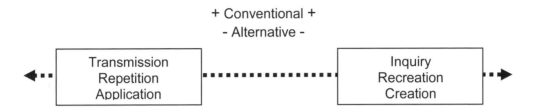

Source: Author.

There are some teaching and learning processes that seem most suitable for use as guidelines in the construction of new educational models, from the point of view of the innovation required for educational systems to comprehend the learning needs of current society. These processes encourage the intellectual involvement of the student through inquiry, recreation of personal, local and global knowledge and the creation of more complex visions of the subjects and problems studied.

One of the most difficult school dimensions to address and at the same time one of those considered to be in most urgent need of change, is the *knowledge* legitimised by the school curriculum. The alchemical conversion of scientific disciplines into subjects (Popkewitz, 2000); the fragmentation of knowledge and skills (Hernández, 2001; 2006); the lack of relevance and connection with the interests of the different children and adolescents and the problems they have to face (Hargreaves, 2003), among other factors, have led to design proposals that are aimed at encouraging the integration of school knowledge (Delors *et al.* 1996; Postman, 1996; Morin, 2000, among others). Nevertheless, it is difficult to find significant changes in school.

In my view a learning model can be seen as an incomplete constellation of the factors that shape learning processes, including the challenges confronting it. The centre of this constellation should contain the concept of the child or adolescent as someone who – as well as having the right to education – has the capacity to learn irrespective of their physical, family, economic, ethnic or social conditions. Placed around this central concept are several dimensions influencing, with a greater or lesser degree, the learner. Along the same lines, this time on the outer part of the graph, the series of challenges that these innovations must confront needs to be included. Figure 6.2 shows a draft representation of the dimensions and challenges of an emerging learning model.

Figure 6.2. Dimensions and challenges of an emerging learning model

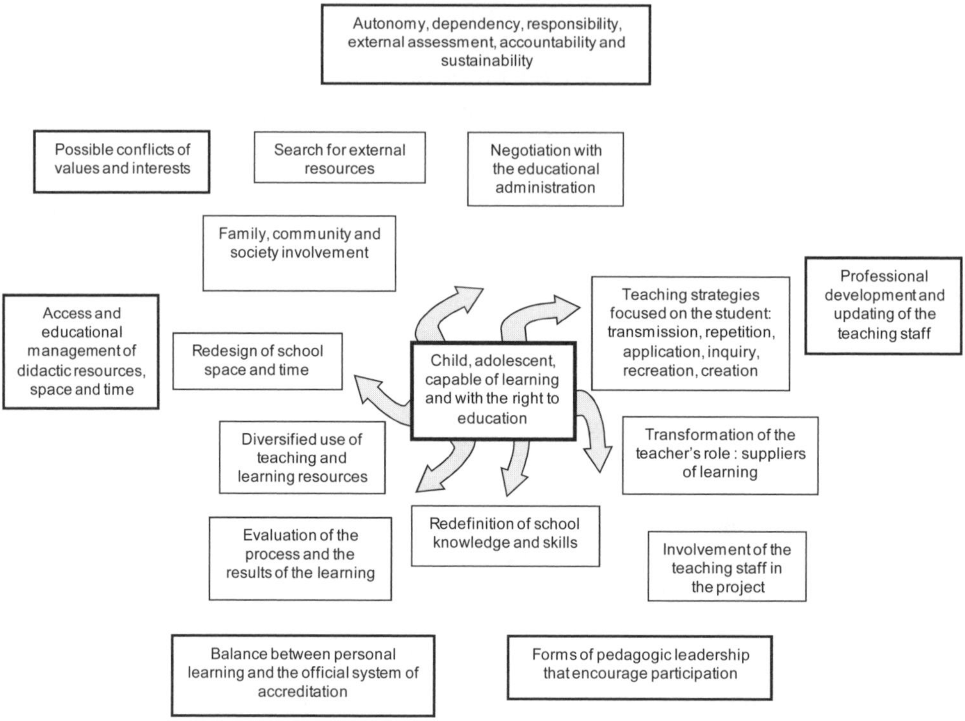

Source: Author.

6.2. Needs and emotions as driving forces
Juan Casassus[3]

Over the last twenty years, the main theoretical source for the formulation of educational policy has been structural determinism. Structural determinism is the basis of management in its behaviourist and neoclassical form and we can clearly see that educational policy over the last few years has largely been focused on measures relative to the management of the system.

The focus in **interactionism** is different. In this approach, behaviour is not determined by the structure. On the contrary, it is the interaction that

_____

[3] Sociologist and former International Education Specialist for UNESCO.

determines the structure. When we speak of structures here, we make reference to real, not normative structures. That is why if we want to study a situation with the intention of obtaining sustainable change, it is necessary to understand how it really functions. We need to understand the type of relationships and interactions of the individuals – each with their own circumstances or each individual with each other – that make things happen in the way they do. Therefore, if we want to introduce changes in behaviour so that they may be sustained over time, we first need to understand elements such as the nature of the relationships, linkages, culture, identity and climates in the classroom, in schools and in the community. This does not disregard the fact that structures do exist and that they exert influences. The point is that their influences are always regulated to a greater or lesser extent by interactions within the system. These are the processes that make it clear that in the last instance events take place in a certain manner and not in another.

In addition to this we can say that these interactions happen in specific *circumstances*. These can be defined as events that happen within a context,[4] events that are in themselves empirical data but have no greater importance than that. What is significant is that those events are important for some people and that they provoke a reaction in those persons. The importance lies in the meaning that the event subjectively has for individuals as well as in its potential to trigger a reaction in them. It is this reaction that generates an innovation. Because of this, it is necessary to identify what it is that makes certain persons, individually or collectively, react in a specific way to these circumstances, whereas when at the same time, the same circumstances do not trigger the same reaction in other persons or stimulate an innovation. Then it is also useful to define what a **driving force** is.

In its most fundamental expression, the forces that propel an action are **emotions** (Cassasus, 2006). An emotion is – as indicated by its etymology – a force of movement. If we pay close attention to the basis of any action, we find one or more emotions that are the elements that predispose us to undertake action. Accordingly, as held by behaviourist tradition and with

---

[4] Situation must be differentiated from context. Wherever we are, we are in a situation. To be in a situation is to be in a "place" where "something" is situated. The individual and their actions are the situated elements. Where the reality is located and how it is experienced by that person, is relative to how it acts and what it does to that person. If more individuals are involved in the same occurrence or event, there will be other situations. Situations are constructed according to the actions undertaken and positions occupied by those persons in that reality. The context is the content of the situation which functions as a condition for those individuals.

greater or less sophistication, emotions determine action (Skinner, 1954). In this tradition, action tends to be seen as a conditioned reaction.

Conditioned reactions are recurrent patterns of response that we enact when we are in the presence of certain events. Somehow, for reasons of protection or otherwise, we incorporate these patterns of response when we face these particular phenomena. We then fix these repeated recurrent patterns in our bodies as a way of reacting. Although it is usually a reaction to a social event, we do so as part of our personal experience, as well as part of our socialisation within – and belonging to – a given culture. From this behaviourist perspective, we expect that each time we are in the presence of these events or circumstances, there will be a typical response. However, this formulation, although it can explain many actions, cannot explain innovations, precisely because an innovation[5] – a *nova action* – is not a typical pattern of response in reaction to an event. On the contrary, it is an atypical response.

Fortunately these recurrent patterns of response to certain events – no matter how fixed they may be within our muscular and nervous systems (Lowen, 2000) – can be modified when a person becomes emotionally mature (Casassus, 2006). Diverging from the behaviourist theory of conditioned action, the approach used here is that action is not predetermined by emotions. Rather, actions are predisposed by emotions, but emotions do not predispose us to just *any* action. When we are affected by an emotion, it allows us to be ready for action, albeit a limited range of possibilities of action. If we are angry, we are predisposed to act in the way a person acts when he or she is angry, *i.e.* violently and destructively. However we can regulate and modulate our anger in order to act in a productive way and carry out non-destructive actions. If we were angry and emotionally immature, anger would determine our way of reacting according to the pattern of recurrent action already registered in our muscular and nervous system.

Frequently there is something else underneath or preceding the emotions. Most of the time, emotions emerge from the universe of **needs**. When needs are met or satisfied, certain emotions appear. When needs have not been met, other types of emotions appear. Since emotions propel action, it is important to understand the relation between needs and emotions. For example if we need security and safety and we can meet this need, then we will feel free, calm and confident in proposing our ideas. On the contrary, if

---

[5] Innovation could be defined as the introduction of an idea into a system of relations – made with the appropriate rhythm – which allows for a transformation in the way a given practice is active within that system of relations.

we have not met our need for safety, we will feel scared, vulnerable, depressed and disconnected. We will tend to retreat from these emotions and devalue ourselves; we will not be inclined to provide our ideas, we will try to escape. There are many examples of this kind, but understanding the mechanism of the dynamics of the **needs-emotions-actions sequence** is important; these three elements comprise the **pillar of innovations**. In illustration of this needs-emotions-actions sequence, some driving forces that are at the core of the teaching profession, both in the case studies as well as in many other innovative initiatives, are included here below.

The **recognition of diversity** is a fundamental need at the basis of many innovations, since many see this as the only way to confront the limitations of the one-model homogenising approach. The standard model of schooling operates fairly well under certain conditions: where there are effective schools, with highly qualified teachers, many financial and material resources and where teachers have the time available to meet, community and school cultures are in harmony and the overall living standards are high. However this does not work well when the conditions are different: for example in schools in low-income areas, with a culture that is not in tune with that of the model and where teachers have low incomes, low qualifications and no free time. There is more than one way of dealing with diversity in education. Thus it is necessary to explore different institutional arrangements and ways of organising schooling in order to ensure that boys and girls find the method adequate for their learning needs, even though that may not necessarily imply different standards, norms and finalities.

The need to have an **identity** is another driving force that encourages innovation and is related to diversity. To affirm the identity of a group is to meet the need that people have to generate a sense of community. This could be seen in other more postmodern identities such as: Internet interest groups, sports teams, artistic groups, gangs and suchlike. The more marked the identity of that community, the more gratifying it is to be identified with that group. They also meet the need for feelings of safety and for communicating. When the need to belong to a community is met, other emotions emerge that nurture and sustain the innovation over time.

Another driving force that we can find in many of the innovations related to teaching and learning practices is that of being part of an active and challenging **professional community** (Brown and Lauder, 2001). These communities encourage teamwork, the capacity to listen, multidisciplinary teams, recognition of the trajectories of its members, observation of reality, flexibility and methodological adaptations, group reflection and trust in the strategies adopted by each member. This has been called collective intelligence. To be part of a recognised professional community, especially in a challenging environment, is stimulating and meets many fundamental needs such as: the need to be accepted, safety, to be heard, grateful, connected, relaxed and stimulated. This allows the revitalisation of emotions based on personal empowerment, trusting others and being alert and engaged. These communities are particularly of value in the contexts of vulnerability and risk because normally they tend to concentrate in the other extreme, in elite schools.

The notion of community has disappeared from the discourse of educational policy, which has tended to focus on themes such as management, evaluation, standards, productivity, accountability, incentives and punishments; these are all terms that come from economics. Policy and schools have concentrated on the development of human capital and there has been no focus on what has been called **social capital** (Hargreaves, 2003). However, social capital, which has been described as "an informal set of shared values that allows people to co-operate among them" (Fukujama, 1995) is the basis of the generation of trust, an emotion considered crucial for the future development of civil society, without which there would be no mediations between individuals and the state. The isolation of schools from the community and the disappearance of the notion of community from the discourse of educational policy will have no other effect than to destroy social capital, consequently increasing social fragmentation. In the case studies, there are abundant references to the re-establishment of traditional ties between school and community, ties that are seen as a strength. This driving force is rooted in fundamental needs such as a sense of belonging, brotherhood, the need for company, connection, to know and to be recognised. The emotions of confidence and trust and the will to co-operate emerge when these needs have been met.

The improvement of education cannot be a neutral process; it requires policies and decisions guided by principles as Jeannie Oakes (2000) confirmed when analysing the failure of educational policy in the 1980s and 1990s in the United States. She found that values such as social justice and caring for children – all powerful emotions – are fundamental needs of human beings and it is precisely these needs that are found at the core of the teaching profession. The obstacles to the development of education do not derive only from one model approach. They also derive from the intent – frequently unconscious – to expropriate from teachers what is the essential role of their professional life: to help in the development of human beings.

6.3. Building a meaningful learning model
Marcela Tovar-Gomez[6]

The four cases studied during the *exploratory phase* invite us to ponder those aspects that might contribute to the construction of innovative learning processes, due to their significance. These learning proposals are contextualised and developed differently in each of the experiences. They combine what is revealed by the teaching practices, the situation of the recipients of educational action and the situation in which they are immersed. This reflects the existence of a range of possible alternatives that may be built.

The innovations studied share some common characteristics, but each of them defines these in different ways. Most of actors involved consider their proposal **meaningful** because they see it as an element of their reality and space that complements other realms of individual daily life. This implies the construction of a space of participation, value-sharing and guidance that gives meaning to everyday chores. These examples respond to one of the true challenges of education, which is to build an educational action that is meaningful for those actors involved in its implementation without neglecting other design and organisation elements.

Another important aspect of building a quality education proposal is the **inclusion** of actors as members of a learning community. This is a dynamic where actions imply involvement in decision-making, co-responsibility and participation of those actors who have had – in Mexico's case – a weak presence frequently reduced to its instrumental aspects, such as the role of parents. Through this, learning centres extend their effect into other social realms. They allow and make participation possible in different ways and at different levels for other actors, who at best were merely passive observers of teaching activities and the work of teachers and students. Besides those who are responsible for the creation and maintenance of learning environments, the learning process implies the intertwining of different views and actors within it. The teacher who facilitates learning is not the only one involved; he/she also receives the support of other professionals who, in a mediating or immediate manner, make up a collegiate body co-responsible for the learning proposal, whose insertion evolves around the problematic and perspectives, rather than around the discipline in which they have initially been trained. This interdisciplinary dimension, as

---

[6] Research Professor of the National Pedagogical University (UPN) (Mexico), in the field of education of teachers from indigenous backgrounds, and responsible of the investigation "The cultural determinations of the production of the knowledge: cosmovision, culture and pedagogy".

revealed by the experiences, is feasible when knowledge integration is based upon **collaborative processes**.

The experiences studied reveal processes focused on the subject and on collaborative learning. The aim of an educational proposal is learning, which is why the ways in which learning environments and experiences are defined constitute its central point. In addition to this, the intervention methodologies of the study cases do not reduce education to the school context, but embrace all those learning forms and opportunities that link knowledge with practice and the transcendence of actions with everyday living experiences. In the same way, they emphasise the incorporation of knowledge to enhance other dimensions of individual development. While distinguishing instrumental, procedural and theoretical knowledge, organising learning experiences and environments requires the insertion of the teacher into the context, along with the articulation of his/her work around the interests and needs of the actors of the learning experience.

Linking theory and practice into the organisational aspects of teaching requires special attention. Knowing what has to be done or building theoretical concepts is not always accompanied with the necessary knowledge about how to achieve this, especially if enthusiastic involvement is required of the actors. A potential solution is to foster **Counselling-Research-Action Circuits** (CRA circuits). These circuits are cycles of different activities that aim to help teachers put their theoretical knowledge into practice and constantly to improve this process. First the circuit includes the creation of teams of professionals who support teachers through counselling, so they can explore different ways in which to address their particular challenges. These teams could also support those students who have severe difficulties in reaching their learning goals. Fostering enriching professional opportunities where teachers can practise and research what they have learnt would be a further step. Access to materials that allow them to address the most complex aspect of teaching would also help. Such a perspective allows for integration, as well as recognition of the different learning capacities, culture, styles and rhythms that make up students' backgrounds, as well as the construction of a perspective in which teachers visualise their duty as the creation of learning environments in diverse contexts.

An interesting exercise comes from combining strengths from each of the experiences with the intention of balancing the weaknesses of others. For instance, an inspiring sign is that the cases encourage the design of student-learning **evaluating mechanisms** within a methodology that emphasises autonomy. In other words, this is a methodology that allows the individual to develop the skills required to help him/her learn how to learn, rather than to manage preconceived contents with doubtful value for the formation of the individual. Nevertheless it seems that the sequences and rhythms of the paths that students have to follow are still rigidly established in most of the education options. In order to enhance the mechanisms that allow a student-training capable of meeting learning needs, careful revision of the negative effects of current **certification** mechanisms is necessary. The design of rigid school terms and of curricular contents mandated for all environments and situations becomes an obstacle for the continuation of the substantial objectives of the learning experiences. It is important to highlight that in three of the cases, certification requirements negatively affected the learning proposal.

The last aspect requiring consideration is the need for **flexibility and adjustment of the regulation** of teaching practice. Institutional regulations become a burden for those experiences that do not originate or develop within the institutional environment, even becoming a difficult obstacle for those experiences inserted in the defined regulations. An innovative experience requires a legal framework to guarantee the suitability and quality of the education service, as well as flexibility and openness in defining the institutional policies whenever the expansion of the experience requires. It is necessary to find an adequate balance between institutional follow-up and the development of situated and meaningful learning experiences. This should come along with a referential and flexible regulation framework that recognises the diversity of learning environments.

6.4. Finding routes for change
Lilia Perez-Franco[7]

Families, students, teachers, school principals and local and federal education officers face real demands and conditions that very often become obstacles in reaching those goals officially established by the education system. In some countries, these goals do not necessarily take into account those difficulties because they obey a "standardisation" logic that tries to boost the coverage of education demand on different levels. In the heterogeneous Mexican education field, actors try to meet the demands of the system while making outstanding efforts to design working and interaction strategies – in practical and pragmatic ways – that will allow them to meet the real needs of all those involved.

In spite of increasing internal diversification of the system over the last decades, this still remains inflexible with regard to the formal regulation of

---

[7] Research Professor at the Department of Sociology of the Autonomous Metropolitan University (Mexico).

those processes associated with a sizeable bureaucracy. However, based on the cases analysed, we see that there is a sector of education actors, at government level and working directly in schools, that is flexible and receptive enough to the conditions, needs, limitations, abilities and shortcomings of those they serve. Thus they are able to fulfill the pedagogical and education goals entrusted to them. However the goal of the education system should not be defined as the creation of *ad hoc* opportunities to match the needs of every person. Instead, the goal should be to accompany those actors who have found "new routes" to respond to their learning needs, to design with them realistic policies that can guarantee these routes. In this way the *blind spots* of education work could be identified and reduced, opening up trends towards equity and plurality.

As shown by the four cases studied, impulses for innovation could come from *public policy* through reforms in the organisational structures of education duties, leading to a new shaping of goals and strategies. In others, the power derives from the urgent and fundamental needs of *communities*, such as: demands for specific services for children (daycare or better quality care), in relation to other actors (working parents who do not have sufficient means or job security), etc. Changes are also related to *social forces with real negotiation power* capable of creating different education patterns. These patterns can be based on cultural identity principles or specific needs relating to future working life or the requirement to involve youth deeper in community life.

Following the reports of the cases studied, it is possible to have an initial idea of the forces that boost the development of these experiences, the "routes" they follow and the main profile they achieve in order to exist within the system. The local community is the main driving force behind Case 1 (Friendship Centre). The centre obtained a civil and independent profile for pedagogical, financial and self-management capability. The route it followed in order to "exist" went from its creation in the community and its recognition by its members to the education system. After obtaining the recognition of the formal education system, not without difficulties, they returned came back to the community with a stronger and larger learning offer. Now it seems there is a confrontation of views between what the community and the education system would like to see in the near future at the Centre.

Case 2 (Support Unit: USAER 8) has a specific education reform as its first learning and development factor. The Unit consolidated a complex operating profile within the organisational frame of the formal educational system. It went from this system to a professional organisation; from here it went to the schools and to management within the system. From there it became a social reference for the community.

Today Case 3 (Intelligent Classroom) has a pedagogical profile that pursues clear and precise objectives within the framework of the compensatory programmes of education policy. This initiative has also gone through different phases; from the recognition of a critical situation of low achievement among immigrant children and the structural problems regarding the design of a pedagogical strategy (that some specific public servants consider "theirs"), it progressed to implementation in the field (which included negotiating financial resources with the government and companies), to its current legitimacy within the institutionalised system.

Case 4 (BICAP) has existed since the establishment of a plural policy that recognised ethnical diversity as the basis of an education model that was considered appropriate in the town of Santa Maria Tlahuitoltepec. This learning centre consolidated a profile of political participation that led to curricular flexibility and a local education system that was more open to the values of tolerance and cultural and ethnic plurality. The route it followed passed from the dynamics of the standard political system to the design of a particular curricular model. They are now facing difficulties in defending this ethnic approach since the political and social system has not become more flexible in view of the ethnic diversity.

The peculiarities of the routes followed by the actors and their objectives show the social complexity of education work. The motivation and objectives of the experiences arise from and in different levels of the education system. Even though the scope of the results is different, the four cases have given themselves specific periods for the interpretation of their objectives and the definition of their operating opportunity contexts. They have designed strategies and tested and modified them immediately. They have reflected on their results and on their future. Their results, however positive they are, will not easily be replicated in other contexts.

6.5. Looking for pertinent education responses
Margarita Zorrilla-Fierro[8]

Paulo Freire (1972, 1973) affirmed we all educate each other by means of experiencing the world. This suggests that the interrelationship among children, young people and adults "happens" in a social and natural context. Ausubel, Novak and Hannesian (1987) advise us that "there are things that pupils already know and find out and these needs to be considered when teaching". To recognise and assume that pupils are not a *tabula rasa* when

---

[8] Professor at the Education Department of the Autonomous University of Aguascalientes (Mexico).

they first come to school, but that they possess previous knowledge and experiences, could be easy to understand but very difficult to apply. It is in fact a radical change with regard to how school learning and education are conceived. Nevertheless the cases studied show that in the daily life of communities and educational institutions, it is possible to construct **pertinent education** responses for both individuals and society in which they live. Thus we would like to highlight some issues and questions that we consider important, in order to trigger reflection, and thereby to encourage some actions.

In general, there is a need to reread and renovate the pedagogical principles that contribute to answering *the* question: **what do we educate for?** As a teleological activity, education should define and pursue its specific purposes and once this is clearly defined the scaffolding processes and institutions built around these goals. The relevant actors should also become scaffolding agents. In this sense the quality and equity of the education proposal are central issues. Muñoz-Repiso (1999) says that **quality** implies paying careful attention to the results of education that need to be observed and measured, "taking into consideration the context and starting point; furthermore they will have to refer to the totality of the pupils without exclusion".

With this idea in mind, the author quotes Mortimore's definition: "a quality school is one which promotes the progress of its students within a broad scale of intellectual, social, moral and emotional achievements, taking into consideration their socio-economic level, their family environment and their previous learning. An effective school system is one that maximises the capacity of schools to achieve these results". It is possible to appreciate in this sentence the necessary links between learning and educational systems, between pedagogy and management and how both dimensions need each other and are necessarily connected. Thus what kind of education and for whom are not pointless questions. At the very least, the four cases analysed represent an affirmation that education is for everybody; that the right to learn, as a human right, demands the design of creative and pertinent forms that ensure their relevance and guarantee opportunities of human development for all persons.

Veronica Larrain (2005) agrees with Keith Sawyer (Chapter 2) when he affirms that during the 20th Century great progresses have been made in our understanding of how people learn. However, school practices have not been modified to reflect this new knowledge. UNESCO (United Nations Educational, Scientific and Cultural Organization) explicitly re-formulates these concerns in its Delors Report (1996), saying that education and learning are processes that occur over the course of a lifetime. Likewise it states that schools in particular must have to promote "the four pillars of today's education": learning to know, learning to do, learning to live together and learning to be. However many questions remain unanswered: which theory and learning model should be followed? What contents and skills are most appropriate, taking into account the different contexts in which different education initiatives take place? For and by whom should these be formulated? How can the necessary human, operational and structural resources be obtained?

Furthermore, as Marcela Tovar explained previously in this chapter, research on learning in particular does not seem to be available to educators. Teachers, principals, public servants and parents are aware that research is progressing and most of them would be willing to acquire new tools in order to carry out their task. However they are rapidly discouraged when scientific findings are difficult to decrypt and apply, or are too far-removed from their daily realities. Thus a more general and urgent question is: how could the learning scientists share their findings and make them available to teachers in a way that is really useful? This issue could be addressed partially as a fundamental matter for training teachers (both those starting out and those already in service). Case 1 (Friendship Centre) has already taken some steps forward with its educator-mothers model. However, this may not be sufficient or easy to do. Thus new and creative forms of sharing learning-sciences outcomes, at different levels of the education system, need to be enhanced.

Another relevant element for further reflection is Feuerstein's concept of the **teacher as mediator**. The notion of mediated learning experience is at the heart of Feuerstein's social interactionist learning theory which states that the way in which *stimuli* are emitted by the environment are transferred by a "mediating" agent, usually a parent, sibling or other care-giver. This mediating agent, guided by his/her intentions, culture and emotional investment, selects and organises the world of stimuli for the child (…). Through this process of mediation, the cognitive structure of the child is affected (1980, pp. 15-16). The force of this mediation approach may only be understood in the light of Vigotsky's notion of a *close development zone.* Vigotsky (1978) sustained that every child has, in any sphere, a real level of development that can be evaluated, as well as immediate developmental potential within this scope. In the words of this author, the difference between real and potential development is a *zone of close development*. This zone is the distance between the real development level – as determined by the capacity to solve problems in an independent way – and the level of potential development, determined by the capacity to solve problems under the orientation of an adult or in collaboration with more qualified peers.

Collaboration with another person – whether an adult or a more qualified peer – in the zone of close development, places the notion of development within a culturally appropriated form. The context in which the interaction occurs then has decisive importance for this development and the effect of these approaches in the instruction based on the school is evident. Thus the valid and urgent questions arise: how could teachers become facilitators or mediators of the learning processes? How could the education system as a whole (drawn from central authorities, teachers unions, community, etc.) contribute to it? Who else should be enabled to become mediators? What could current, future and potential teachers/mediators say about this, from a field perspective?

The comprehension of the nature of the knowledge that needs to be learnt and taught is also essential in order to construct spaces of learning and development for everyone. The key question is: what learning should be promoted in our pupils and how? Today, more than ever, it is vital not only to accumulate information but also to know how to handle it and identify how it can be used. Linda Darling says that in the choice between the extent and the depth of contents, the emphasis should be put on the latter. "To develop comprehension in students requires both the time and pace that can make comprehensive learning possible with the right orientation of the teacher, who may construct a framework for key ideas and anticipate conceptual mistakes or stereotypes, while also designing learning experiences that takes the pupils' way of thinking into consideration, as well as showing the parameters that research on a certain discipline should follow" (2002, p. 161).

The cases analysed help us to think about **institutional learning**. This new form of functioning for educational systems at macro and *meso* levels may support the micro or institutional development of every school (see also Chapters 8 and 9). A significant issue for consideration is that the experiences studied and many similar to them should manage to build themselves and be successful because they are born and grow outside the system. Does this suggest the need to escape the administrative and bureaucratic environment in order not to be held hostage kidnapped by nevertheless relevant requirements and therefore be able to create good education?

6.6. Reforms built from the field
María de Ibarrola[9]

In almost every country, the goals, policies, projects and programmes that aim to improve the quality of education systems are constantly being renovated. More often the actions implemented by a government are analysed and the results achieved are evaluated. In most of the cases, better diagnoses of the condition of national education are obtained. These diagnoses normally come with new changes, different intervention methods, and management strategies.

Nevertheless, it is evident that there is no magic formula for educational change. It has been demonstrated, as Juana Sancho mentions in this chapter, that large-scale education reforms barely come into being, and that some of them seem to die as soon as they make contact with reality (Tyack and Cuban, 2000, p. 120) and that failure is easily predictable (Sarason, 1990). On another note, some of the schools that put reforms into practice arrive at a completely different interpretation of what was originally proposed (Tyack and Cuban, 2000, p. 121), or they produce complicated dynamics that are "more sophisticated and difficult to register through the application of the traditional conceptual frameworks" (Rodríguez-Romero, 2003; p. 79, 2006).

In order to understand the elements that have facilitated the possibility of improvement, particularly the inefficiencies of the current education system, we should look at the reality of the complex historic puzzle. Change requires the careful reconstruction and restoration of multiple elements. The task is then to identify action plans that are suitable and to recognise for each of them the obstacles, gaps, digressions or contradictions present, then resolve them. This would produce a great number of proposals and specific actions.

In the case of Mexico, as in other OECD countries, a current transcendental phenomenon is the emergence of new and very different actors with real capacity for action that attempt to respond the countries educational needs. Some of these actors seem more able to conduct changes than the two main actors of the 20th Century: the federal Ministry of Education (SEP) and the Teachers Labour Union (SNTE) (Loyo, 2006). In addition to the federal government, local governments, municipalities, congresses and several civic society organisations – some of which are highly qualified – have a relevant role to play.

---

[9] Researcher at Department of Education Research of the Research and Advanced Studies Centre of the National Polytechnic Institute (CINVESTAV–IPN) (Mexico), former member of the Mexican National Council of Specialists in Education.

The Mexican cases discussed in this volume are – as previously mentioned – marginal, specific, local and at the micro level. However their educational and learning achievements seem promising. In Chapter 8, Aguerrondo reminds us that a key phase of all innovations is the effective interaction of the (local) innovations with the regular education system which is a "hard negotiation with reality". OECD's work on learning environments does not pretend to find a way of automatically generalising these experiences or to replicate them on national scales. A more relevant contribution would be to identify those innovation dynamics that harmonise the key elements of learning processes as a response to immediate problems, as identified by local authors. This means imbuing learners and teachers with a very active interaction role in a dynamic where everyone can learn and to assure the compromise of all actors.

The OECD proposal also seeks to rethink the content of education options based on its pertinence for the cognitive structures of the groups to which these are addressed to and to reorganise them in accordance with this goal. It looks at the value of local cultures; at transforming the use of time and spaces in education; at introducing new didactic material, formative assessments and encouraging certifications based on real learning outcomes.

Achieving these goals requires careful consideration and the identification of and making visible those concrete experiences that have been built by those actors at the foundation of the system. Some of them are in the margins and sometimes even in open opposition to the policies dictated by the national structures. Taking into account the enormous dimension of this task, one starting point would be the full participation of a fundamental group of actors: the teachers.

In the search for better learning environments, the goal of CERI should be to encourage the system to look at their foundations in order to discover and encourage the rich learning initiatives they will certainly find. Then the subsequent aim should be to learn from these and build the transition towards more flexible national policies that promote respect, autonomy and the responsibility of – and for – the actors on the ground.

References

Ausubel, D., J.D. Novak and H. Hannesian (1987), *Psicología educativa: un punto de vista cognoscitivo*, Trillas, Mexico.

Bransford, J.D., A.L. Brown and R.R. Cocking (1999), *How People Learn: Brain, Mind, Experience, and School*, National Academy Press, Washington, DC.

Brown, P. and H. Lauder (2001), *Capitalism and Social Progress: The Future of Society in a Global Economy*, Palgrave, Basingstoke, Hampshire and New York.

Casassus, J. (2006), *La educación del ser emocional*, Cuarto Propio Indigo, Editorial Castillo, Santiago de Chile, México, April.

Cuban, L. (1993), *How Teachers Taught: Constancy and Change in American Classrooms, 1890-1990*, Teachers College Press, Nueva York.

Darling-Hammond, L. (2002), *El derecho de aprender. Crear buenas escuelas para todos*, Biblioteca para la Actualización del Maestro, SEP-Ariel, Mexico.

Delors, J. *et al.* (1996), *La educación encierra un tesoro*, Santillana, Madrid.

Eastman, M. (1941), *The Atlantic Monthly*, John Dewey, December, pp. 671-678.

Feuerstein, R., Y. Rand, M. Hoffman and R. Millar (1980), *Instrumental Enrichment. An Intervention Program for Cognitive Modificability*, University Park Press, Baltimore.

Freire, P. (1972), *La educación como práctica de la libertad*, Editorial Siglo XXI, Mexico.

Freire, P. (1973), *La pedagogía del oprimido*, Editorial Siglo XXI, Mexico.

Fukujama, F. (1995), *Trust: The Social Virtues and the Creation of Prosperity*, London Hamish Hamilton, London.

Hargreaves, A. (2003), *Teaching in the Knowledge Society: Education in the Age of Insecurity*, Open University, Buckingham.

Hernández, F. (2001), "El curriculum integrado: de la ilusión del orden a la realidad del caos", *Cooperación Educativa*, No. 59-60, pp. 79-85.

Hernández, F. (2006), "¿Por qué decimos que estamos a favor de la educación si potamos por un camino que deseduca y excluye?", in J.M. Sancho (ed.), *Tecnologías para transformar la educación*, AKAL/Universidad Internacional de Andalucía, Madrid, pp. 51-76.

Larrain, V. (2005), "Visiones sobre el aprendizaje", *Revista Kirikiki. Comperativa Educativa*, No. 75-76, December 2004-May 2005, Barcelona.

Loyo, A. (2006), "El sello de la alternancia en la política educativa. México 2000-2005", *Revista Mexicana de Investigación Educativa*, Vol. 11, No. 30.

Lowen, A. (2000), *Narcisismo o la enfermedad de nuestro tiempo*, Paidós, Barcelona.

Morin, E. (2000), *La mente bien ordenada*, Seix Barral, Barcelona.

Muñoz-Repiso, M. (1999), "Calidad divino tesoro", *Crítica*, pp. 22-25, *http://www.mec.es/cide/espanol/investigacion/rieme/documentos/files/cri ticacalidad/criticacalidad.pdf*

Oakes, J., K. Quartz, S. Ryan and M. Lipton (2000), *Becoming Good American Schools: The Struggle for Civic Virtue in Education Reform*, Jossey-Bass, San Francisco.

Popkewitz, T.S. (2000), "The Denial of Change in Educational Change: Systems of Ideas in the Construction of National Policy and Evaluation", *Educational Researcher*, Vol. 29(1).

Postman, N. (1996), *The End of Education. Redefining the Value of School*, Vintage, New York.

Rodríguez-Romero, M. (2003), *Las metamorfosis del cambio educativo*, Akal, Madrid.

Rodríguez-Romero, M. (2006), *Aprendiendo de la experiencia: los estudios de caso y las perspectivas del aprendizaje y la enseñanza que promueven.*

Sarason, S.B. (1990), *The Predictable Failure of Educational Reform: Can We Change Course before It's too Late?*, Jossey-Bass, San Francisco.

Skinner, B. (1954), "The Science of Learning and the Art of Teaching", *Harvard Educational Review.*

Tovar, M. (2006), "El modelo educativo emergente: la práctica educativa como fuente de innovación", working document for the OECD-Mexico International Conference: "Emerging Models of Learning and Innovation" held between 14-16 June 2006 in Mérida, Yucatán.

Tyack, D. and L. Cuban (2000), "En busca de la utopía. Un siglo de reformas en las escuelas públicas", SEP/FCE, México.

Vigotsky, L.S. (1978), *Mind in Society: The Development of Higher Psychological Processes*, Harvard University Press, Cambridge, Mass.

Chapter 7
What Makes Innovations Work on the Ground?
by
María Cecilia Fierro-Evans[1]

This chapter outlines ways in which we can view innovations as managerial processes, and how the various factors inter-relate. Three sets of innovation processes and features of innovative educational processes are defined, forming a theoretical scheme through which the innovative field experiences as the four Mexican cases can be analysed.

7.1. Innovation as a managerial process

As a form of educational change, innovation may be constructively approached as a managerial phenomenon (Ezpeleta and Furlán, 1992; Díaz Barriga, 1995). From this perspective, it is possible to address the manner in which regulatory, managerial and organisational factors, as well as those of a political, pedagogical and cultural nature, become manifest and inter-relate. Such an approach also allows us to observe structures and operations, as well as the internal configurations of work teams. From the moment an innovation is conceived, designed and implemented, it gives a "new foundation" to ideas, since the successive experiences and actors involved imprint their own perspective – adapting, enriching, diluting, publicising, bureaucratising or recreating their original purpose. Thus, the life-path of an innovation is a process of successive reinterpretations of a set of initial ideas by which those responsible for implementing them have the "last word" on contents and scope.

---

[1] Researcher, Universidad Iberoamericana, León (Mexico); Coordinator of Education Research, Education Programmes and Research Directorate.

For an educational institution, innovation can be perceived as change processes constructed by actors who begin by understanding and adjusting their practice. From this perspective, the primary purpose of innovation is to find the most adequate response to practical needs or problems (Fierro, 1996). The underlying assumption then is that innovation follows a critical analysis of an educational practice that takes place within specific performance contexts and is carried out together with others that share the task. Indeed, it is within these institutional spaces that the substance of innovation is defined. Within each innovation, different mechanisms will be used to adjust, create and/or consolidate activities and relationships leading to more valid educational results for their target population. In this sense, innovating is equivalent to educational management and it entails interpreting, negotiating and decision-making at the school level.

By considering innovation as a process of educational management, three main sets of processes can be highlighted:

- *The model of intervention*: In terms of design and methodological conception, it is relevant to analyse the proposed intervention models and to understand the routes they have followed for their implementation and sustainability. This includes their proposals, conception, structure, scale, decision processes, resources available, communication mechanisms, flexibility and adjustment capacity.

- *Innovation agents and the political processes related to their efforts*: Innovation agents need to be defined according to their identity, interests, ideas, alliances, proposals and platforms for action, negotiation capacities and ability to take advantage of favourable political and educational opportunities, along with their capabilities in configuring the spaces for the diverse participating agents and management of conflicts that arise.

- *The innovation's institutional and formative processes, considering the context and the professional culture in which they are to be developed:* Time-analysis for innovations is not carried out from the point of view of the project's management logic, political opportunities and timing, but from their agents, who are the central figures of the innovations and not mere implementers of externally created projects. Therefore the elements that require consideration from this perspective include individuals' reflection and adoption of the contents of innovation in medium- and long-term processes, assuming that cultural change implies changing existing visions in an institutional performance context.

Innovation may thus be understood both as a process and as the outcome of actions taken to introduce new elements into a situation in order to improve it. It involves a critical review of practices influencing performance from a managerial, training and financial standpoint. Through this review, legitimacy and support for the innovation is obtained and diverging perspectives are given an opportunity to be considered. The likelihood of procedures being harmonised and appropriate, and that the target population participates genuinely in the innovation are thus increased. The following sections of this chapter describe these innovation processes more fully.

7.2. Features of innovation: building the intervention model

Design and growth path

The first dimension in describing and understanding innovation focuses on how the proposal is designed. This covers such aspects as: the content and scope of the proposed changes, the structure and context of the intervention, its expected evolution and the size of the target population. These elements communicate the complexity of an innovative experience, the type and quality of the resources it will demand, as well as its time horizon, all of which affect its feasibility.

Projects may have three possible levels of origin: *i)* local, with no government or external intervention; *ii)* local, with only limited government or external intervention; or, *iii)* regional, ministerial or even international origin, with diffusion to the local sphere (Havelock and Huberman, 1980, p. 48; Huberman, 1973). While some might label microlevel proposals as "models for local change or of limited relevance", to do so is paradoxical if we consider that these "limited relevance" changes are usually the most permanent and with a deeper impact than other forms of change. In this sense, they are the models with the broadest scope.

The four cases studied (see Annex A) are all microlevel initiatives designed as geographically limited interventions that are – at least in their initial stages – limited in scope. This model for local change contrasts with more common models of large-scale projects that follow very rapid growth curves and involve a large number of components. These larger projects can be subject to the so-called "dilemma of greatness", "controlled expansion" or "cross expansion" behavior.[2] As local change occurs almost exclusively

---

[2] In the *dilemma of greatness* model, growth occurs quickly, followed by a fall that is either equally quick or slower, after which there is stability or paused fall. Under this model there is a "logic of rupture", given the aim of breaking radically and quickly with the past. The

at the pace suited to the project and its needs, it is first imperative to establish what these are. A whole set of other strengths, which we will deal with shortly, derives from this step.

The agent and the change process

A way of considering innovations is to take into account the role of agents and the change process their actions privilege through their defence of an initiative's aims. In their analysis of educational innovation, Havelock and Huberman (1980) consider that the success of an innovation is dependent on personal contacts and that the unit of analysis should be the individual at whom the innovation is aimed. The innovation's development is thus determined by the **social interaction** of group members through the successive stages of: awareness, expression, interest, trial and evaluation, trial period and, finally, adoption. This characterisation fits Case 3 (Intelligent Classroom), in which interaction is orchestrated by the leadership of the innovation's central promoter. The co-ordinating team's response has enabled the project to operate for several years, albeit while remaining vulnerable. Likewise, the education experience in Case 4 (BICAP: Ayuujk Polivalent Integral Community High School) relies heavily upon social interaction. The robustness of the initial project as well as awareness of its relevance explains why the innovation survives, although with diminished support from its initial players.

The **problem resolution** model of innovation insists that target populations must solve problems by themselves: thus, they are the starting point of any innovation. From this perspective, the diagnosis preceding the search for solutions is crucial, since the problems must be analysed as a precondition to their resolution. If there is an external "agent of change", it is non-directive. The individual and collective knowledge accumulated by the target population is more useful in addressing the problem than imported knowledge. It is also assumed that there is a higher likelihood of assimilating an innovation that is "owned", *i.e.*, assumed as a personal

---

controlled expansion model features a quick rise, followed by levelling and then gradual fall, or a gradual rise, with points of stability and regression. In this model the "gradual" logic prevails, with proposals for setting goals or carrying out transformations in the medium or long-term and by means of accumulating resources, conditions or partial achievements. The *cross expansion* model implies that the growth curve is steep and sustained and is followed by stabilisation. This type of project is rare, since it demands exceptional political conditions: not only being guided by a charismatic personality, possessing ample popular support and an unequal managerial infrastructure, but also being appropriately linked at national and local execution levels (Havelock and Huberman, 1980, p. 48).

decision, because it responds to a clear need. Case 1 (Friendship Centre) falls into this category, since the solution responds to the experiences of a community that is gradually being assimilated by the surrounding urban environment. The Case 3 (Intelligent Classroom) project also responds to the lack of consideration for the diversity that prevails in the schools and its inequitable consequences.

Types of intervention

Another useful categorisation is to look at the "content" of innovations (García, 1988, pp. 55-56). In this sense, **pedagogical innovations** are oriented towards education's qualitative aspects, such as improving teaching, efficiency, performance and new equipment. The key variables are the teacher, the environment, the students, their parents, etc., or those integral to the daily performance of the educational institution. Cases 1, 2 and 3 fall within this category. The **structural innovations** are political-educational actions that generate fundamental change inside schools. They harness political circumstances, such as government changes and the implementation of new political or educational arrangements. Although pedagogical content is at the heart of Case 4 (BICAP), through community activities the project's curricular change incorporates a political and social demand that has economic implications:

> The demand of the indigenous populations is to design public policies that allow them to influence, formally and without limitations, the decision-making and budgetary exercise of the schools in their jurisdiction; to address matters required by the indigenous peoples for their development and teacher and student roles based on community values; they also advocate the existence of an educational space where children and youths do not suffer from discrimination because of their identity and their culture.

Legislation aiming at education change is a common motor of innovation. In García's view "innovations in state systems are characterised by involving **pedagogical aspects simultaneously with political and institutional stances**, which undoubtedly makes analysis more difficult and complex" (1988, p. 61). Although none of our cases falls directly into this category, two have been developed under changes in educational legislation, *e.g.* Cases 2 (Support Unit: USAER 8) and 3 (Intelligent Classroom).

7.3. Strengths found in the cases' origins and operations

Taking into account the origins and operational models of the cases studied, a list of strengths can clearly be identified (see Box 7.1).

Box 7.1. Strengths derived from the cases' origins and operation modes

- *Short operative cycles*: A relatively short time span from detecting a need, designing and then implementing interventions, in contrast with the complex mechanisms and the extended timeframe of innovations on another scale.

- *Needs-adjusted operation:* The planning logic is strictly related to the particular needs and problems of the project in its specific development context and in consideration of the availability of agents to respond to them. This stands in contrast with planning, operative and resource assignations that respond to managerial agendas exogenous to the project. These latter require approvals and human and material resources that either paralyse or unduly quicken the pace and timeframe of development.

- *Flexibility and adaptability:* Operational strategies permit the resolution of tensions in discrepancies between plans and practice. The scope of action gives the flexibility to adjust objectives, contents and tasks gradually in order to adapt to new circumstances, widening or closing their intervention margins and reorienting them when necessary.

- *Financial and support diversification:* All of our cases succeed in articulating adequately an operational strategy guided by local human resources, but one that is backed, in different ways, by external financial support, either through philanthropic or entrepreneurial sources or by means of state advice or participation in terms of regulations, financing or certification.

- *Close communication and exchange:* The operational structures of the projects enable the maintenance of clear communication and exchange mechanisms, the ability to solve problems that arise and linking capacity with different external bodies. This contrasts with the frequent signalling of communication, co-ordination and problem solution hurdles experienced by innovations implemented in other levels of the system.

- *Adequate resource management:* Resources are critical to the project and its needs. In none of our cases were financial management problems or resource loss or waste reported. Nor were actions suspended due to lack of resources, although this might represent a challenge to project continuity.

- *Clear leadership:* The projects include clearly defined operational schemes stating actions and goals.

- *Stability of the teams committed to the projects.*

- *Regulatory support.* Two cases, Case 3 (Intelligent Classroom) and Case 2 (Support Unit: USAER 8) are strong in terms of educational policy definitions. Case 1 (Friendship Centre) has faced changes in this regard, while Case 4 (BICAP) confronts one of its greatest challenges in this sense: "The regulations were there; we chose to be different".

- *Consistency between purpose*, the intervention chosen and the strategies employed. Due to their dimensions and operational modes, the cases succeed in orienting purposes, actions, resources and operations in the same direction. Inconsistency between these processes can be a major handicap.

7.4. Innovation targets and their action spaces: agents and the political processes

This second section focuses on the actors and the relationships between them. It acknowledges the relevance of power and its dynamics. It also analyses the successive negotiations involved in each stage of the project: from design to operation. Finally, the "virtuous circle" of attitudes that foster innovations is examined.

Rationale and legitimacy of the proposal

Whether an innovative project has the capacity to respond to problems depends on the degree to which it is accepted by its promoters and target population. In some instances, a consistent diagnosis and solution proposal mechanism is required. Often though, proposals respond to problems or purposes external to the needs that practitioners identify, which explains a reluctance to participate. Hence the rationale and orientation of the proposals influence the project's legitimacy among those in different positions on whom success depends. In this respect, all four cases are explicit: the relevance of the needs addressed is convincing both for the target population and for other agents. This is important both for making these experiences not only inspiring, but also largely successful, as adoption follows conviction, moving actors to add their efforts to the cause.

Political conditions: willingness and reality

Political conditions may be understood as being the extent of the political will that supports a project, the situations – at local, regional and national levels – that make it more or less relevant and from the specific combinations of forces, specifically those agents and groups that support an innovation and those who are indifferent or antagonistic. It is important to gain the political will of those responsible for its approval, as well as granting the necessary resources and staff to undertake the planned activities. They can also help during the adjustment process while the project is implemented. In order to survive, innovations must be supported by those with power in an active way rather than through merely formal or legal channels. It is equally important that managers and target populations agree on the basic purposes and central elements of implementation activities, since one of the main challenges of the project is to reach and maintain consensus. At the same time, this is a condition that poses serious challenges at other operational levels, which have not always been resolved.

Every educational change project calls for co-ordination involving:

- Alliances between the key stakeholders.

- Agreements on labour concessions, commitments, rights, benefits and opportunities for the different agents concerning their involvement and power.

- Actors who might not be able to reach consensus or negotiation.

- Consensus-building among planners and the target population on the project's objectives and their implementation, aimed at reconciling different positions and expectations among the groups involved; and

- Ability to negotiate with different sectors throughout the life of the project, through reviewing those matters previously agreed upon as well as to be able to confront unforeseen situations.

However, reaching agreement is not only essential at the beginning of the process, but also throughout the entire life of the project, particularly when new possibilities for action appear or when it is necessary to make decisions within more limited time frames – or with fewer resources – which inevitably favours some aspects or players over others. Case 4 (BICAP) is an example of effective negotiation, where the participants have developed the ability to address and negotiate the changes demanded by the official education system through curricular adjustments, while maintaining the essential nucleus of contents.

7.5. Real room for conflict management and for different actors to make decisions

Beyond the formal distribution of tasks, each innovation project builds participation spaces whereby the intervention of certain actors is privileged over others. To the extent that the spaces agreed upon match those that have been granted *de facto* constitutes a strength, since any mismatch would undermine support from those involved. In contrast, decreasing interest among different groups at different levels weakens innovation projects since they will not have sustained adequate participation levels despite the political will to do so at a higher level. Commitment from intermediate and/or ground level evaporates, thus diluting and eventually undermining the invitation to change. Committed engagement is a feature of all the cases; for example, this is clearly seen among the teachers working with migrant children and in the voluntary participation of high school teachers and students. All of them vouch for a horizontal type of participation, with a high and lasting degree of commitment generating cohesion within the teams. For instance, Case 2 (Support Unit: USAER 8) is sustained by the participation of different agents in changes in practice, along with acknowledgement that the idea of inclusion means that everyone is different.

Conflict management indicates that the ability of innovators to negotiate is closely related to the above, meaning that a workable climate and timely problem-solving mechanisms must be established. In Huberman's words, innovations depend on the ability to solve problems. There are different ways of solving them and their solution depends, to a great extent, on those in leadership positions. Innovations are thus highly revealing of the different workings and intertwined aspects of the school system (1973, p. 26). Case 4 (BICAP) makes some of these conflicts explicit; this has been a complex and difficult process, since most of those involved did not have elementary education levels. Over a period of six months, meetings were held between the community and the BICAP's multi-disciplinary pioneering team, with the participation of other Mexico City officials and scholars. Dialogue with the national education authorities ended during the mid-1990s because what was offered by them – *i.e.* contents that were consistent with the cultural context and a different role for teachers and students – was not required by the community. Initial support was lost when policies changed direction. Nevertheless, they decided to proceed, either with or without official support. Ministry of Education management changed in 2000, at the same time as the government. The changes that subsequently took place in the education sector favoured technical education based on mastering abilities that were transferable to other contexts, which meant curriculum centralisation. The 2004 curricular reform clearly confirms this tendency since it provided only a minor space to change the official curricula. BICAP needed to manage this conflict of interest in order to survive and achieve its goals.

Consistency between aims and contents and decision making

Establishing spaces for participation – consistent with those aims expressed – supports the authority legitimised through innovative practice and maintains the commitment of those involved. For instance, in Case 2 (Support Unit: USAER 8) undisputed strength is drawn from the consistency of the project's inclusive philosophy and its own work as a team: "Each practitioner contributes her/his strategies based upon the tasks at hand, thus making them complementary in terms of the approaches and knowledge of the schools themselves. The balance between the number of teachers, psychologists and specialised therapists has resulted in the appropriate mix.

Their diverging training paths and the experience accumulated configure the team's capital, which is highly valued by its members".[3]

All this offers the chance to build moral authority, which is among the most valuable resources with which to influence schooling. The same is seen in Case 4 (BICAP). Its very operation is subject to its philosophy, *i.e.* "the supremacy of community values – particularly those related to social and political participation – implicit in building ethical citizenship."[4] This implies a social and political position of community control over the schools in their territory so that there is permanent interest in educational opportunities and their relevance. Each community has a parents' committee that monitors school activities in response to a mandate from the community assembly and as part of a community service within the authority structure. Case 1 (Friendship Centre) is similarly authorised by the community. Its work in favour of the children symbolises the process by which the community gains strength and addresses its problems. The Centre embodies how matters should proceed in order to achieve joint social action. "…the community members acknowledge that the Centre generates the context in which they can identify, as neighbours, their ability to organise their leadership and commitment towards improving their living standards, in the same way that they solved the need for building dignified spaces to care for their children".[5]

7.6. Attitudes that foster innovations

We would like to underline some of the key attitudes that appear to reinforce the innovation processes that emerge from analysis of the dynamics between agents, their action spaces, political processes and the four cases studied. These are presented in Box 7.2.

---

[3] Analytical Report of Case 2: Support Unit: USAER 8 (Spanish Version): *www.oecd.org/ edu/learningenvironments*

[4] Analytical Report of Case 4: BICAP (Spanish Version): *www.oecd.org/ edu/learningenvironments*

[5] Analytical Report of Case 1: Friendship Centre (Spanish Version): *www.oecd.org/ edu/learningenvironments*

Box 7.2. Virtuous circle of attitudes that foster the "As" of innovations

- *Amazement:* So-called "problematic" situations arise from human encounters that are constantly changing. While these entail a degree of vulnerability, they also demand that the cognitive, moral and affective discomfort associated with them lead to the exchange of indifference for discovery.

- *Appropriation:* Responding to a shifting reality can lead to an initial decision that might gradually allow the assumption of a greater commitment with others. These experiences are inspiring because someone has committed her/his efforts to intervene in collaboration with others so that they can improve their situation as regards exclusion and vulnerability. As a result leadership emerges and expands towards a group of individuals; it is not handed down but built together with others, establishing a shared mystique that is recreated, re-elaborated and enriched each time a new member enters. This provides the moral capital and source of strength for innovations.

- *Audacity:* Since this strength derives from their personal commitment and the relevance of the task that moves them, there is no hesitation in negotiating the resources, necessary approval and support required in the most diverse environments. No one works just for themselves but thinks more expansively in the context of their particular environment.

- *Ancestry:* The cases are strengthened by their community bonds – acquiring roots and being locally relevant and welcomed – as well as through the participation and support of parents, teachers or authorities.

- *Authenticity:* There is genuine interest in working on a shared social need. It is immediately clear when other stakes come into play that they may risk distorting the direction of the innovation. Authenticity is generated through consistency between what is intended and actual operation.

- *Authority:* The legitimacy of the action is acknowledged – its viability and the commitment of those who lead it – which translates into respect and recognition. Based on this commitment, actions that achieve positive results gradually allow higher-level negotiations in the pursuit of project needs. Technical and moral authority is the ultimate factor that sanctions the actions of genuine innovators.

The analysis presented here is based on a theoretical scheme that considers innovations as managerial processes. Its employment as a reflection tool of cases based on other logics is insufficient in certain aspects. On the whole, however, it is a relevant exercise, since – in addition to helping identify relevant matters associated with the development of these experiences – it offers explanations for their significance. From the point of view of their origins and *raison-d'être*, all four cases, analysed during the Mexico *exploratory phase*, aim at equity. Nevertheless, it is through the way in which they organise their actions and guide the participation and training of the agents involved, that this purpose comes alive as their ultimate power.

References

Avanzani, G. (1985), "Inmovilismo e Innovación en Educación", in C. Delorme (ed.), *De la Animación Pedagógica a la Investigación-acción*, Narcea, Madrid.

Baez, A. (1977), *L'Innovation dans l'enseignement des sciences: Synthèse mondiale*, UNESCO, Paris.

Ball, S. (1989), *Micropolítica de la Escuela*, Paidós, Barcelona.

Cabrero, E. (1995), *La Nueva Gestión Municipal en México. Análisis de Experiencias Innovadoras Engobiernos Locales*, CIDE/Porrúa, Mexico.

Cabrero, E. (1996), "Capacidades Innovadoras de Municipios Mexicanos", *Revista Mexicana de Sociología*, No. 3, Vol. 58.

Delorme, C. (1985), *De la Animación Pedagógica a la Investigación-acción*, Narcea, Madrid.

Díaz Barriga, A. (ed.) (1995), *Procesos Curriculares, Institucionales y Organizacionales*, COMIE, Mexico.

Escudero, J.M. (1988), "La Innovación y la Organización Escolar", in R. Pascual (ed.), *La Gestión Educativa Ante la Innovación y el Cambio*, II World Basque Congress, Narcea, Madrid.

Ezpeleta, J. (1992), "Problemas y Teoría a Propósito de la Gestión Pedagógica", in J. Ezpeleta and A. Furlán (eds.), *La Gestión Pedagógica de la Escuela*, UNESCO/OREALC, Santiago.

Ezpeleta, J. (1996), *Reforma Educativa y Prácticas Escolares. Avance y Perspectiva*, No. 15, CINVESTAV, Mexico.

Ezpeleta, J. (1999), "Federalización y Reforma Educativa", in M. Pardo (ed.), *Federalización e Innovación Educativa en México*, Colegio de México, Mexico.

Ezpeleta, J. and A. Furlán (eds.) (1992), *La Gestión Pedagógica de la Escuela*, UNESCO/OREALC, Santiago.

Ferry, G. (1974), "Rôle de l'enseignant dans un échantillon d'écoles novatrices en France", *L'Enseignant face à l'innovation*, Vol. I, OCDE, Paris.

Fierro, C. (1996), "Fortalecimiento de la Gestión Pedagógica de la Escuela a Través de los Consejos Técnicos", M.A. thesis, Universidad Iberoamericana, Mexico.

Fierro, C. (1999), "La Participación de los Maestros en los Procesos de Innovación desde la Escuela. Un Desafío de la Reforma Educativa Mexicana", *Cero en Conducta,* No. 47, p. 14.

Fierro, C. (2000), *La Gestión: Una Perspectiva para el Análisis de Procesos de Innovación en los Sistemas Educativos*, DGIE/SEP/Fondo Mixto, Mexico-Spain.

Fierro, C. and G. Tapia (1999), "Descentralización Educativa e Innovación. Una Mirada desde Guanajuato", in M.C. Pardo (ed.), *Federalización e Innovación Educativa en México*, El Colegio de México/Ford Foundation, Mexico.

Furlán, A. and A. Rodríguez (1995), "Gestión y Desarrollo Institucional", in A. Díaz Barriga (ed.), *Procesos Curriculares, Institucionales y Organizacionales*, COMIE, Mexico.

García, W.E. (1988), "Innovacoes nos Sistemas Estatais de Educacao", *La Educación, Revista Interamericana de Desarrollo Educativo*, No. 103, XXXII.

Gimeno Sacristán, J. and A. Pérez Gómez (1994), *Comprender y Transformar la Enseñanza*, Paidós, Barcelona.

Havelock, R.G. and A.M. Huberman (1980), *Innovación y Problemas de la Educación: Teoría y Realidaden los Países en Desarrollo*, UNESCO, Paris.

Huberman, A.M. (1973), *Cómo se Realizan los Cambios en Educación: Una Contribución al Estudio de la Innovación*, UNESCO/OIE, Paris.

Hummel, Ch. (1977), *La Educación hoy Frente al Mundo del Mañana*, UNESCO, Paris.

Husen, T. (1976), *Las Estrategias de la Innovación en Materia de Educación. La Educación en Marcha,* UNESCO/Teide, Barcelona.

Husen, T. (1986), *Nuevo Análisis de la Sociedad del Aprendizaje*, Paidós, Barcelona.

Janne, H. and M.C. Roggemans (1975), "Tendances nouvelles de l'éducation des adultes", *L'Éducation en devenir*, UNESCO, Paris.

Marmoz, L. (1985), "Innovation et rénovation", in C. Delorme (ed.), *De la Animación Pedagógica a la Investigación-acción*, Narcea, Madrid.

Muñoz Izquierdo, C. and S. Lavín (1988), "Estrategias para Mejorar el Acceso y la Permanencia en Educación Primaria", in C. Muñoz Izquierdo (ed.), *Calidad, Equidad y Eficiencia de la Educación Primaria*, CEE/REDUC, Mexico.

Núñez, I. and R. Vera (1990), *Participación de las Organizaciones de Docentes en la Calidad de la Educación*, UNESCO/OREALC, Santiago.

Pardo, M.C. (ed.) (1999), *Federalización e Innovación Educativa en México*, El Colegio de México/Ford Foundation, Mexico.

Popkewitz, T.S. (1994), *Sociología Política de las Reformas Educativas*, Morata, Madrid.

Rivas, E. (1984), "Cambio e Innovación Educativa: Metodología para su Consecución", *La Educación, Revista Interamericana de Desarrollo Educativo*, No. 94-95, XXVIII.

Schwartz, B. (1979), *Hacia otra Escuela*, Narcea, Madrid.

Tedesco, J.C. (1987), *El Desafío Educativo. Calidad y Democracia*, Grupo Editorial Latinoamericano, Buenos Aires.

Tedesco, J.C. (1992), "La Gestión en la Encrucijada de Nuestro Tiempo", in J. Ezpeleta and A. Furlán (eds.), *La Gestión Pedagógica de la Escuela*, UNESCO/OREALC, Santiago.

Chapter 8
The Dynamics of Innovation
Why Does it Survive and What Makes it Function
by
Inés Aguerrondo[1]

This chapter explores the various dynamics of the processes of innovation and change. The author suggests that it is through the examination of actual endeavours that truly innovative procedures may be successfully activated. To this end, she defines four phases of innovation in the context of the transformation of education, which are illustrated utilising the four Mexican case studies.

The paucity of results obtained from most of the attempts at reform throughout the world brings into question the possibilities of change in education. However, research on the subject indicates that a broad variety of innovations offer an interesting field of inquiry with regard to the application of public policies. One of the aspects requiring consideration is related to the process of change itself and to the possibility that existing experiences can be used to understand better how to instigate genuinely innovative procedures with successful results.

The starting point for this is the fact that the school system is a complex organisation, where – from the specific to the general – instances range from classes, institutions and intermediary echelons, to the level of federal or national management. The dynamics of this system are structured on a classic model (to which some authors refer to as a as paradigm, see also Keith Sawyer's "standard model" in Chapter 2) of what could be called education know-how or the "basic technology of the production of

---

[1] Training Unit Coordinator at IIPE-UNESCO, Buenos Aires, former Undersecretary of Programming at the Ministry of Culture and Education of Argentina, and professor at San Andrés University (iaguerrondo@iipe-buenosaires.org.ar).

education" (Oszlak, 1999). This basic know-how can be represented by the didactic triangle: namely the knowledge transmitted, the learner or learning process and the teacher or teaching process.

From that standpoint, innovation is genuine when applying an alternative technology of production of education, which necessarily entails the structural redefinition of the didactic triangle. This means that each of its three elements can be re-conceived within an alternative conceptual frame. In simpler terms, it can be said that when knowledge ceases to be understood as being "scientific" by redefining it within the model of "research and development", the student ceases to be passive by becoming active (constructivism) and the role of the teacher ceases to be one of transmission, becoming instead a facilitator of the experience of learning.

The transformation of education supposes that this re-conceptualisation or paradigm leap must go beyond the level of discourse and affect all the instances of organisation of the school system, modifying likewise the structure of the class, the institution, the intermediary echelons and the central management of the system. This posits the idea that, in order to achieve the objective of education consistent with the 21st Century, these redefinitions and subsequent changes must be verified in all these instances, while still maintaining adequate cohesion between them through the major principles that are their foundation.

The dynamics of innovation can be understood in terms of four phases that are at times in sequence and at other times overlap each other, in such a way as to create a sort of spiral growth (or decrease). These phases, described in the following sections, are:

1. The processes prior to innovation: *Genesis* or *Gestation*.

2. The initial stage or early steps: *Setting in Motion*.

3. The interrelation with the classic education system; this step requires a negotiation with reality: *Development and Evolution*.

4. The challenge of survival: *Effects and Sustainability*.

The cases included in Annex A are used here to illustrate some of the main concepts.

Box 8.1. First phase: genesis or gestation

1. Existing pressures

2. Gaps requiring innovation (or "the window of opportunity")

   - Conditions of the structure

   - Conditions of the current situation

3. Development of the proposal, preparation and participation

---

In practice, the inherent dynamics of education and diversity of potential responses available define a series of innovating answers that are drawn either from the basis of the system – at schools – or from the very top, in the shape of political strategies such as plans, programmes or projects. In order to make these impulses concrete, there is a series of previous processes that can be considered to have triggered innovation itself. These can be grouped into three categories: existing pressures, the gap requiring innovation and the characteristics of the development of the proposal.

8.1. Existing pressures

The pressure prior to innovation is determined by the detection of a problem requiring a solution and the existence of a critical mass of developed knowledge which diagnoses and accounts for a possible solution. The interrelation between these two dimensions provides the components that generate an idea of how to develop new proposals. In many cases, the **problem detected** is related to the inadequacy of the classic education proposal, as seen in the characteristics of social groups that have been incorporated as a consequence of overcrowding of the education process. The problem detected in Case 1 (Friendship Centre) is the existence of unattended children at kindergarten and in Case 2 (Support Unit: USAER 8), the requirement to include children with special needs.

Early knowledge or ideas about how to treat education problems and the exhaustion of the traditional education proposal provide sufficient elements for action in many cases. In some cases there is no certainty that genuine innovation presupposes the discovery of theoretical advances, but rather the ability to put into practice knowledge that is already accepted in the academic field. This is no minor development, since it is clear that even though these ideas are available today for all education actors, they are not generally considered a sound support for carrying out changes.

Case 1 (Friendship Centre) is based on two main sources of early knowledge: the first is the Montessori method, which advocates respect for the individual and training in autonomy, along with the development of individual decision-making capacity and the capability to share. The second is based on the development of the students' mothers as individuals in their own right. Its relationship with UNESCO (United Nations Educational, Scientific and Cultural Organisation), UNICEF (United Nations Children's Fund) and OECD allows it to be supported by the overall context of the use of international and national policies as proposals for the paths and destiny of community efforts and the networks they have developed. The Centre's concern to uphold the convocation of the women of its own community is a priority stemming from the commitment and determination that has empowered women with a sense of identity and belonging, constituting the major potential to shape a better future for the children and themselves, despite the lack of professional profile that is traditionally expected.

8.2. Gaps requiring innovation (or "the window of opportunity")

The tension between the problem and its solution acts as a latent trigger in the search for the instance required to put a proposal into practice. The right spaces in the system are sought in order to find the appropriate gap for change. For this to be possible there must be a current situation in which the processes of the structure and their adequate articulation need to be combined:

- As regards the structure, there must be a political and administrative space for innovation.

- As regards the current situation, there are three elements: the driving forces in action, one or several actor(s) in charge of being the bearer(s) of change, and a specific trigger or catalyst that combines all these elements.

Conditions of the structure

In the cases studied there seem to be different situations concerning the structure which provide the window that enables these innovations to come into being. Two cases contain a structural element represented by the decisions of the general education policy (federal state), which – jointly with what takes place in the rest of the region – has turned towards change in education in preceding decades. In these cases there are federal programmes allowing the introduction of innovation.

The existence of these programmes provides a possibility space or a general political gap that allows the existence of the innovations. In parallel it also shows the administrative openness (or flexibility or space) that a programme must have in order for innovation to be included in the general education system. Changes in the education system structure and the processes of decentralisation also provide open spaces of autonomy for the local authorities that help the process.

Conditions of the current situation

The historical process of educational evolution gives rise to spaces that are susceptible to the emergence of innovations, along with others that are more resistant. Different situations present different opportunities for innovation.

The **driving forces** are usually found in the groups directly interacting in the current situation; these can be external agents, philanthropic institutions, professional or political institutions, various actors of the same community or political actors interested in resolving a specific education problem. Powerful actors in the local environment can, for diverse reasons, also be interested in solving the problem.

Innovations demand one or more actors – whether individuals or groups – to become **bearers of change.** Leadership of the process, upkeep of the line of change and negotiation of emerging problems all seem to demand a specific task that is usually undertaken by a single person, even though, in some cases, the conductor of the experience is a group. The role of these bearers is of utmost importance as they are in charge of the initial tension and take advantage of the window that is presented. Very often, they not only take advantage of it but they also devote their efforts to the "building" or "expanding" of the window, which although already a significant process in this phase, is all-important for the adequate handling of the feasibilities in the next phase (*i.e.* development of the innovation).

Apart from **leadership**, two other elements seem to be common traits in those playing this role in the surveyed innovations. The former involves **expertise**, which means having full command of the theoretical aspects of the proposal to be carried out and, at the same time, having extensive personal **experience** in the handling of similar situations to those that are to be solved by the innovation. The latter has to do with the continuity of duration.

In general, the person appointed as manager is fully experienced, offering his/her services in the conviction that they can be used to advantage. He/she tries to give different answers to those that he/she has already used. In both Cases 1 (Friendship Centre) and 2 (Support Unit: USAER 8), the bearers were for the most part both educated and experienced. In Case 2, the principal worked for a long time with disabilities and now feels much more useful in this situation where there is an unemployment threat to the group. The bearer is also characterised by his/her interest in the issue. One of the main managers and leaders in Case 3 (Intelligent Classroom) is majoring in psycho-pedagogical intervention as part of her postgraduate studies which, together with her personal commitment, have allowed her to combine both professional career and academic development within this proposal. The next significant aspect for consideration is the possibility of durable continuity for the leader to be able to carry out the innovation. However, the question of continuity presents liabilities in that it can present problems with sustainability. Who will be in charge later on, or who will undertake its expansion? How do you put together new teams?

Besides the agents or driving forces and the bearer or leader of the innovation, a **triggering factor** can also appear in a specific situation; this is sometimes an unexpected event that makes all the other elements combine to start the innovation. In Case 3 (Intelligent Classroom) it would appear that the trigger element occurred when one of the leaders participated in an international conference and heard a specific project presentation that addressed the same educational challenges as those to which she was trying to respond. In the Friendship Centre (Case 1) a series of accidents befalling some of the children who were left alone at home gave rise to the need to have someone look after them when their mother was working.

8.3. Development of the proposal, preparation and participation

In many cases the proposals have long **preparation periods**, mainly because of the process of maturation that results from the application of previous processes. Nevertheless, this is not always the case in all education experiences. Literature registers cases where innovation policies have been **improvised**, although lacking the necessary qualifications. From the standpoint of its beneficiaries, no matter what the degree of development, what determines whether there was improvisation or not is the degree of knowledge/diffusion/acceptance that the proposal has enjoyed among teachers on one hand and the community and parents on the other.

The diffusion of the proposal can be improved through a true **participation** process in achieving joint construction, thus ensuring greater feasibility. In the cases studied, two appear to be models of participation in the development of the proposal. The first situation can be traced to Cases 1 (Friendship Centre) and 4 (BICAP: Ayuujk Polivalent Integral Community

High School). In these, we find community construction occurring through a wide-ranging process of consultation carried out by the actors who were later in charge of innovation. In Cases 2 and 3 (Support Unit: USAER 8 and Intelligent Classroom), this construction acknowledges participation, but only of the professional individuals who are responsible for the experience. The community is understood to be another actor with which to work in order to develop various activities.

Box 8.2. Second phase: early steps – setting innovation in motion

1. The politico-cultural feasibility

2. The feasibility of knowledge

    - The scientific-professional dimension

    - The organisational-administrative dimension

3. Concrete feasibility and resources available

The second phase in the process of genuine innovation is the setting in motion or putting the innovation into practice. The characteristics of the application are framed during this early stage. From the previous stage there are a number of concrete elements to start with, including a decision (political, administrative, communal, or any of these variables), a delineated and developed proposal and a leader willing to take charge.

In terms of process, this stage comprises two levels: the initial setting in motion and the ensuing first steps that initiate the application. It is at this stage that a series of real restrictions appear in relation to true difficulties, as well as to the development of any resistance. Tackling these problems demands strategies to confront and resolve them. We call these strategies: *feasibilities*. The idea is to create the conditions to *do* and these conditions can be grouped into three areas: to want to do (politico-cultural feasibility); to know what to do (feasibility of knowledge); and to be able to do (concrete feasibility) (Prawda, 1995).

These feasibilities have their own dynamics and respond to diverse characteristics – whether political, cultural or material, etc. – and can be constructed or amplified as they are produced during interaction of the innovation with the system's routine and with the resistances developed. A major task for the leaders of the innovation is related to the premise that "conditions are not awaited but are brought into being" (Hirschman, 1991).

8.4. The politico-cultural feasibility

This feasibility represents the "permission to act". It is the "want to do" dynamic of the non-bearers of the innovation. In the education system, this permission to act comes from two instances: the political echelons of the local and federal authorities on one side (political feasibility) and the community in general into which the innovation is inserted, as well as from the parents whose children are involved (cultural feasibility).

Many innovations are not set in motion, or fail in their early stages because they do not comply with the social representations of the parents and the community about what education ought to be. The expectations and representations of the parents and the community are usually framed through their own experience of education and thus are in accordance with the classic school culture. In these cases the **cultural dimension** does of course render difficult the introduction of genuine innovations for confronting difficulties in redefining the places and objectives of regular education. In the case of all the experiences studied, there is permanent co-operation with parents and the community, either because they have inspired the basic ideas of innovation or because their co-operation as co-participants in the education of their children is necessary.

The **political dimension** of the feasibility concerns the express permission that is required to carry out innovations in education. The present frame simplifies this aspect, as there is a generalised consensus on the need for change in education and public policies have expressly encouraged such change. Nevertheless, the political dimension plays a significant role in the innovations as they are genuine, meaning they go even further than what is usually accepted, thus breaking certain already established rules, making the decision still more difficult to put into practice.

The most common case in the experiences analysed is the existence of an important public official who has been approached to act as facilitator, or contacted in view of the fact that he/she is interested in making decisions that will solve the old problems of quality in education. In the experiences outlined in Cases 1 (Friendship Centre) and 2 (Support Unit: USAER 8), political authorisation was automatic as long as the conditions of current federal programmes were satisfied. In Case 3 (Intelligent Classroom), the political management changed and now there is a new administration that desires to help this migrant population; in Case 4 (BICAP), there is a high-level official related to the Ministry of Education who supports and finances the project.

8.5. The feasibility of knowledge

This feasibility refers to the immaterial aspects related to the quantity and availability of knowledge required to solve the problems of innovation. Further to keeping available the ideas for which adequate solutions already exist, it is also necessary to rely on them and make them available to share with the group in charge. These could be strictly related to new (scientific-professional) knowledge or to the managerial know-how necessary to carry out complex (organisational-administrative) operations, as is the case in education.

The scientific-professional dimension

An innovation demands alternative knowledge to that used on a daily basis and is generally represented by emerging ideas in academic and professional spheres. However, in order to be useful, these ideas must be adapted professionally to the specific situation at stake. This means it is important to take into account not only the previous experience of those undertaking the innovation, but also any professional and scientific training that allows them successfully to resolve everyday situations. Accordingly, leaders now actively try to increase these knowledge resources. It is common to have debates during special sessions about students with problems, as well as commentaries about new bibliographies, workshops or talks/lectures in order to update topics of interest. In short, the feasibility of innovation finds ongoing conscious feedback in the growth of the resource of knowledge. The innovations studied are assured in this feasibility mainly by their leaders who ensure that this resource is present and who themselves also grow with the experience.

Another aspect of the "resource of knowledge" found in all the experiences could be referred to as the "resources of professional competence", meaning full capitalisation of the existing professional experience of the personnel in question. The personal and professional capabilities and abilities of the team members have been duly appraised. The different training backgrounds and accumulated experience are a team assets greatly acknowledged by its members.

The organisational-administrative dimension

This non-material dimension is not usually regarded as being exceptional. However, it is particularly important in the case of innovations that encompass large groups of schools. It deals with the broad variety of proceedings and norms that allow the insertion of innovative institutions within the education system in order to solve the different administrative and ruling problems that emerge. The breakthrough of the established order produced by the innovation withdraws it from routine proceedings and creates problems when it is set in motion. As concerns the political "authorisation to act", it is understandable that different ways of placing the experience within the rest of the education system are employed.

In general, there seem to be three possible ways of inserting innovation into the administrative structure. The first is to make an exception in the established order; the second is to make it fit the present structure with specific conditions and the third is to create an *ad-hoc* parallel administrative structure. Each one has its pros and cons, depending not only on the innovation and its contents, but also on the number of learning centres involved, the time it takes to apply the innovation, whether or not it affects certification of the students and other variables. There are no records from which to infer which are the preferable options and which short- or long- term effects are, in each case, to be produced.

Each of the ways to solve this articulation presents its own liability for the future, which will add to the probabilities of generalising innovation. From an interpretative perspective, using special supervision or an assisting technical team could "isolate" these experimental units, causing a loss of the fluid relationship with the rest of the education system.

The "boycott" is the apparent risk in the case of ordinary supervision, which is still more dangerous than the former situation, as it implies an active position of hindering possible transformation. Finally, the "scuba effect"[2] appears when there is excessive support for innovation, creating certain conditions that are difficult to extend to the rest of the education system.

8.6. Concrete feasibility and resources available

Finally, concrete elements and resources are required to innovate. Some experiences do not demand different **human resources** to those already available in the education systems, as is shown by the cases studied. They involve regular professors, psychologists, psycho-pedagogues, etc. The weight of the main responsibility still lies with the tenure teacher, even in Cases 2 (USAER 8: Support Unit) and 3 (Intelligent Classroom) where innovation acts as a remedial aid for slower students. Interestingly, in these two cases there are outlines for special education tutors that show that all teaching must be capable of accommodating these contents.

---

[2] In the original Spanish version this is called: *efecto escafandra*.

Though previously we have developed some of the issues related to the acting human resources, there are still certain questions regarding professional competences and knowledge, training and its variables, teaching conditions, specific norms and the process of selection. These as yet unanswered questions include whether special personnel are required, whether education can be carried out by any teacher in the system, whether there is much rotation of personnel and if this is the case, how is this problem resolved? The case concerning the educator-mothers (Case 1: Friendship Centre) who somewhat obviate the need for professional training in order to undertake teaching responsibilities themselves, is one of the most interesting aspects of the study. This must be considered in relation to the complexity of contents to be taught at higher levels of schooling, but at the same time, this creates an opportunity for reflection on the different functions that need to be undertaken in order to facilitate the experience of learning.

Since innovation is a process, the management of **time** in this context is essential. This allows anticipation of the sequence of the different stages, how long each of them might be and how to judge what is going to happen. This also helps explain why something functions (or not) and how long it will take for the crisis to arrive, or in Prawda's words: "to be able to foresee the flood" (1995).

The **material resources** encompass the premises – the building and its equipment – and the other aids or support materials as a financial flow requested to back the innovation. Though references are scarce, it is possible to infer that a modification to enhance working strategies should include infrastructure and different materials other than those currently in use in the cases studied and therefore more resources. However, nothing different was observed in the classes, with the exception of one (Case 3: Intelligent Classroom). There is not always an innovative use of traditional resources and in general, material conditions do not appear to be inherent to innovations.

Box 8.3. Third phase: development and evolution – the negotiation with reality

1. The role of background and general context

2. Available courses of action

3. The process of consolidation

    •   Appropriate atmosphere for innovation

    •   Flexibility in the development of innovation

This section refers to implementation and calls attention to the dynamics of the process. Once innovation is in motion, its interrelationship with the rest of the education system, with its traditions and existing routines, begins. In order to move forward in the description of this moment, it is necessary to go back to the idea that innovation takes place inside a complex system, whose components are in permanent dynamic relation, which also interact with social components outside the teaching institution or the education system. At this stage, then, it is important to know what effect external relations have on innovation, what its context is, as well as its history and background.

8.7. The role of general context and background

The cases studied reveal the role of past history in each proposal. These experiences do not come from nowhere. In order to innovate, the existence of ideas and conceptual frames that help with finding creative solutions and, furthermore, the dynamics of the education process based on a trail of past attempts at change, must be taken into account.

A second issue for consideration is related to emerging alternative processes. Interrelation with the community, the general context and the rest of the education system produces concrete effects on innovation. The school centres, being different, become special objects that must **negotiate with the environment** in order to develop and grow.

External situations to the experiences also exist, at school or in the general context of the education system, which create conditions susceptible to different courses of action. A genuine innovation appearing in the context of general transformation of the education system has better chances of taking a successful course of action than another that develops in the context of generalised routine. Thus the existence or absence of a strategy in education reform at federal or local government levels will have an impact on the development of innovation. In the former case, there is an opening for innovation in the system; in the latter, there must be a series of defence mechanisms in place to preserve it (see Tom Bentley's Chapter 9).

During implementation and development, a range of transactions emerges which determines the way in which this can relate to the rest of the education system. This mode of relation can be seen through an **isolation/non-isolation axis**. In the routine context in education, many innovation experiences resorted to isolation in order to protect and consolidate themselves. In these cases, isolation can be positive as it allows innovation to survive and to strengthen itself within the framework of being an exception or a special case. However, there can also be negative isolation that gives rise to or even aggravates resistance to innovation, eventually making it disappear.

The isolation/non-isolation axis plays an important role in opportunities for development of the experience. If the external and internal political current situation in the education system is adverse (politico-cultural feasibility), the only opportunity it then has to survive is by isolating itself and not spreading. If the external situation is favourable and has been satisfactorily negotiated with the different sectors of power, the transformation can be somewhat generalised as long as there are constant feedback mechanisms, which – on the whole – presuppose the rupture of the isolation.

The most widespread defence mechanism in the context of non-generalised reform is the isolation of innovations. In such cases, apart from "underground planning" which may hide innovations from regulatory agents, many other creative options could emerge. This could mean negotiating special administrative norms or implementing the special exemption of current ones. It could also mean generating human resources through the training of teachers among graduates, or obtaining independent financial resources from foundations or philanthropic associations. In general reform contexts, or when top-down decisions to change have been made, for example, with federal programmes, it does not appear likely that the innovation has to isolate itself to survive. Time here plays a pivotal role as, in these circumstances, what is essential and what is redundant must be absolutely clear in order to establish adequate priorities at the time of adjustments and feedbacks, confirming that which is fundamental to retain and when to make concessions.

8.8. Available courses of action

After an innovation has been set in motion, three main processes can be discerned: consolidation, bureaucratisation and/or interruption. Contrary to the components of previous stages that are important because they either have a specific impact on the process or have conditioned the following step, here we consider there are different alternative courses.

Consolidation is produced when innovation strengthens and enriches itself. It is the process by which it moves forward according to plan and functions, giving the desired results by addressing and resolving the expected current problems. It entails a continuous process of enquiry, monitoring and assessment, meaning a full awareness of the actions being carried out. It implies teamwork of crossed controls through which the original proposal is enriched in a process of ongoing team-learning in order to resolve the problems that have arisen. In the next section, this process will be analysed in more detail.

Bureaucratisation takes place when the erosion of the innovation in the transaction process transforms itself internally, keeping its shape but not its innovating content. In other words, the innovation formally exists, but not in reality. The designed activities are carried out but the result does not vary in relation to traditional products stemming from classic proceedings. Adequate monitoring and follow-up of these aspects will provide us with the clue that the innovation secures itself or bureaucratises. However, the awareness that it is paving the road for bureaucratisation allows the possibility of rerouting the initiative and reinstalling the innovation. This is a typical crisis in the process of innovation, where the handling of time can provide benefits as long as the right strategies are taken to confront bureaucratisation and put the initiative back on its initial course.

Interruption takes place when a formal decision determines that the experience ceases to exist. In some cases, it comes at a later stage to bureaucratisation, when there is a realisation that there is no more innovation in reality, or it can appear in the course of its development. According to who is responsible for deciding the interruption, this may or may not be traumatic for the actors or the institution. If the decision stems from external resistances and it is the authority that makes it, a problematic and contentious situation is likely to be unleashed. If, however, the decision comes about as a result of the will of those involved in implementation – although this always leads into difficult situations – it is much less traumatic.

8.9. The process of consolidation

All the experiences studied thus far have endured the course of time, so they may be regarded as cases of consolidation. They represent an interesting opportunity to observe the processes that have allowed its sustainability. Two characteristics are worth mentioning in particular. One is the "atmosphere" of the innovation, encompassing the quality of interpersonal relations all the way through to a sense of the mystical and of belonging. The latter refers to a particular mechanism of negotiation with reality, far beyond the classic "all or nothing" approach that frequently characterises the manner in which it is regarded, to a certain degree determining the belief that reforms have failed. This mechanism of flexibility expresses itself in various ways.

Appropriate atmosphere for innovation

The atmosphere of the innovation is expressed in terms of interpersonal relations that go far beyond the individual, representing a characteristic that transcends it. It is an organisational trait, noticeable not only in some of the people or institutions involved, but also as such in the innovation itself. One dimension of this atmosphere susceptible to innovation has to do with **clarity of vision**. The people involved in the innovations build up a common image-objective, with well-defined traits, which accounts for a common ground for everyday exchange and even allows the justification of delays or unwanted results. This shared vision provides a new "sense" to the task, in accordance with what Fullan calls moral purpose (1993).

A second dimension of this atmosphere is the **quality of interpersonal relations**. Sharing a common vision that is hard to achieve and is different from the rest of the schools, with results highly appraised by its members, gives way to a positive interpersonal relation. Without ignoring the different responsibilities of each of the members, the interchange is framed by its horizontality and by the possibility of teamwork. This basis provides broader possibilities for the adequate processing of conflicts that are obviously also present and allows collaborative work and the constitution of true communities of practice (Wenger, 2001).

A third dimension of this atmosphere is the "**appraisal**" of the actors. People feel well and this increases their self-esteem. They find a personal sense of belonging. By rescuing traditions from the beginnings of the education system, it would seem that, in the professional development of education, there is a motivational recompense found in personal reward and individual growth. It is evident that participants are fully attracted to the fact that they truly see that what they are doing is worth doing, that it is effective and that they achieve goals that are not feasible in other proposals. This feature turns out to be pivotal in a context that has always been marked by a process of teacher dissatisfaction, whilst not appearing to be related directly to material conditions (Esteve, 2001).

This atmosphere susceptible to innovation has concrete consequences in that it enhances personal commitment and makes team members capable of collaborating with experience and with much more than their work. The mystical element is created by the shared responsibility of those who contribute to overcoming the problems. In some cases this becomes their "mission" and helps develop a sense of belonging.

Flexibility in the development of innovation

A second characteristic of the consolidation, as visualised in the four cases studied, is the scale and flexibility with which the task is undertaken. Contrary to normal development of the education system where routine prevails, here there are more open models of operation that are capable of processing upheavals and of finding new ways to meet difficulties. Although there is clarity in the sense that it is expressed in a shared vision or image-objective, this vision does not function as a norm to fulfil, but as a direction to follow. The image-object allows us to visualise how far it is meant to go and is taken not as a restriction or hindrance, but as a dynamic which allows continuation, arising from many different and repeated attempts to arrive at a solution.

Flexibility is expressed in different ways along the development of the innovation. In some cases, particularly when initiatives aim to be expanded into other fields or scaled-up to other learning centres, flexibility could better be identified after a "long" period of existence. In the process of **permanent progressive advances**, phases are usually identified and could be compared to a "cycle of life".

Another mechanism of initiation and negotiation is **concerted bargaining**. This refers to interaction with an administrative education control system that imposes its models on the innovation. This concerted bargaining, although allowing the innovation to continue, creates a zone of risk in that it opens up possibilities for the experience to deteriorate, or simply disqualifies it. Perhaps concessions to reality restrict the innovating components and facilitate the road to bureaucratisation.

Case 3 (Intelligent Classroom) entails concerted bargaining between the needs of the federal and regional states in order to enforce the constitutional principles of equal education opportunities for all, along with the need for manpower and competitiveness among local entrepreneurs. As with the actions of local education multiple agents (technical-pedagogical advisers, school and teacher advisers or supervisors), education agents with very meagre salaries are motivated to participate in the project by a profound civic conviction, a great social commitment and the will to serve. In Case 2 (Support Unit: USAER 8), concerted bargaining does not seem to be embodied by the authority that proposes it, but rather by a set of social representations.

Concerted bargaining can be interpreted as an example of the effects of isolated innovations and their interaction with the environment. If the innovation is isolated, the interaction could either reinforce the characteristics of the innovation and probable isolation, or strengthen relations with the environment and probable loss of its distinctiveness and, in the case that the innovation prevails, its bureaucratisation. This could be the case for BICAP (Case 4) as regards the latest curricula negotiations, where some of the modules characterising the experience are suppressed.

There is a mechanism that is neither related to the historical process of permanent advances nor to the negotiation with the political or administrative context: this is the **trial and error process**. This process is the negotiation between theoretical knowledge that serves as a reference and the mechanism by which the adjustment between the theoretical conceptions aims to be applied, producing concrete restrictions. These restrictions could be related to available knowledge, the professionalism of the human resources, the characteristics of the students, or the theories to be applied.

When an innovation is initiated, no matter how much theoretical knowledge has been accumulated, it is impossible to resolve everything in advance. Evidence shows that this process is jointly built up in tandem with the development of the experience. It is not a case of lacking the necessary knowledge beforehand, but involves the increase of change possibilities as a result of the interplay among needs, expectations (what can be and is known to do) and what actually happens. This trial and error mechanism allows construction of the complex competences of the participants and enactment of the vision. It also defines the everyday activity and sequence of this action. Time here plays a pivotal role, as in these circumstances it is all-important to know what is fundamental and what is not, as well as when feedback and adjustments are needed. Priority must be given to those aspects that are understood to be essential, whereas concessions can be made about others.

The education performance carried out in Case 3 (Intelligent Classroom) by the various education agents is affected by constant changes in administrative and technical-pedagogical rulings. This is due to ongoing experimentation and the irrelevance of those education proposals derived from federal frameworks that aim to respond to the educational needs of internal migrant boys and girls. The origin and implementation of Intelligent Classrooms is the result of some school managers and local education services attempting to offer efficient institutional and psycho-pedagogical support alternatives for these children. In Case 4 (BICAP) there are tensions between the national norms and the possibility of an education proposal with local cultural pertinence. BICAP has been able to organise its operation by reframing the norms. The external changes contradict its education proposal, specifically in two respects: the completeness (or integrity) of the education and training educative programme and strengthening the identity and culture of the students. In the former, spaces in the curricula have allowed the insertion of education and training programme links with the community reality; the latter includes training elements that reappraise indigenous Ayuujk local culture, with the due consensus of the community.

This appropriation and re-evaluation of the main lines of the proposal of knowledge play an important role in the internal appreciation of the innovation, as well as in the general atmosphere of change. The aim is to accomplish an institutional management capable of appraising itself while providing clear guidelines on how to do things. There is evidence of this in Cases 1 (Friendship Centre) and 2 (Support Unit: USAER 8).

The trial and error mechanism allows the appraisal of achievements and places within what should (and can) be improved, as well as of problems and inadequacies. This is significant in contexts where the notion of achievement and failure have an extremely rigid definition, where achievement is interpreted solely as having obtained ALL the expected results.

Box 8.4. Fourth phase: effects and sustainability – the challenge to survive

1. Functionality of the innovation

2. The open roads (sustainability)

   - Responding to changes in context and avoiding the onset of routine

   - Reacting to the pressure of institutionalisation

   - The challenge of expansion

8.10. Functionality of the innovation

Functionality is a reading of reality that establishes the reason for the innovation by providing clues, so that an education system capable of overcoming the "debts of the past" can be constructed. A first interesting function of innovations is the **building of concrete knowledge**, proceedings and work related to population sectors for which education was not initially considered, or to which it has not been capable of responding. In particular, new educational systems that need to respond to these issues, have in turn faced the most problems. Innovations should help to answer questions such as: how can the protection of children growing up with high social risk exposure in unfavourable social environments be guaranteed (Cases 1: Friendship Centre and 3: Intelligent Classroom); how to detect children with "differences" early on and redefine those who are different (Case 2: Support Unit: USAER 8); and how to respond to cultural diversity and needs (Case 4: BICAP).

A second group of positive elements is related to the **enhancement of the "performance" of the system.** Some innovations aim at (and succeed in) introducing proceedings in order to reduce drop-off or over-aged students, thus optimising the education pyramid. Some initiatives (Case 1: Friendship Centre) try to encourage students to continue their development, using it to build a solid educational background. Others try to increase inclusion in the education system as shown in Case 4 (BICAP).

Many innovations look far beyond that which is strictly pedagogical. This **cultural "training"** includes issues such as: the improvement of the quality of life of individuals and their neighbourhoods (Cases 1 and 3); increasing awareness of prejudices and the real needs of those who are "different" (Case 2); encouraging the positive aspects of cultural diversity and bilingualism, as well as personal and community self-esteem among minority groups (Case 4). Some innovations are also linked to more practical issues such as how to acquire the knowledge and skills in order to get specific jobs and develop the ability to foster productive projects (Case 4); or more general ones such as the preservation of the environment or the development of regional and national levels.

There are many elements in relation to new proposals of teaching and learning in the cases studied. Outlined here are just some issues related to the **pedagogical practice** that these innovations underline as being important and to which they are trying to respond: the transformation of regular education into a real model of integration and inclusion (Case 2); models of curricular flexibility and teachers' technical and formal capacity to adapt curricula (Cases 2, 3 and 4); and the acknowledgement of differently structured ways in which to stimulate children to learn (Case 3). Some of the initiatives also question some of the basic principles of traditional education systems, that for many years it has seemed impossible to change. Among these are: the accreditation (certification) procedures (Cases 3 and 4); the consolidation of different types of class groups and strategies (multi-graded classes, personalised programmes and rotating/temporary classes as well as the need for fun, inspiring strategies and the benefits of personalised assessments).

An issue which tentatively appears in those cases studied concerns the concrete ways in which **personnel training and development** participate in the experience. This is of utmost significance when considering the difficulties encountered in finding non-traditional training strategies in most education reforms. Case 1 sheds some light on how to provide community educators with a sound personal and professional training. Two examples of in-service professor training are found in Cases 2 and 3. Another matter of equal importance is the search for alternative ways to organise educational **government and administration**. Some of the issues that arose were:

collaboration with the private sector (Case 3) and strengthening the school-community relationship (Cases 1 and 4). In particular, Case 3 explores ways in which to organise supply to provide services in places nearby to where the parents work ("people go to school" vs. "the school goes to the people").

8.11. The open roads (sustainability)

The major variable to consider when analysing the sustainability of an innovating process is time. This is because it reveals differences in the processes in action and also because it allows the results of the almost mandatory interchange of the innovation with the environment to be demonstrated. The main issue appears to be "the risk of deterioration". Two of the cases analysed have sustained their existence for long enough to provide an interesting point for revision: Case 1 (Friendship Centre, 32 years) and Case 4 (BICAP, 10 years).

The progression of "the innovating force" can be analysed in these and other innovations. Some "typical" phenomena could emerge: decrease in pro-activity towards the innovation, the rotation of human resources, the diminution of commitment and consequently a hypothetical decrease in the quality of the results. Thus 3 challenges have been identified as being the most obvious. Firstly, what should be the response to changes in the early characteristics of the context? Secondly, what should be the reaction to the pressure of institutionalisation? Finally, what are the challenges and potential of expansion? These issues are discussed below.

Responding to changes in context and avoiding the onset of routine

Long-established innovations confront the consequences of **global changes** in context and their influence in the environment in which they function. The passage of time, mainly in decades as is the case of the Friendship Centre (Case 1), may imply severe modifications of the original conditions that, somehow, threaten the ongoing continuity of the innovation. Time also seems to act as a moderator of the conditions of pro-activity, which was indicated as a characteristic of the developing phase. The novelties and initial problems fall into a type of proceedings that will probably transform the innovation into a **routine**. Further related to this, another restriction in being part of a system is the scope of material provisions available. Other than the financial aspects, restrictions related to the training of new personnel or the need for special equipment can create problems in the long run and facilitate the development of routine.

Two important changes shape the current situation in Case 1 (Friendship Centre). First, the expectations of the families approaching the service have changed. The report pointed out that their "commitment and passion is different from those found in the participants at the beginning and throughout the years of construction". Second, these have modified their demands, going from requesting very basic day-care services to more advanced academic services, including the teaching of English and ICT. These requests may be more difficult to satisfy than the previous ones. In Case 4 (BICAP), there are also references to changes in the motivation of the students.

The introduction of this issue aims to determine whether or not some of these changes are altogether part of its success, a new external menace to it or even just the evidence of its deterioration. In any case the main challenge would be that the innovation may evolve in response to these changes, having a (new or similar) strong proposal, while retaining its innovating spirit. The report for Case 4 (BICAP) indicates some signs of the onset of routine. The report on this case especially refers to the need for innovating pedagogical responses and to the question of how to prevail over time, as well as how to find the human and material resources to carry on the different strategies.

Reacting to the pressure of institutionalisation

The report for Case 1 (Friendship Centre) says: "…the pressure exercised by public authorities is undeniable and among them the Ministry of Education (SEP) is under legal requirement to lead towards a progressive uniformity". Also Case 4 (BICAP) reports that the pressures of institutionalisation involve its erosion. Institutionalisation is in fact a very complex and the most threatening issue in the long term. Normally the central levels of governments are not conscious (and/or capable of recognising) that these innovations are real opportunities to improve the education system and to identify some of the most important obstacles and ways to solve them. When there is a serious attempt to reform, these opportunities can be extremely valuable since there is a strong need to ascertain more precisely what has to change and how. Neglecting them should be seen as a high price to pay.

A deeper and more careful analysis of these cases and the legislation and rules is needed in order to evaluate the possible ways forward. However there are enough elements available to encourage the authorities to look at these cases to understand their current challenges and the problems they have resolved, as a source of inspiration and analysis. For instance Case 1 may underline the urgency of the creation and formal recognition of new actors (*e.g.* the community educator in addition to kindergarten bachelors); or the need for alternative modalities in education programmes and infrastructure that could offer flexible services (ranging from short-term to "home extension" programmes). Both issues (learning facilitators and flexible education programmes and infrastructures) refer to the core of what could potentially be a viable model for Latin America. Because of increasing demands in education and its budget limitations, today this region needs new ideas that allow the use of new paradigms for the solution of problems.

The challenge of expansion

Despite agreeing that no social process can be reproduced strictly, we can definitely accept the existence of a "demonstration effect" that could inspire the will to replicate the innovation. In Case 1 (Friendship Centre) this question clearly appears as a consequence of the results accomplished, a strong determination to improve the conditions of the neighbourhood and the accumulated experience of its leaders. Case 4 (BICAP) presents another very well-known dimension of this question: "The introduction of new professors to the philosophy and functioning of the project, including kindergarten training and professional development of the professors…" is usually a decisive point of inflection in all innovations.

The dilution of the innovation seems to be an unavoidable consequence in the processes of expansion functioning "in cascade", when in each progressive instance there is a partial decrease of the vision and know-how about how to solve problems. It is perhaps related to the fact that in every innovation it is usual to find great dependence on the leaders and the fact that there are no strategies to generate alternative leaders who can take charge of the new expansion. Nevertheless, this is a central issue in the debate about changing the system in general and concerns the difficulties proven by generalisation of the changes.

Box 8.5. Looking to the future

1. A new paradigm: under construction?

2. Organisation of the administration

3. Transition towards generalisation (or the vicious circle of the "two sets of logic")

Most of the research teams that analysed the cases faced major difficulties in attempting to describe holistically the model of learning organisation fostered by the different innovations. However when trying to find elements that will help us to imagine better forms of organisation of teaching and learning, an interesting question arises: what lies behind these innovations which may help in the envisaging of a new model of learning and/or education supply, that is capable both of resolving the debts of the past and meeting the challenges of the future?

8.12. A new paradigm: under construction?

The frustrations of attempting education reform over the three or more past decades introduce a key question: what particularity is inherent to the education system that inures it to change? My hypothesis is that the mismatch between the demands for education and their answers is so great that it is no longer a question of how to improve what we know, but of how to invent an alternative education production model (see also Tom Bentley's Chapter 9). In order to fulfill this prerequisite, it is necessary to redefine the foundation from where the education proposal is generated and then, to imagine the concrete instances of the system (learning units, institution, supervision, central management, etc.) arising from this **new paradigm**. This change of vision must include both the pedagogical proposal and the process of change. It should also consider the most problematic contextual conditionings such as budget, the quantity and quality of the teachers, the existence of labour unions, etc. Another possible response is the reconsideration of the popular idea that "all reforms fail". My impression is that at the basis of these judgments there exists an "all or nothing" approach to reality, which ignores the intermediary stages and the logic of the dialectic process with which social reality functions.

A new paradigm presupposes a **dual re-conceptualisation**, firstly of the education proposal (the didactic triangle) and secondly of the process of change (the dynamics of the education change). The first of these issues has been discussed briefly at the beginning of this paper. In fact this is a very well-known and much-discussed aspect and is one about which there is fairly generalised agreement. The other aspect of central importance, but which paradoxically has been less debated, is the dynamics of education change. I believe that interpretations of the failure of change in education happen to be conditioned by how social dynamics are conceived. I quote Rodríguez-Romero's interesting conclusions where she warns about "the mutable nature of knowledge in social sciences…" and "…projects an image of education change focused on instability and mutations, far from the ideal of control pursued by the traditional visions of change in education" (2003).

Thinking of educational change from the viewpoint of a concept of "hard" knowledge, where a cause is definitely followed by an effect, does not reveal the process. We have noticed an interesting condition in these cases: flexibility as a condition "to keep on constructing".

Some examples of the issues that have been analysed and that could redefine the process of change and nourish this new paradigm are:

The redefinition of success and failure in the process of change. The important role of background in these experiences reinforces the idea of failure of the change processes in education. Do the processes of change fail or do we fail in not being able to see the advances? We are focused on the final product and we do not see the process of change which is hazardous and difficult, but which allows us to approach the goal or, at least, to advance in the right direction. The traditional representations and deterministic conceptions of cause and effect are not solely a question of theoretical debate, because they also provide nourishment for public opinion, which disqualifies many political strategies as these create unrealistic expectations.

Establishing an alternative for the most disadvantaged? In a new paradigm, it is not a complementary proposal for the most disadvantaged sectors that should be envisaged, but instead a general alternative education proposal that includes these sectors as part of a whole. The four cases studied reflect how education can provide a solution for the groups that have more problems when faced with the classic proposal. However, are these solutions only applicable in the case of the less advantaged? Or are we able to see them as an invitation to think about another education model that must not only encompass these groups, but also the whole of the population? The Ayuujk indigenous community of Case 4 (BICAP) tries to find a way of not setting aside their traditions while at the same time trying to fit into a more universal society. To do so, do they have to invent a new education system or another education supply? This is also the case for many valuable Latin American experiences, as shown in the case of the Escuela Nueva (New School) in Colombia or the Active School of Paraguay (see Anne Sliwka's Chapter 4). These are seen as models for solving the problems of those who cannot accommodate the traditional system, but it is unfortunately not a starting point for thinking about another system. This raises the fact that the proposal created in the West has a hegemonic vocation and does not provide room for any variation. This lack of flexibility, which apparently cannot be set aside, has become the real crisis in question in past decades.

ICT as part of the strategy. Considering a change of paradigm does not mean having to think of a traditional school enhanced with ICT, but instead of an alternative education proposal that includes the use of ICT and other innovative didactic resources. There are already too many experiences in all types of countries and regions and too much time and money invested in these types of strategies, allowing us to confirm that future challenges will not be solved with "computerisation" of the classic school. It is time to start thinking about using another school or organisational model to distribute education in accordance with the demands of society, using these new tools that have already given ample examples outside the education system that different results can only be achieved by implementing structural changes.

Communities of practice as an option of in-service training. As Hopkins (1996) correctly points out, the problem with teacher training is that all the proposals still seem to be more of the same. Thus in a new paradigm, it would be very important to revise the models of teacher training. The cases studied prove that the strategy of change is a collaborative work and they have developed and explained concrete procedures that can be traced back to the Communities of Practice. The goal of a community of practice is to develop skills and the creation and interchange of knowledge among its members through a collaborative atmosphere and team-work (Wenger, 2001). The conditions for its development are sustained by adequate management of the knowledge that already exists in the organisation. These communities are social groups built up with the aim of developing specialised knowledge, through the sharing of learning based on reflection shared over practical experiences. Specialisation provides the object of study, whereas the process of learning is achieved through the participation of a group of individuals experimenting, in diverse ways, with the object of study in question. This model demonstrates that communities of practice make explicit the informal transfer of knowledge within the networks supplying a formal structure and allow the development of further knowledge through shared experiences. Finally, the identity of the group is empowered when learning is reinforced as a shared process of participation and leadership.

8.13. Organisation of the administration

Another aspect that is present – although not profusely – in the cases studied, refers to a new model of the distribution of political, administrative and financial responsibilities in education between the state, private sector and civil society. This issue – which is truly relevant to Latin American reforms today – has no space in debates about new education and there is little concern about it in the world of specialists. This is perhaps because it is wrongly considered to be an issue that has emerged, not from the needs of countries, but from the interests of certain foreign credit financing organisms.

Here we find mostly doubts and questions that need further reflection and answers. For example, in a new education system model (and a new model state), which legal and administrative entity status should education institutions have? In a decentralised system, do schools have to be legal and administrative "agencies", "entities" and/or "civil associations"? What would differentiate them? The experiences of good decentralisation are generally found in countries of Anglo-Saxon tradition, whose education systems were decentralised from the outset. Which process should be adopted for countries with a centralised tradition, like those in Latin America?

8.14. Transition towards generalisation (or the vicious circle of the "two sets of logic")

A third area of reflection opened up by these innovations concerns transition processes. Learning how to manage the process of change in terms of generalised public policies is as important as being able to re-conceptualise the didactic triangle. Moises Naim (1995) acknowledges the difficulties of transition during institutional changes precisely because, contrary to macroeconomic changes, they include the factor of time. The image he uses is that of the opposition between what he calls shock strategy and chemotherapy strategy. In the former, change is resolved rapidly with few actors and decisions, whereas in the latter, there are many actors with many decisions (which hopefully will be concurrent) to make over a long period of time. Education is clearly placed within the second situation.

A greater risk is added when the duration of **co-existence of both sets of logic** is prolonged. It is traditional for changes to be thought about "progressively", but understanding this progressiveness is like starting the first year in first grade, then going on to the second year in second grade and thus progressively incorporating a further grade every year. This is a strategy that would continue for as many years as the number of grades present in the reforming sector. There are two main inconveniences with this strategy. First, as time passes, pro-activity towards the innovations decreases. Second, it extends the duration of the co-existence of two systems, with the additional problem at the beginning being that when the new one needs to gather strength, the traditional one is already stronger. Furthermore, it also divides the participants – since a professor who teaches two grades is part of both systems at the same time – which is divisive and impractical. The co-existence of both sets of logic operates against the possibilities of change. When both exist, it is difficult to reinforce the idea that the "regular" model is exhausted and another one will substitute it. It is not easy either to reinforce the message that the new model will retain the good elements of the previous one (*e.g.* to reach all children) but will also include other new and better elements (the policies for the elimination of exclusion).

One last aspect related to the implementation phase has to do with the levels of the education system that are involved. In many cases, schools want to introduce innovations and supervisors refuse them, or they accept them but they do not have the support of the upper levels. We may imagine that innovation would benefit from a coherent and coordinated interaction among the different institutional levels in the education system. This **transversal mode** strategy is the one expected to function in order for the changes to be able to move forward and be sustained.

References

Aguerrondo, I. (1993), "La calidad de la educación, ejes para su definición y evaluación", *La educación. Revista Interamericana de Desarrollo Educativo*, No. 116, III, OEA (Organización de Estados Americanos), Washington DC.

Aguerrondo, I. (1997), "¿Es posible impartir educación de calidad con menores costos?", *Perspectivas, Revista trimestral de Educación Comparada*, Vol. XXVII, No. 2, UNESCO.

Aguerrondo, I. (2003), *La escuela del futuro. Como piensan las escuelas que innovan*, Papers Editores, Buenos Aires.

Aguerrondo, I. and P. Pogré (2000), *Los Institutos de Formación Docente como Centros de Innovación Pedagógica*, IIPE-Buenos Aires/Ed. Santillana, Buenos Aires.

Brunner, J.J. (2000), *Educación: Escenarios de Futuro. Nuevas Tecnologías y Sociedad de la Información*, PREAL (Partnership For Educational Revitalization In The Americas), Documentos No. 16, January.

Esteve, J.M. (2001), *El malestar docente*, Paidós, Barcelona.

Fitoussi, J.P. and P. Rosanvallon (1997), *La nueva era de las desigualdades*, Editorial Manantial, Buenos Aires.

Frigerio, G. (1991), "Curriculum: norma, intersticios, transposición y textos", *Curiculum presente, ciencia ausente*, Bs. As. Miño y Dávila editors.

Fullan, M. (1993), *Change Forces*, Palmer Ed., London.

Hirschman, A.O. (1991), *The Rhetoric of Reaction: Perversity, Futility, Jeopardy*, Cambridge Mass., Harvard University Press.

Hopkins, D. (1996), "New Rules for the Radical Reform of Teacher Education", in A. Hudson and D. Lambert (ed.), *Exploring Futures in Initial Teacher Education. Changing Key for Changing Times*, Institute of Education, University of London, Bedford Way Papers, September.

Matus, C. (1976), *Planificación de situaciones*, CENDES (Centro de Estudios de Desarrollo), Caracas.

Matus, C. (1978), *Planificación, libertad y conflicto*, CENDES, Caracas.

Naim, M. (1995a), "Latinoamérica: la segunda fase de la reforma", *Revista Occidental. Estudios Latinoamericanos*, Año 12, No. 2, México.

Naim, M. (1995b), "Latin America's Journey to the Market from Macroeconomic Shocks to Institutional Therapy", International Center for Economic Growth Occasional Papers, No. 62.

Oszlak, O. (1999), "De menor a mayor, el desafío de la 'segunda' reforma del estado", *Revista Nueva Sociedad*, No. 160, Venezuela.

Pedró, F. and I. Puig (1998), *Las reformas educativas. Una perspectiva política y comparada,* Paidós, Barcelona.

Prawda, J. (1995), *Logros, inequidades y retos del futuro del sistema educativo mexicano*, Grijalba, México.

Rodríguez Romero, M. (2003), *La metamorfosis del cambio educativo*, Ediciones Akal, Madrid.

Wenger, E. (2001), *Comunidades de práctica: aprendizaje, significado e identidad*, Paidós, Barcelona.

Chapter 9
Open Learning
A Systems-driven Model of Innovation for Education
by
Tom Bentley[1]

This chapter introduces the idea of a systemic approach to open innovation: one that is driven by demand from learners and those funding learning. The author details the way that in this approach, innovative practices can be incorporated directly into systems at a small scale and then diffused such that they influence governance and, in turn, larger scale reform. He furthermore cites recent examples in which this approach to innovation is applicable.

9.1. Introduction

Over the last decade education has become even more central to progress – social, economic, civic and cultural – across the world. Education reform, raising the attainment and participation of an ever-broadening constituency of learners, is therefore pivotal to the political prospects of governments and the growth prospects of economies. For OECD countries, education is the focus of investment for raising productivity and competitiveness, for meeting citizens' aspirations, and for attempting social cohesion. In developing countries education is looked to for the same goods, albeit in often different circumstances: recognised as essential for achieving primary health outcomes, population stability, stable governance and economic growth.

---

[1] Senior policy adviser to Julia Gillard, Australia's Deputy Prime Minister and Minister for Education. Former Director of Demos, UK, and Director of Applied Learning at ANZSOG, the Australia and New Zealand School of Government (t.bentley@anzsog.edu.au).

Global change puts education in the spotlight. In the richest countries, it is seen as the route to sustained prosperity. In those catching up, it is the spur to development. As economic competition and social dislocation intensify, so the pressure on publicly funded education systems to improve their existing performance and to meet new needs will continue to grow. Given these pressures, it is remarkable how resilient the bureaucratic model remains.

In general, industrialised (and now developing) countries have moved towards more explicit outcome standards and performance measures for students, teachers and schools, while devolving control over other resources directly to schools and allowing greater local flexibility. In some countries, including the United States and Australia, this has been accompanied by the liberalisation of school supply through a mix of deregulation and funding policies to cultivate and incentivise the growth of non-state schools. But even where marketisation has gone furthest, the range of basic schooling models, and the structures used to coordinate them, have changed little.

A new educational paradigm has been anticipated, its features hotly debated, for at least a generation. In this paper I argue that the challenges and needs being placed before schooling are making the dominant forms of system and reform intervention gradually obsolete, and set out an emerging model of system change which may come to replace them. In a new way, school-age education systems can become the fuel of economic prosperity and the binding agent of social well-being. Achieving this goal in the 21st Century depends on identifying and harnessing a particular approach to innovation and system change to recreate the parameters of teaching, learning, participation and organisation. Doing this successfully requires that we understand properly the sources of bureaucratic and systemic resilience.

The systemic approach I am articulating is one of open innovation, driven by demand from both learners and funders of learning, and carried through collaborative learning networks, in which new practices, organisational methods and specific models of schooling are generated at smaller scale across the system. Then, through a process of continuous diffusion and adaptation, these practices and methods are incorporated directly into the whole system of governance and school organisation, influencing larger scale reform. In this model, schools operate with a high degree of flexibility, but are governed through frameworks which create strong interdependencies with each other and with other institutions and sectors. The design of governance regimes therefore helps to create powerful shared responsibilities and accountabilities, but explicitly seeks not to discriminate between different sectors of schooling. Schools are not the only (and in some cases, not the main) institutions of education provision. Change is driven not so much by the constant imposition of external requirements to comply with, as by the continuous process of innovation and adjustment by organisations and teams within the system itself. The focus of policy and strategy is to ensure that such adaptation is guided and shaped by long term learning outcomes, and not by vested interests or survival values within the existing institutions.

The crucial features of this approach to innovation are: first, that the "innovation system" on which education rests is an open, not a closed system; it can draw better knowledge and practices from anywhere and test them against its desired outcomes, and it can treat resources beyond the formal organisation of schooling, such as family engagement and community structure, as factors within its reach. Second, rather than trying to incorporate innovations into the standard institutional model of schooling through the tri-level structure discussed below in this paper, governance and coordination structures can adjust and update themselves in response to shifts in practice and emerging patterns of activity, as in the best systems of continuous learning built in other sectors. If we can recognise and develop the essential dimensions of this approach to educational innovation, we can also begin to locate within it other more specific features, such as the role of ICT platforms, of desirable assessment practices, of cross-organisational networks and clusters and of evaluative data. But without the right kind of approach to system design, none of these other components will be able to achieve what they promise for learning outcomes.

9.2. Multiple dimensions

The strain on current systems arises from twin pressures.[2] The first pressure is to ensure and demonstrate better attainment across *all* students and schools, and narrow the gap between the highest and lowest achieving students. The second pressure is to respond to the ever-growing range of need and demand, expressed as social and cultural diversity; changing student, family and employer expectations; growing economic inequality and geographical polarisation. The major challenge therefore is to build systems able to reflect the heterogeneity and diversity of the societies they serve, without sacrificing the quality of learning outcomes or the public fairness of their distribution.

This observation could also be put another way; education systems are multidimensional – affected by many different factors, resources,

---

[2] By system I mean the dominant institutional and governance designs for resourcing, structuring, coordinating, holding accountable and driving change in publicly funded education.

connections and relationships. Those under the formal control of policy makers or of educational professionals represent only a fraction of the whole. Changing schooling systems to improve learning outcomes for every student requires strategies which can act on the same complex range. That the systems are complex is obvious to anyone who works in them. But the focus of much research and policy has avoided the fact for at least a generation. Our starting point for understanding a new model of innovation must be the way in which the interrelated institutional structures and practices of schooling create multiple, overlapping forms of value.

First, and perhaps most important, schools apply pedagogical principles to the process of teaching and learning. Whether teaching has a didactic or a constructivist turn, is culturally nationalistic or cosmopolitan, seeks to draw directly on experiential learning or relies heavily on rote learning and mnemonics, will be influenced in part by the origins of the school in the cultural history of each society. But teaching and learning are also inseparable from their social context, meaning that the organisation of schooling also reflects wider patterns of social power and identity, shared cultural and civic commitments, and the distribution of wealth and status.

The role of social geography is particularly powerful here; in the United States, local control of school boards means that school funding reflects local tax income. In many cities around the world, house prices are correlated with the popularity and performance of schools in the neighbourhood. The role of Catholic schools in Spain and Portugal, or of private schools in Korea and Israel, has significance specific to each society, but is common in its reflection, and reinforcement, of social stratification and cultural history.

Public schooling systems and their composition also reflect "state-making"; the process through which government has built its role in financing, regulating and directing key public services and the relationship with other sectors, including religious, philanthropic and private sector institutions. For example, the terms of incorporation through which schools have joined public state systems, or been established by governments, have an ongoing influence on their character and their role in the wider system.

Equally, the presence and strength of religious schools, and the level of prestige and autonomy that they receive, reflect the religious, social and military history of each country, and the evolution of its civil state. In France, state schools reflect a strong, secular, republican history, creating famous tensions over whether students can wear religious symbols. The hierarchical nature of the French state is also reflected in the elite academies and training institutions towards which the highest performing students are channelled. Religious schools in different countries have played very different roles, according to the cultural and political context.

Schooling systems are also intertwined with the economy, not just in the sense that they provide future workers and influence their pathways towards different kinds of work, but also in their reflection of wealth, class and economic status. Different tiers of school provision, the availability of elite academic school places, and the nature of vocational courses are common manifestations of this issue.

All of these dimensions, and how they vary and interact, influence the performance of our education systems; regardless of the reform priorities and levers that are applied to them. They also influence each system's evolution; the "critical path" it takes in response to new pressures, stimuli and resources. These multiple dimensions and their complex inter-relationships are crucial for understanding how education systems change, and simultaneously resist change. Even when many people agree that better educational outcomes are desirable, the range of factors influencing how and why the school system functions are spread far beyond the control of one institution or social group.

9.3. Creating human capital: a new global narrative for schooling?

This is particularly important because of the breadth, depth and intensity of global change and the centrality of education to any response to that change. These changes influence the pressures and challenges that young people and families present to schools, the social and economic geography of communities, the nature of the teaching workforce, the other resources available to public education, the rewards that people can expect from educational achievement, and so on. The key global drivers are:

- The growth of an international knowledge and service economy, and emergence of rapidly industrialising economies from Brazil and Russia to China and India, changing patterns of trade, employment and educational achievement. India is currently producing 2.5 million graduates in science, technology and engineering each year.

- ICTs, especially the impact of digital networks, underpinned by the Internet, on patterns of economic and social organisation and flows of knowledge around the world.

- Consequent growth in the flow of people; mobility, migration and a steady increase in ethnic diversity within OECD countries, and the emergence of an integrated global labour market for those with recognised skills.

- A slow, global, gender revolution, with female workforce participation still rising, and younger women outperforming men in tertiary qualifications in most OECD countries.

- Urbanisation, with a majority of the world's population now living in cities, new patterns of city growth and inequality, and new planning and infrastructure pressures.

- Ageing, with a bifurcation of demographic challenge between industrialised and developing worlds, reproduction below replacement rates for most of the OECD, and a huge boom in the youth population of many intermediate economies, including middle Eastern states, and China currently the most rapidly ageing population in the world.

- Growing economic inequality, with Gini coefficients having grown in most nations over the last twenty years, and diverging rates of economic development between the wealthiest and poorest people on the planet.

These changes will have deep and unpredictable long term effects; in the short term, their combined effect is to place ever greater strain on the existing bureaucratic paradigm of schooling, stretching its resources more thinly across a greater range of need.

However, they are also driving a new narrative of global progress, in which education investment becomes the centrepiece of a "human capital" approach to competitiveness, and the solution to the cultural and social challenges of radical diversity and interdependence. In this story, governments can no longer guarantee rising standards of living through traditional public services and welfare provision. Instead, our chances in life are most influenced by the "human capital" that we accumulate as individuals and carry, freshly exposed, into the global marketplace and culturally diverse societies.

Investing, through education policy, in human capital, is therefore becoming the central way to improve long term competitiveness and well-being (OECD, 2001). The approach is well summed up in the findings of a recent Canadian analysis, which suggest that:

> *"A country's literacy scores rising by one percent relative to the international average is associated with an eventual 2.5% relative rise in labour productivity and a 1.5% rise in GDP per head. These effects are three times as great as for investment in physical capital. Moreover, the results conclude that raising literacy and numeracy scores for people at the bottom of the skills distribution is more important to economic growth than producing more highly skilled graduates."* (Coulombe and Tremblay, 2005)

These are important correlations, repeated consistently around the world. The Australian Productivity Commission recently estimated that raising literacy and numeracy rates would generate billions of dollars in increased economic output and government revenues. On the face of it, they suggest some obvious priorities for education reform. Governments are emphasising literacy, numeracy, workforce skills and participation as priorities for future productivity growth. But responding to these intensifying levels of economic competition and widening inequalities by seeking to push up the attainment outcomes of students solely within *current* schooling systems is, unfortunately, inadequate for two main reasons.

The first is that educational qualifications are used as positional goods, not just as absolute markers of attainment or capability. While not meeting literacy and numeracy thresholds at an early age provides a strong indicator of later educational failure and labour market marginalisation, it is not automatically the case that a rising tide of literacy and numeracy will raise everyone's boat by enhancing their future employment and life outcomes. If more people meet minimum outcome standards, then the selection criteria for participation in work will also be adjusted. Overall, economic growth rates are higher, suggesting that more people are likely to be economically active, and that their work is more productive. But whether everyone benefits also depends on how the work and the growth are distributed; if there is heavy competition for high status educational places or secure employment, shifting numeracy and literacy scores up may not change the eventual distribution of opportunity and benefit.

The role of education in productivity growth is fundamentally important, as any examination of the trajectory of different societies shows. But it is a process of *complex* causal interactions, in which institutions, cultures, markets and many other factors all play their part. The multiple dimensions we discussed above return with a vengeance. This complexity should not be used as a defensive measure to deflect ambitious reform or the demands of accountability. It does, though, defy efforts to reduce the process to an artificially small number of elements, or impose reductionist models of coordination and improvement onto complex systems.

The second reason why simply increasing formal educational attainment will not straightforwardly generate better social and economic outcomes for all, is that in most countries, inequality is widening. While human capital endowment makes more of a difference to life outcomes that it used to, the countervailing influence of other factors can mean that simply improving the output performance of school systems, point by point, year by year, may not be enough to improve the overall picture. The biggest effect of these global changes, at least currently, is to create self-perpetuating dynamic of *human capital* investment that will widen the gap between and within many societies. In many places the wider landscape is changing faster than the pathway of reform, helping to undermine the positive effects of new investment, increased capacity and better educational performance.[3]

This returns us to the challenge for reform and innovation strategies: they must learn how to support higher levels of differentiation, or diversity, while combating the tendency to harden patterns of socio-economic stratification, in which the distribution of disadvantage reproduces and amplifies the likely distribution of opportunity for the next generation, locking those behind into last place. OECD analysis has done much to illuminate how these levels of stratification and inequity vary around the world; how early academic selection and streaming appear to harden it; and how the world's highest performing school systems, especially those of the Nordic countries, combine excellent attainment with equitable socioeconomic distribution of outcomes.

It is not simply the level of private provision in a given system that determines this stratification, as the OECD's PISA analysis shows. Instead, it is the more complex interaction between the formal distribution of educational opportunity (the range of schools and their quality) and wider factors such as social geography, class divisions, social network structure (in particular parents' education), labour market conditions, access to books and information technology. These drivers are distributed widely across communities; they are not directly controlled by policy makers or public authority; but they nonetheless coalesce into patterns which have a consistent, enduring effect on who gets what from learning.

To borrow an economic metaphor, both human and social capital are subject to compound growth; if you start with a higher endowment, and continue to invest in their development, the gap will only grow. The most effective route to compound growth is to combine high quality formal education with the other, wider, informal factors which have positive impact on learning.

So schooling and school reform have joined the competitive race of nations; the performance of each school system is itself a reflection of economic and social progress, and a future contributor to it. Countries seeking to enhance their own development, and to secure future prosperity, are well advised to invest in schooling, but the idea that school reform, as it is currently defined (see below), will change the terms of economic competition and social cohesion within and between societies is over-optimistic.

---

[3] For a clear illustration of this dilemma see the discussion of ICT policies in Ibero-American countries, in Benavides and Pedro (2007), *Revista Iberoamericana de Educacion*, No. 45.

9.4. The dominance of the bureaucratic paradigm

In virtually every country, rich and poor, political leaders are now on record declaring that education is their number one priority. It is hardly a vote loser, after all. What is equally striking, however, is the commonality of reform goals adopted from country to country. In the second half of the 20th Century, education policies focused on achieving universal coverage for the core years of schooling. In its last two decades, the focus shifted towards pushing up its quality through standards-based reform. Most countries aspiring to advanced economic growth have national education policies clustered around the following themes:

- Standards based strategies to improve attainment in essential outcomes, especially numeracy and literacy.

- Frameworks for reporting, assessment and accountability based on key performance indicators.

- New infrastructure, including the overhaul and modernisation of school buildings and the introduction of ICT hardware and networks.

- Reduction of class sizes and training of new teachers.

- Finding, training and rewarding high performing educational leaders.

- Funding and growing childcare and early-years places.

- Increasing post-compulsory participation, through expanding higher education and creating new school-work pathways and higher vocational qualifications.

- Reshaping the educational workforce to emphasise flexibility, professional development, specialisation of professional and para-professional roles, and performance management.

- Civic engagement and citizenship among young people.

- Targeted strategies to tackle underperformance among specific, deprived social groups and in marginalised urban or rural areas.

There are many different ways to tackle these challenges. Yet with few exceptions, the basic approach across OECD nations revolves around the same governance paradigm, and the ongoing dominance of public bureaucracies in managing schooling and school reform. In this model, responsibility for educational management and improvement is coordinated through a tri-level structure of central agencies, local authorities or school districts and individual schools with their own senior management.

Standards-based reform uses a simple, powerful set of tools to pursue better outcomes. They are:

- Creating formal performance objectives and standardising measures of performance.

- Targeting resources and prioritising key outcome measures.

- Strengthening and simplifying accountability structures.

- Building professional development and continuous improvement strategies.

- Centralising control over investment budgets, performance measures, curriculum specification, accountability structures and inspection systems.

- (Often) decentralising and deregulating other aspects of school resourcing and organisation, including school budgets, support and ancillary services, curriculum and professional development, creating new managerial flexibilities for school leaders.

The major policy trend, therefore, over a generation, has been the creation of a single framework for state-funded schooling through which to pursue continuous improvement in school performance, by identifying standards, resourcing schools to meet them, and making schools, students and professionals accountable for their attainment. The aim of the reform strategy is to ensure that each school has an appropriately focused strategy for improving its own performance, on the basis of its participation in a single system of governance and accountability. Resourcing, management and pedagogical decisions at every level are driven by transparent, consistent educational standards. In other words, the principle is that form should follow function; the organisational character of schooling should follow the best available evidence about what kinds of practice will be effective. This focus has never, as far as I know, resulted in the replacement of the traditional bureaucratic model of schooling.

9.5. Why are bureaucratic models so resilient?

One explanation is that the familiar model of schooling has become so entrenched that it is simply impossible to overturn it, because of the vested interests and centuries-old habits that hold it in place. But even where these interests are weak, or have been swept away, for example through industrial relations reform or the introduction of market competition, the model has not changed radically. Successful private schools rarely stray from the organisational form or the regulatory methods found in state sectors. Across countries and cultures, the received definition of a "successful school" has become remarkably similar, increasingly influenced by both the international research movement on school improvement, and the internationalisation of performance indicators and measurement through the OECD and other international organisations.

It revolves essentially around the idea of a stable, high performing, continuously improving learning organisation, as set out by Dean Fink and Louise Stoll in their characterisation of effective schools, and helpfully summarised by Juana M. Sancho Gill.[4] It is also bound up with the idea of a strong, positive and self-sustaining set of social values, an "ethos" which influences the motivation and identity of individual students and creates a collective identity in which parents and surrounding communities want to invest. This effective school is characterised by:

- Strong, purposeful leadership.

- A shared vision that provide a collective mission, practical coherence and professional coordination.

- An ordered, stable setting that enables sustained focus on learning by staff and students, held in place by a clearly defined hierarchy of organisational power.

- Reliable systems for the collection and interpretation of data.

- Purposeful, high quality teaching activities and materials.

- A culture of continuous and structured professional development.

- Clearly established relationships, rights and responsibilities.

- Strong behavioural norms, reinforcing the values of the school as a community and the motivation to learn.

There have been many variations and inflections on this basic framework; developing schools with a curriculum specialism that makes them distinctive and marketable, schools driven by exceptionally dynamic and entrepreneurial individual leaders, schools developing distinctive products or franchises that they offer to families or to the wider community in some way. But in all these cases, the thrust of the reform model has been to achieve higher, more consistent performance in output by building up

---

[4] "In Search of Learning and Teaching Models that Meet the Changing Needs of Education", Juana M. Sancho Gill, OECD Mexico International Conference, "Emerging Models of Learning and Innovation", June 2006.

schools as focused learning organisations within these well established parameters.

This model of the individual school then fits neatly into a governance system which relies on very similar principles to provide it with structure and reliability. That is the model which breaks school organisation and management into a three-level governance structure, with the centre making policy, setting rules of accountability, and allocating funding; a layer of local or regional authorities conducting planning and coordination; and, individual schools operating elsewhere. This basic **tri-level model** is almost universal, though the relative power of each layer varies. What is most striking is that the model applies to the internal organisation of the typical school as well as to the wider system; indeed, to many different kinds of organisation, especially in the public sector. By and large, other educational innovations are channelled through and absorbed into this institutional paradigm.

Figure 9.1. Tri-level bureaucratic model

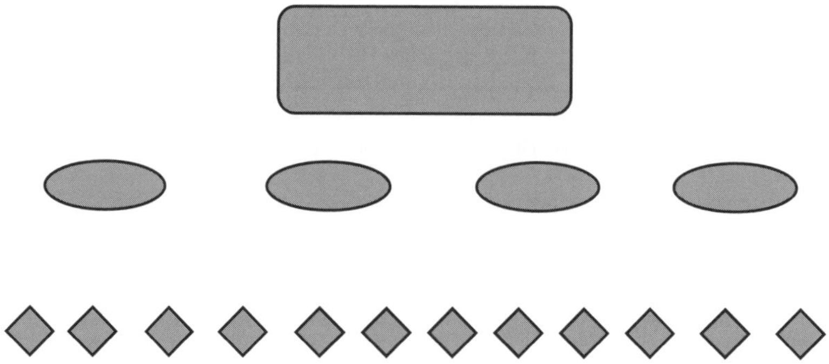

Source: Author.

Traditional models of bureaucracy are usually characterised as rigid, rule-based, and internally focused. But perhaps the explanation for their **resilience** in fact lies in their peculiar flexibility. Rather than the formal, rational objectives and accountabilities of the institutional system, which is the focus of so much school reform, much recent thinking about the nature of social and economic behaviour has focused on the evolution of complex adaptive systems. That is, human behaviour is adaptive in that it continuously adjusts to changing environments and new experience, even without conscious decision-making. A burgeoning literature on game theory, behavioural and institutional economics provides a rich new source of insight into how and why people and organisations behave in the way they do under different circumstances (Homer Dixon, 2006; Douglass, 2005).

Similarly, evolution in both natural and social systems leads to increasingly complex patterns of specialisation, interdependence and self-organisation which hold together different needs, functions and interests in diverse systems. Such systems contain many diverse parts but still operate as coherent wholes which generate more than the sum of those parts (Chapman, 2003). An ecosystem is an example drawn from the natural world. A school system can be characterised in the same way, except that its evolution is directed by human intentions and norms, and not simply by competition and natural selection. Nonetheless, the value that it produces as a whole should be more than the sum of individual efforts and outcomes within it.

My argument here is that the bureaucratic model is adaptive, but that it is not necessarily designed to optimise learning outcomes for all of its participants. Instead, it is adaptive in the sense that it allows its members – schools, administrators, teachers and so on – to coordinate the process of continuous adaptation to changing student identities, changing socio-economic conditions, and changing policy requirements, through an ordered, incremental process of adjustment, refinement, and organisational learning. The bureaucratic model is not impervious to change because it is inflexible, but because it offers a particular kind of flexibility: it makes continuous adaptation manageable, as long as the changes can be accommodated within its own organisational parameters. The system is implicitly geared towards maintaining the integrity of *its own* design.

This layering allows reliable organisation of teaching and learning, and progression of cohorts of students, simultaneously with the day to day adjustment and improvisation needed to accommodate changing needs and behaviours – each box in the figure represents a domain of local knowledge and authority with its own leadership, power structure, informal social relationships, shared culture and so on. The durability of these parameters in the face of change is remarkable, but it may be explained partly by the mutual dependence of policy makers, administrators and practitioners on its orderly structure for the implementation of their central objectives. In other words, these functional organisational structures simultaneously make ordered learning possible by creating the predictability and responsibilities needed in order to organise at large scale. They produce boundaries which limit the possibilities of learning, because they limit the scope of inquiry, interaction and information flow, in teaching and learning activities.

Many teachers would like to find ways around these limitations, but most remain within the boundaries of classrooms, year groups and a pre-set curriculum. However some of the new approaches require radically different patterns of organisation, using time, space, information and people differently in the learning process. But as Richard Elmore has persuasively argued, this multiple layering of organisational systems and authority, and the strong separation of the core technical and practical knowledge of teaching from the organisational knowledge and authority of educational administration, creates a potent "buffering" effect in practice. Thus policy makers and experts are insulated from the classroom, and individual teachers are insulated from the expertise, decision making, innovation and exposure that might make them directly accountable for generating the best possible outcomes (Elmore, 2000).

This creates a deep **systemic tension** that focusing performance regimes in pursuit of higher standards from the centre requires strengthening of vertical chains of command, and reinforcement of the structures which implicitly create functional standardisation and fragmentation. At the same time, meeting the needs of an increasingly diverse student body, deploying a burgeoning range of expert knowledge and evidence about effective learning practices, requires much greater levels of flexibility and direct collaboration with the wider world. The likelihood is that while there is a core routine of teaching and organisation to pursue, and incremental gains in value to be generated from it, schools and teachers will continue to channel their energy into preserving and extending it, regardless of the limitations that it imposes on what learning outcomes are possible. After all, what else could they do?

This combination of stability and incremental change allows the traditional model of schooling, and of bureaucratic school systems, to adapt continuously to all kinds of external change, and therefore to deflect the disruptive potential of almost any innovation, whether it comes from above, below, or around the corner. While reform strategies rely on the ongoing consistency at the core of the system – such as those required by standardised reporting processes, outcome measures and benchmarked features of effective schools – they will help to reinforce and embed the core institutional design, even when they are seeking to improve its performance. Meanwhile, the adaptive resilience of the wider system is just as likely to be filtering and interpreting the signals being sent from the policy centre, and in the process reducing their impact.

The lesson is that, rather than seeking to subvert or bypass the adaptive capacity of existing systems, new reform strategies for improvement need to harness them. But at the same time they must connect them with the relentless, open-ended pursuit of better learning outcomes, rather than to the implicit preservation of their own core values and underlying structure. For that, we need a new view of innovation and its relationship to system design, and a refreshed sense of the global context into which we should put education.

9.6. Liberalisation and specialisation: responses to rising demand

Standards-based bureaucratic reform has not been the only policy trend of the last twenty years, however. In many systems it is also supplemented by a growing focus on specialisation, diversity of provision and responsiveness to demand. In tune with the times, education policies have followed a market-based liberalisation, seeking to extend new choice to parents and stimulate improvement through competition. This has taken very different shape in different jurisdictions, ranging from charter schools in the United States to federally subsidised independent schools in Australia, accredited specialist schools in the United Kingdom to the publicly regulated and funded private schools in the Netherlands.

Although liberalisation has been a pronounced trend, nowhere has it bled into full-blown privatisation. In virtually every country, publicly managed state schools remain the defining element of "the system", and barriers to large scale entry by alternative providers remain high. Rather than leading inexorably towards retail markets in schooling, liberalisation should instead be understood as one part of a deeper attempt to respond to social diversity. A combination of more specialised knowledge about teaching and learning, demand for greater responsiveness, and a growth in social and cultural diversity is fuelling ongoing efforts by education services to support more differentiation. This means different types of school in different communities, offering greater choice and flexibility for individual students and families, greater variation in curriculum methods and teaching practices according to student need, and greater accessibility and flexibility of access arising from the use of ICTs.

The main expressions of this trend in education policy have been:

- *Choice-based* strategies, given parents and students new access to alternative provision, such as charter schools.

- Investments in *specialisation*, designed to deepen excellence and to give students more flexible access to specialist resources, such as England's quest to make every secondary school an accredited specialist college excelling in one or more curriculum area.

- *Engagement* strategies, designed to increase motivation, commitment and ownership of educational endeavour by students, families and local communities.

The big challenge to these movements, regularly thrown down by sceptics and opponents, is whether greater differentiation can *avoid* fuelling systemic inequality, particularly given the trends we discussed above. If access to and take-up of educational opportunities in part reflects the unequal endowments of human and social capital that different individuals, and societies, bring to the process, then is it not inevitable that the higher value, higher status, higher quality learning services will end up being systematically dominated by those who are already more advantaged? The evidence is always complex and often inconclusive. A greater diversity of provision should stimulate more innovation and be capable of serving a greater range of need, but the OECD data suggest that many of these changes *can* reinforce the stratification of already unequal societies, but that this hardening is not inevitable. Whether they do or not, the modest variation created by current reform models is unlikely to produce radically different patterns of learning outcome on its own. If we want models of schooling which genuinely serve the full potential of each society, and which overcome entrenched patterns of inequality, a deeper, more ambitious shift is required.

One major expression of the desire for this long term shift is the growing focus on personalised learning (Leadbeater, 2004; OECD, 2006). This emerging idea is that systems capable of achieving universally high standards are those that can personalise the programme of learning and progression offered to the needs and motivations of each learner. Personalisation can mean adopting a more holistic, person-centred approach to learner development, as well as more demand-driven, market-friendly approaches to system change. In part, it reflects a change in social climate, driven by the affluence and value change that arise from sustained economic growth: as Parker and O'Leary recently put it:

> *"Innovation, productivity improvement and prioritisation are the keys to escaping from the trap of rising demand without heavily increasing taxation. But they are also the key to dealing with a second set of social pressures that is starting to bear on public services. This is the demand from populations for more attention to their diverse personal needs, and their increasing ability to express those needs in personal terms."* (Parker and O'Leary, 2006)

Therefore a combination of changing demand patterns, cost pressures, and technologies of supply help to explain why personalisation is coming into focus. Yet can it actually be achieved within the framework of schooling? In one sense, we can see clearly emerging new strategies which aim to build on school effectiveness and standards-based accountability frameworks to create differentiated interventions, both for students and for individual schools.[5] Individual performance data and report cards, as seen most brutally in the United States under the *No Child Left Behind* legislation is one example. School self-evaluation and benchmarking based on detailed comparison of individual schools with similar characteristics serving similar populations, as is increasingly practised in England, is another. However these are still limited responses that operate within the standardised context of schools and bureaucratic school accountability. And even moves towards encouraging competitive markets, for example by giving parents vouchers, still work within the same heavily regulated set of institutional designs. Sometimes these policies include an explicit effort to address the attainment gap, for example by targeting those most disadvantaged with additional funding, and by focusing accountability regimes on narrowing the distribution of attainment between highest and lowest, as now happens in many American states, at least on the basis of their standard testing data.

To question them is not to dismiss either the intention of these policy designs or the positive marginal impact that they can create. Yet as Stahlberg (2006) of the World Bank makes it clear in a recent paper, varying the level of funding per student does not produce any guaranteed outcome for attainment, either in level or distribution, because the performance of different schooling systems does not simply reflect different levels of funding. Inequality of resourcing is one part of the explanation for variation in educational achievement, but perhaps it is as much a symptom as a cause. What appears to matter more is how funding, admissions, teaching, learning, assessment and reward fit into a deeper organising framework, or system, with its own adaptive capacities and underlying resilience.

As we have seen, these systems limit the possibility of innovation because of the organisational boundaries that they put around learning and around the use of resources. And they limit the transfer of innovation because they maintain relatively fragmented organisational units, largely insulated from the pressures of competition and market incentive. Schooling also tends to be insulated from innovation because of the perceived risks of responding directly to the voices and demands of younger generations without losing the socialising role that most society wants education to play. The real question, therefore, is whether it is possible to develop systems which are directly responsive to personal need and capable of reconfiguring themselves in response to feedback from learners and outcome data, while *simultaneously* working within a long term framework of outcomes and principles of equity that reflects the collective choices about public fairness deemed desirable by each society.

---

[5] Use of value added data, specialist school accreditation, segmentation of school performance, individual school development plans, etc.

9.7. Innovation through collaboration: learning from open systems

Melbourne is known as one of the world's most liveable cities. Yet the city of Hume, a local government in the Melbourne metropolitan area, is characterised by huge ethnic and cultural diversity and by a widespread economic marginalisation. Hume exemplifies many features of the new global economy: diversity, inequality, dynamism, and economic activities which do not neatly fit into an idealised, traditionally planned definition of place or community. Thirty-five different languages are spoken by its people. Jobs are limited and learning opportunities are difficult to access; and Hume face the impact of economic disadvantage and social fragmentation. School reform to drive up standards would be an obvious way to tackle this challenge, and improved learning outcomes are high on the agenda of both the State government and the local council. But Hume has also chosen a different kind of response: the Hume Global Learning Village™.

The Global Learning Centre, a sleek steel and glass building in the town centre, is a deliberately designed hybrid: it houses the Council Chamber, a welcoming café, and a public library. It provides seminar facilities and Internet services for local learners, whether teenagers using them after school, mothers learning English, or workers looking to improve their ICT skills. The centre is just the hub of a much more ambitious strategy to link together the traditional elements of Hume's educational infrastructure – schools and colleges – with many other activities and sites of learning that can impact positively on the achievements, aspirations and life-chances of Hume's residents. *Learning Together*, Hume's introduction to its strategy, sets out a vision of "a learning community where people embrace learning as a way of life, for all their life, thereby creating a community that values learning as the key to strengthening individual and community well-being." The evidence shows that learning can achieve all these things; but not necessarily when it is systematised and institutionalised by our current models of schooling and governance. Hume's strategy is to transform and enhance what is achieved within its education institutions by linking them to its wider communities in new ways.

This means myriad projects, organised around a series of themes; inspiring lifelong learning; learning in community settings; language, literacy and numeracy; ICT uptake, and village networking. Threaded through them is a hard, practical focus on developing skills and learning with tangible benefit to learners. However the activities reach into places where the traditional bureaucratic model rarely gets; recruiting women from new migrant communities to create digital records of songs, stories and oral history; attracting teenagers in to download, create and exchange their own learning materials; holding an annual State of Learning research conference; mentoring and "inspiring learners" programmes that put high profile individuals who grew up in the area in touch with Hume's current youngsters.

Many of these activities are familiar to education practitioners. But there are few places in the world where such a range is systematically connected to the development of formal education services and infrastructure. Hume's model for doing so is to have built a wide-ranging partnership of institutions, a network capable of coming together to raise money, offer shared services and plan new infrastructure collaboratively. As part of the same regeneration process, many of Hume's government schools are being rebuilt and reconfigured into a smaller number of "learning centres" designed to offer higher quality pathways to all students.

The Global Learning Village does not act as a traditional corporate or bureaucratic centre; when it needs a legal entity to form a partnership or bid for funding, one of its network members steps forward. It is not a direct replacement for the existing governance institutions or service providers, but by designing itself to further the whole population's learning interests, it can bring these other institutions together in ways that create entirely new possibilities.

The Hume Global Learning Village is an illustration of how open systems of governance and learning can support more ambitious educational objectives. It uses practice-based innovation to generate collective and institutional action to change the *context* in which personal experience and service delivery occur. It does this by seeking to adjust the broad institutional parameters within which the ongoing, incremental processes of educational attainment are organised. Crucially, it connects the workings of formal education providers with the many other dimensions of learning and sources of innovation that exist beyond their formal boundaries. It seeks to create community, as well as to serve it.

This approach, in turn, depends on a distinctive form of *innovation system,* which reflects recent thinking about the innovation process which draws explicitly from the study of systems. The dominant assumptions about innovation, and its sources, which have dominated the educational debate up to now, are threefold:

- Innovation arises from competition between schools, or from "quasi market" policy measures which replicate the effects of open competition, such as publishing performance league tables.

- Innovation arises from new knowledge, primarily created upstream from teaching and learning in the fields of basic research. For example, advances in neuroscience or in ICT create insights about the nature of learning which can be fed scientifically into the design of curriculum, teaching and assessment programmes.

- Innovation arises essentially from the interaction between teachers and learners; it is context-specific, and cannot be generalised in ways that go beyond professional judgement and discretion; it therefore emerges from the bottom up, and should be recognised and rewarded by policy makers.

Each of these has some truth. Yet none has proved itself capable of fuelling the kinds of innovation that learners need, given the schooling systems that we have got.[6] More likely is that each needs to find its place within a larger, more robust schema of how multiple source of innovation can work as part of a more robust *innovation system*. Such a system would work to resource, share the risks of, evaluate and scale up new knowledge and practices in a given field of operation.

Innovation can come from multiple sources; but it is best understood as the product of dissonance or incongruity; the clash between expectation and reality, or the gap between the ideal standard and the particular form. Hume's innovation is perhaps a response to the gap between the diversity of its community and the institutional capacity available to support its development. In successful learning systems, dissonance is not screened out or neutralised, but incorporated as the stimulus for a continuous pattern of experimentation, evaluation, collaboration and exchange which leads the system on to ever more successful configurations.

As we argue in a recent pamphlet, making the most of potential discovery and innovation in education requires a system which:[7]

- Is clear about long term, system-wide priorities.

- Invests in rigorous basic research without attaching the wrong strings to it.

- Expects multiple failures and incentivises continuous experimentation, but ensures that valuable feedback from users flows through the system.

- Harnesses the benefits of central direction, market competition, and open communities of collaboration in appropriate ways.

---

[6] See the interesting explanation of *research-based innovation* by Bereiter and Scardamalia in Chapter 3.

[7] S. Gillinson and T. Bentley (2007), "A D&R System for Education", Innovation Unit, 2007, *http://www.innovation-unit.co.uk/*

- Makes knowledge and new applications available and transparent in quick, easy, and interactive ways.

- Makes the most of user-driven innovation and demand to shape new methods and create knowledge that centrally driven discovery and development would miss.

These characteristics will be familiar to many educators and policy makers, but they are rarely brought together systematically. My closing argument is that it is becoming possible to design and develop large scale systems for innovation and learning which harness the benefits of open participation and still manage to focus on identifiable, long term, public goals.

It is possible because the study of adaptive systems is coming together with the emergence of more open models of participation and innovation, typified by the open source software movement, but extending far beyond the world of computer science. A huge range of fields and institutions, including schools and universities, are now actively developing "open" methods and models of coordination and exchange on a large scale. As Chesbrough (2003) puts it: "Now it's about harnessing the most effective sources of innovation – from wherever they are derived. This is not just about ideas – it's about their realization. Organisations are porous, creating start-ups to exploit new technologies or bringing them into the fold." Charles Sabel, the US political scientist, argues that "These federated organisations respond to the problem of bounded rationality not primarily by decomposing complex tasks into simple ones, but rather by creating search networks that allow actors quickly to find others who can in effect teach them what to do because they are already solving a like problem."[8] This kind of thinking is reflected in the focus that CERI, and some OECD member states, have put on growing collaborative learning networks, such as the Networked Learning Communities programme in the United Kingdom and the many other examples emerging around the world.

As I argued earlier, if we want to understand properly the interrelationships between education, society and economy, we have to view school systems as part of a more open set of relationships, characterised by complex causal development. These systems are increasingly open; unbounded, interconnected, and driven by patterns of exchange – both competitive and collaborative – which emerge from the interaction of millions of participants.

---

[8] Charles Sabel, "Beyond Principal-Agent Governance: Experimentalist Organizations, Learning and Accountability", WRR discussion paper, see *http://www2.law.columbia. edu/sabel/papers/Sabel.definitief.doc*

A famous corporate example is Toyota's employee suggestion scheme, which generates over 2 million ideas a year. More than 95% of the workforce contribute; over 30 suggestions per worker per year. Perhaps the most remarkable figure, though, is that over 90% of the suggestions are implemented. Some argue, rightly, that private sector practices cannot be easily transplanted into public systems, and that the outcomes of education should be compared so lightly to productivity in car plants. Yet these reactions are too simple. The point is not that shareholders and performance measures dictate "improve or die" imperatives, but that Toyota and similar systems have evolved a highly complex, collaborative infrastructure for pooling effort and knowledge towards a set of shared learning goals.

Similar lessons can be learned from the growth of the open-source software movement, and its ability to harness the participation of millions of users and experts, often giving their time for nothing, to the invention and improvement of new designs and products. As Yochai Benkler, the legal and information theorist, has recently argued, the possibilities of knowledge and cultural production using these network-based models of interaction and coordination, are extraordinary. They make it possible to contemplate a far wider range of simultaneous responses to the needs of different participants; exactly what a higher performing education system needs to do. However, in so doing, they inevitably challenge the dominant institutional structures, definitions of ownership and methods of knowledge transfer bound up in the existing bureaucratic system.

It is striking, in reviewing other examples and case studies of innovation, including those produced through CERI work on innovative learning environments, to see how many of them share the same features, of offering a more active and interactive role to the learner by building experiences and environments which bridge the distance between the formal, classroom-based curriculum and the wider forms of knowledge and learning bound up with other settings; the natural environment, social and community-based knowledge, workplace participation and so on. Open source educational repositories, seeking to share learning resource and design learning environments through open collaboration, are now rapidly appearing around the world. Organising these forms of learning at scale requires us to develop open systems of coordination and development. Open source projects are not entirely spontaneous or anarchic; they depend on clear design rules and hierarchies of decision making, and their variations are rigorously tested by users. It is these characteristics which offer greatest potential to education system reform, because they point to the development of a new, open, institutional architecture able to harness all the resources described above.

Such an architecture would make use of specific educational innovations such as:

- Individual digital record keeping and portfolios.

- Formative assessment and peer to peer exchange.

- Open access curriculum standards and specifications, and open archives of curriculum content, learning resources.

- Network-based user communities, both of educational practitioners and of students, clustered around specific shared interests.

- Area-based information about social and economic outcomes, services, and community structure, integrated across different public agencies and openly available for community use.

- Funding and regulation of education providers which did not discriminate by sector or function, for example between private schools or public technical colleges, but which explicitly sought accountability for public outcomes for any kind of organisation receiving public subsidy or protection.

- Opening up of educational infrastructure and facilities to wider, plural forms of community use, as many jurisdictions are now doing.

- Harmonisation of regulatory regimes designed across different countries and jurisdictions to encourage diversity of practice and model, but make possible higher levels of mobility and "interoperability" between systems.

- Development, research and innovation strategies based on the development of open, collaborative platforms and specialised clusters of innovators.

- Home-school-community services designed to support the educational "coproduction" of families and informal community networks.

Finland's success at the top of the PISA tables has made it the subject of widespread international attention, for good reasons. Yet it often seems that, in applying our own perspectives to the achievement, we are in danger of learning the wrong lessons. As Sahlberg argues, Finland did not produce outstandingly high outcomes by driving the system's performance with standardised measures, or making teachers accountable from above to narrow measures of outcome, or by prioritising test performance over all other aspects of learning.

Instead, Finland has built up a set of institutional foundations for schooling which promote a specific combination of universal participation, specialist knowledge and flexibility. The system is not driven by instrumental pressures, or by the imposition of standard templates. What drives it is the interaction between a deep investment in participation through the welfare system, and the culture of open, network-based interaction, symbolised by Nokia, which Finland has so successfully developed over the last twenty five years (Himmanen and Castells, 2003).

Finland's success will not automatically reproduce itself, which is why it is actively seeking the next steps in its own economic and educational strategies. But it nonetheless offers a way for the wider world to think about what combination of qualities our schooling systems may need to acquire, and how to go about building them. In doing so, we should learn to apply the lessons of open systems, to ensure that education does not become a global zero sum game.

References

Australian Productivity Commission, modelling of the effects of the National Reform Agenda, *http://www.pc.gov.au/research/crp/ nationalreformagenda/index.html*

Benavides, F. and F. Pedro (2007), "Políticas Educativas sobre Nuevas Tecnologías en los Países Iberoamericanos", *Revista Iberoamericana de Educación*, No. 45.

Chapman, J. (2003), *System Failure: Why Governments Must Learn to Think Differently*, Demos, London.

Chesbrough, H. (2003), "The Era of Open Innovation", *MIT Sloan Management Review*, Vol. 44(3), Spring.

Coulombe, S. and J.F. Tremblay (2005), "Public Investment in Skills; Are Canadian Governments doing Enough?", CD Howe Institute, October.

Douglass, C. (2005), *Understanding the Process of Economic Change*, Princeton University Press, Princeton.

Elmore, R. (2000), "Building a New Structure for School Leadership", Albert Shanker Institute, Washington DC, *www.shankerinstitute.org*

Himmanen, P. and M. Castells (2003), *The Information Society and the Welfare State: the Finnish Model*, Oxford University Press.

Homer Dixon, T. (2006), *The Upside of Down: Catastrophe, Creativity and the Renewal of Civilisation*, Souvenir Press, London.

Leadbeater, C. (2004), *Personalisation through Participation*, Demos, London.

OECD (2001), *The Well-being of Nations: The Role of Human and Social Capital*, OECD Publishing, Paris.

OECD (2006), *Personalising Education*, OECD Publishing, Paris.

Parker, S. and D. O'Leary (2006), *Reimagining Government*, Demos, London.

Sahlberg, P. (2006), "Education Reform for Raising Economic Competitieness", *Journal of Educational Change,* Vol. 7, No. 4.

Annex A
Summaries of the Four Mexican Case Studies

As explained in the foreword and Chapter 6 of this publication, CERI started the analytical work on innovative learning environments as part of the "Schooling for Tomorrow" project. From July 2005 to June 2006, with Mexico in the lead role, a network of national and international experts was selected to reflect together about this issue. The concluding event of this *exploratory phase* was the OECD-Mexico International Conference "Emerging Models of Learning and Innovation" held in Merida, Yucatan, on 14-16 June2006.

As part of the *exploratory phase*, four Mexican cases were chosen and visited by different groups of experts who then prepared a report about their learning proposals and innovative projects. These reports were subsequently used by some of the experts in the project's network to write the papers that were discussed at the international conference of Merida. Most of these papers are summarised in Chapter 6 of this publication, while Chapters 5, 7 and 8 were prepared on the basis of the authors' conference discussion papers. The executive summaries of the reports, as they were discussed at the Merida Conference, of the four case studies are included in this annex.

Some antecedents

The four case studies were selected from a limited list of over 30 initiatives suggested by different Mexican authorities, academicians and experts from the project's network. The selection process was handled over a very short period of time (from September to November 2005) mainly because of logistic and time constraints inherent to this phase. As a result of these restrictions, criteria for the cases were defined as follows:

- All cases had to be learning initiatives aimed at responding to the needs of vulnerable populations.

- They had an evident impact on various "learning dimensions" indentified by the network's experts.

- The origin of the initiative had come, if possible, from the local actors themselves (a bottom-up approach).

- Although cases from several educational sectors were encouraged (initial education, pre-school education, basic education, etc.), initiatives related to the "tertiary" sector or that exclusively target adults as a population were not to be encouraged.

Underlying these criteria, the cases chosen were the following:

- Case 1: The Cerro del Judío Friendship Centre (or as used in this publication: *Friendship Centre*), in Magdalena Contreras District, Mexico City.

- Case 2: Regular Education Support Services Unit No. 8 (*Support Unit: USAER 8)* in Iztapalapa District, Mexico City.

- Case 3: Intelligent Classroom for Migrants (*Intelligent Classroom*) in different farms in Culiacan and Elota municipalities, Sinaloa State.

- Case 4: Ayuujk Polivalent Integral Community High School (*BICAP)* in the community of Santa Maria Tlahuitoltepec, Mixe Regions, Oaxaca State.

The teams that visited the cases were composed of *at least* three experts: one international and one or two national and/or local analysts. For this project, each of the cases chose a local leader who facilitated the visit and production of the analysis. A pre-visit and logistics were co-ordinated by the staff of the Ministry of Education. The official visits to Cases 1 and 3 took place between 21-26 January and to Cases 2 and 4, between 29 January and 3 February 2006.

As the reports demonstrated, the different initiatives share some common characteristics as well as structural differences. Case 1 (Friendship Centre) serves the "initial" and "pre-school" educational sectors. This experience has prevailed during several decades and its origins are clearly linked to the local community. It is located in one of poorest zones in Mexico City.

Case 2 (Support Unit: USAER 8) provides "theoretical and methodological" support to schools and teachers attending to students with special education needs within the regular educational environment. This unit started as a state initiative and offers services to 5 public basic education schools in the urban area of the Mexican capital. The USAER has operated since 2000. Of the four cases, this initiative is not "bottom-up" in its origins.

Case 3 (Intelligent Classroom) is located in the agricultural state of Sinaloa, on the northeast Pacific coast of Mexico. Here, farms usually offer housing and other services (such as health and education) in their own infrastructures to migrants (from different regions of the country) who come to work in their fields with their families. The *Intelligent Classroom* is an initiative that has been set up in several of these educational centres offering basic education courses, to help those children who – due to several factors, including their miserable life conditions – have enormous problems with continuing their basic studies. At the time the report was undertaken, it was the second year of operation of the Intelligent Classroom. This innovation came mainly from public servants from the regional authority who were working directly with migrant children.

Case 4 (BICAP) is an experience in the Ayuujk (Mixe) indigenous zone located in the sierra of Oaxaca, in the south of Mexico. Through BICAP, the community offers high school education to local youth in accordance with their culture, language, principles and local needs. They also try to facilitate their transit to work. This experience has existed for at least three decades.

Case Study 1
The Cerro del Judío Friendship Centre[1]

What does the Friendship Centre represent for you and your team?[2]

"It has given us the opportunity to be trained as professionals and improve our childcare practices, even giving us a chance to bring home some money without neglecting our children."

"We feel fulfilled as persons. It has opened up for us a huge range of possibilities; we are more aware of the value we have in our community and we have changed for the better the role we are expected to have as women in our families. We know our rights and our place."

What would you expect after participating in this OECD initiative?

"First, that the Ministry of Education should certify us as community educators based on our many years of service. Second, that the Friendship Centre education model should be recognised for what it is: a successful practice. Finally, that more resources from the authorities should be reserved for our centre, since current fundraising efforts are too demanding."

Verónica González and Concepción Arista
Local leaders of Case 1

Introduction

The Cerro del Judío Friendship Centre (Centro de la Amistad del Cerro del Judío) is a childcare community project that over a period of 32 years

---

[1] The complete report was written by: Francesc Pedro (OECD-CERI Senior Analyst) and Lizbeth Camacho and Leticia Araujo (Analysts, Ministry of Education of Mexico).

[2] Mar Rodríguez-Romero (author of Chapter 5) interviewed during the Merida Conference the leader of Cases 1, 2 and 3. Some of their comments are included in these executive summaries.

has provided care, feeding, health and teaching services to children up to the age of six. It also promotes the community's culture and development.

It is located in a marginal zone in the west of Mexico City where central education coverage is incomplete; it has generated a self-management system that is operated by the children's parents themselves. It offers the first levels of education and, as an extension of home, provides minors with protection from risk factors to their health and integrity.

This centre is one of a growing number of community initiatives[3] that respond to an urban reality where family structures are disintegrating.[4] These organisations are born from the union of parents, religious groups, political activist groups sometimes affiliated to a political party, or due to the initiative of philanthropic groups. They are generally identified as non-lucrative juridical entities according to the Private Assistance Institutions (Instituciones de Asistencia Privada or IAP), or as civil associations (AC). They are financed by national and international non-governmental organisations and receive contributions from families and – on a smaller scale – from the Mexican government.[5]

The need for an educational programme that responds to community requirements and the learners has fostered an innovative training system for mothers to become educators. This is the reason why the centre has been at the heart of the community and has earned the commitment of its beneficiaries to become actors of their own development from the beginning. The educational proposal is understood as a nucleus that activates and initiates the community's progress in different domains, through the valorisation of the capabilities of its inhabitants, their dignity and collective organisation.

The historical and social contexts of the case

When the Friendship Centre was founded in the 1970s, the Cerro del Judío zone was a semi-rural area with a migrant rural population. The

---

[3] Nearly 250 centres are registered with the Ministry of Education (SEP), which attend to an average of 12 000 children, with the participation of 950 community educators.

[4] 50% of the children registered at the Cerro del Judío Friendship Centre are members of families with only one parent and mothers aged from 17 to 30.

[5] The Friendship Centre is financed by private donations (74%), parents' contributions (20%), the Ministry of Education (3%), in addition to some other sporadic contributions. A small percentage comes from self-generated resources.

Magdalena Contreras Delegation,[6] which belongs to this zone, has undergone great economical contrasts in accelerated urbanisation over the years. Religion is an important influence on the behaviour of the inhabitants. The Jesuits' communitarian, educational and evangelisation work has been present in the area since it was first inhabited, via the existence of grassroots ecclesiastical communities. These communities fostered educational projects aimed at organising and involving the population along with raising awareness in the search for better social justice.

The creation of the Friendship Centre resulted from the awareness of risks faced by children, after some of them suffered serious accidents in houses in the district. A group of women – convoked by Ana María Casares, an educator specialised as a Montessori guide, catechist and member of the "grassroots communities" (*comunidades de base*) – founded the Friendship Centre Trust and established themselves as a team of educators.

Pedagogical methodology and learning proposal

The Centre's learning proposal is based on three main issues: a) an active pedagogy based on the Montessori method; b) the concept of educator-mothers; and c) close links with the community.

The Centre's **pedagogical proposal** is based on an adaptation of the **Montessori method** that follows the principles of respect for the person, training for autonomy, developing personal strength in decision-making and the capability to live in a group. Therefore, the child is considered as a subject to whom high levels of responsibility are assigned and education is integrated around his/her activity. Contents are complemented by psycho-motor stimulation and theatre-related activities. A friendly atmosphere for learning is created in order to stimulate willingness towards activity, where children share under the principle of respect and acceptance of each other. The Centre has "long schedules"[7] as it tries to adapt to the families' working schedules.

The **educator-mothers** are trained at the Centre over a period of two and a half years, during which they are provided with institutional, methodological and theoretical resources, as well as diagnostic tools. The introduction to the Montessori model stresses the importance of the first school experience and relationship with families and explains the child's

---

[6] The federal district is divided into 16 political districts or delegaciones.

[7] Community centre schedules vary from 5 to 12 hours a day. Children are also fed on-site in most of the centres, as with the Friendship Centre experience.

development process. **Training** is complemented by follow-up in practice experiences, which involves and commits the mothers by taking advantage of their experience and knowledge, thereby granting them the institution's trust.

Because of its **links with the community** through workshops, group activities and coaching sessions, the Centre is sustained by the driving force of members of the community who are committed and who act upon acknowledgment of educational deficiencies. Their strength in the self-management, organisation and valorisation of the community's potential improves their capacity to convoke as well as raising their prestige in the eyes of the population and authorities.

Thus, palpable results have attracted support – both financially and in terms of other contributions – as well as social recognition. The Centre has also developed its role locally and become an active agency defending human and citizens' rights, strengthening in particular its relationship with some NGOs. Consequently, the Centre has obtained enough legitimacy vis-à-vis the community and government. However they do not always succeed in being heard and supported by the authorities.

Results

To date – when the report was finished – there have been 28 generations of Friendship Centre graduates, who have maintained a high academic performance at basic and middle education levels. Furthermore, 70-80% of these young people have had access to and finished their university studies.[8] According to their own testimonies, the Centre has been a decisive stage in their life, during which they have assumed attitudes of respect, willingness to participate in group work and mutual help. In this atmosphere of comfort and protection they have acquired self-confidence, improved their capacity for decision making and demonstrated their responsibility and independence. Thus, the educational capacity of a pedagogical model with an active focus is evident, designed from the beginning under completely different social and cultural conditions.

Regarding families, there have been important changes in the dynamics, education and nursing rules. The proposal has been accepted and is significant in their daily life, since it offers a clear educational methodology that has allowed neighbours to take over the project, consolidate it and manage it by themselves in order to improve their life conditions. Therefore,

---

[8] The percentage of the Mexican population between 25-34 years old attaining tertiary education in 2004 was 19%. Thus the figures of the Friendship Centre are very relevant.

it now has recognition and prestige among the area's inhabitants. Training has provided a professional alternative for community women, which shows great potential for innovation when implemented. Furthermore this has encouraged the community in general to do everything necessary to develop urban services and infrastructures with the local authorities, thus creating a positive change in life conditions in the district. In fact the change of mentality in most of the families has encouraged advances in gender equality and equity in women's remunerated work, as well as a civic and democratic co-existence and a culture of non-violence. The importance of dialogue and the acceptance of earlier education for their children have also been incentivised.

As a result of its objectives and achievements, the Friendship Centre has been included in the international context of childhood protection policies promoted by the studies carried out by UNESCO (United Nations Educational, Scientific and Cultural Organisation), UNICEF (United Nations Children's Fund) and OECD.

Replication of the case

The founders of this project have promoted the establishment of similar centres in other regions. This expansion has generated another four centres in Mexico City, three in the indigenous rural zones in the state of Michoacan and one more in the state of Puebla. The reproduction of the experience in other places has also required the participation of an organised community where vulnerability conditions and vital deficiencies lead to collective cohesion. It is important to have leaders with initiative, who convoke and acknowledge the potential of their human resources and the support of non-governmental organisations and public administration.

Challenges

One of the main challenges is rejection of the project by certain professional groups and others questioning the personal origins of project members. This exclusion is reproduced at all levels (towards the woman, towards her children and towards illiterate people), because of enduring traditionally defined feminine and masculine roles and the idea that adults are the owners of truth and knowledge.

However, it is probably the Centre's relationship with the central educational authorities that remains the most challenging. Public authorities urge the Friendship Centre to conform to official norms and introduce pedagogical norms intended to increase the quality of service standards. On one hand, this could incorporate mechanisms that would help to improve operating conditions and the dissemination of results, to provide strategic planning and evaluation and to optimise resources. On the other hand, the imposition of academic training (the new norms demand that all teachers have at least the official title of pre-school education teachers) can alienate the project from the community and denaturalise it, instead of strengthening the specialised education required by marginal communities currently implemented by educator-mothers. Being "officially recognised" is sometimes seen as a danger, since there is a fear that mutations will make them lose their innovative character. For instance, according to the new norms, some efforts have been made to establish the day's work within the (reduced) schedule of the official curriculum, but this does not accord with the conception of the Centre as an extension of home.

A further challenge is related to the growing number of different community centres. Some of these initiatives, which are apparently similar to the Friendship Centre, manipulate the social function that this centre should have by responding to other interests and discrediting those who really respond to their local commitments. Since juridical and administrative references adjust slowly to the new demands of society, creative strategies must be established in order to integrate them with existing needs and experience.

Perspectives

During the past few years, family income has improved significantly in the area and this has created new needs, such as the need for English and ICT teaching. There is also a broader educational offer that obligates the Friendship Centre to redefine and reinforce its role in and its links to the neighbourhood and community. For instance, in the near future it intends to duplicate its enrolment and to extend academic support so that the children also receive basic education. In order to achieve these objectives, better infrastructures must first be built. Also, if the idea is to continue with the innovating role, their proposal should evolve. Thus, the plans are to transform the school into a research and community educators training centre, and to integrate it as a model centre offering consulting services for new projects. This qualitative leap implies systematising training and documenting experience with studies and statistics.

Case Study 2
Regular Education Support Services Unit – USAER 8[9]

What does the Support Unit: USAER 8 represent for you and your team?

"We have learnt how valuable our unit is because of the results we see and this encourages us to continue working in this direction."

What would you expect after participating in this OECD initiative?

"That it would encourage the creation of 'spaces for reflection' and the mechanism to maintain them."

Lucero Azpeitía and Sonia Navarrete
Local leaders of Case 2

Origins: special education reforms

The Regular Education Support Services Unit No. 8 (USAER 8) is an interdisciplinary team in charge of promoting the "transformation of school and teaching practices in order to address the diversity of educational needs of all students, with and without learning barriers, in classrooms and schools despite their social, physical, or cultural conditions." The USAER 8 Unit is located within the General Direction of Education Services of Iztapalapa District, a branch of the Federal Administration for Education Services of Mexico City. During the 2004-2005 school year, this Unit followed 254 students in four out of five schools.[10]

---

[9] The complete report was written by: Zardel Jacobo Cúpich (UNAM – Universidad Autónoma de México), María Lilia Pérez-Franco (Co-author of Chapter 6; UAM Autonomous Metropolitan University) and Inés Aguerrondo (Author of Chapter 8; International Institute for Educational Planning-UNESCO).

[10] Since 2002, Iztapalapa District has implemented a policy for the incorporation of students with different disabilities into regular education groups, turning school into a "school for all". This "Inclusive Education" model is a particularity of this district, since the other districts follow an "Integrating Education" model.

Among the main duties carried out by USAER 8 are the curricular adjustments that the teacher must make for students with different capacities, which in turn involve the rest of the students, providing support for groups and teachers in managing the inclusive situation, both at teaching and emotional level. Parents of "special" children are offered counselling in participative training so that they are able to understand their child's situation. For "regular" children, the Unit's presence implies constant support for overcoming prejudice towards those considered "different". In this way, a new inclusive school model is being generated in which the abilities of children "with" and "without" problems are being enhanced.

This set of goals has resulted in the design of a progressive work plan that has been maintained and improved over five years. The stages correspond to the school years beginning in 2001.

2001-2002	2002-2003	2003-2004	2004-2005	2005-2006
Making of school leaders.	Sustained improvement in schools.	Enhancement and improvement of school management and the teaching-learning process.	Sustained improvement of learning, teaching, and school management.	Follow-up, evaluation and adjustment of actions for education improvement in schools.

Source: General Direction of Education Services. Iztapalapa, "General Route: Main Actions and Projects 2001-2005. Dimension. Professional Advancement for Teachers", p. 52.

The birth and structure of USAER 8

Iztapalapa District accounts for 7.5% of Mexico City's total area, but it holds 20% of the basic school enrolment. In this district, there are 46 different USAERs. Each USAER has five basic schools within its responsibility; each Unit is composed of a director and support teachers who are permanently in regular schools as support teams for teachers, children with educational needs or with/without disabilities and parents. Finally, they have an itinerant team – made up of a psychologist, a social worker and a language and communication specialist – that visits the five basic schools and offers their services where needed.

USAER 8 was created in 2000 as part of the organisational changes in the district's education services. Its headquarters are located in a prefabricated classroom lent by one of the elementary schools.

USAER 8 has come up with a creative way of organising its duties that is also self-critical. This has allowed USAER 8 to search for and achieve successful alternatives in connecting with and linking together schools, adjusting to the singularities and particular needs of each of the institutions in which it works. The Unit has been able to do this in an outstanding and sustained manner within the formal structure of the management proposed by the district education authorities.[11] Nevertheless, the goal of an inclusive education involves other actors. At this level, results become slow and less obvious.

Strategy and functioning

USAER 8's connection to regular education requires the description of a few elements that allow us to distinguish the learning model. Some of these are outlined below.

The inclusive model prioritises a **shared responsibility model** in which the USAER and the regular teacher are responsible for the learning process of all the students in a group. This co-existence favours innovation and creativity within a framework for experimentation.

In the **classroom,** the USAER model offers a creative space where both curricular organisation and teaching methods can be modified. In this sense, the objectives are only partially reached. However, this may be because the teacher's evaluation is carried out under the observation of the official indicators appointed to the programme. In any case, in practice the group dynamic tends to follow the traditional manner.

Teachers who so wish, may ask for support, in writing, from the USAER. In practice a model that is more inclusive than integrating is developed. However the key aspect is perhaps that all the students are in the regular classroom and simultaneously receive help from the USAER. Several **teaching strategies** can be detected that may range from the traditional to the inclusive model. However, we cannot know for certain if teachers are actually putting into practice the recommendations of USAER professionals.

Transformation of working strategies should include different **materials and infrastructure**. This is not visible, but innovation at a conceptual and discursive level where "everyone is different" has been detected, thus

---

[11] The Iztapalapa Education Services Unit (USEI) – formally defined as a *pilot unit for decentralisation* of education services in Mexico City – was transformed in 1997 into the *General Direction of Education Services of Iztapalapa* (DGSEI) and was given the status of "experimental situation".

encouraging the respect of diversity and generating beneficial socialisation not only for "special children" but also for the regular groups as well.

School management has shown that one of the major difficulties is putting theory into practice. At present, all seems to be based on principals accepting USAER support whenever teachers consider it necessary. This initiative implies transformations of education as a whole. In this sense, **parents'** perceptions and the perception that **students** have of themselves have changed for the better. Prejudice and mockery are still present in the interaction of the group and in the playground, although this is socially controlled.

Strengths behind the initiative

Among the main factors of USAER 8's achievements are the following:

- Development of the sense of **leadership** of the team (director, psychologist and education sciences specialist) who, valuing cultural and teaching transformations, are convinced of the benefits of inclusive education. The **persistence** of the group of professionals is noteworthy during the five-year period, knowing as they did beforehand that they had embarked on a slow and gradual endeavour.

- The **duality in the organisation** of duties has also been successful. Team members are under obligation to carry out individual efforts in the schools, as well as collective efforts during USAER central work meetings. This framework is independent from the school's own activities. On the other hand, school officials have learned to incorporate themselves into the Programme for the Enhancement of Education, allowing them to institutionalise their duties.

- **Multiplicity and flexibility** of the ways in which professionals apply the programme have been a beneficial factor in the team's self-appreciation. The horizontal scheme and different backgrounds, as well as **accumulated experience,** have been keys in the community's recognition and the legitimacy of the Unit.

In sum, USAER 8 professionals have known how to present themselves as a "community in practice", where a network of relationships is cultivated allowing the development of experiences, resources and stories, creatively and with criticism, in order to carry out formal duties in schools.

Perspective and difficulties

USAER 8's case is set within a national education problematic, that in turn is situated in an international education policy of inclusive education. The challenge is enormous, implying as it does a far-reaching change in the socio-cultural process based on the model of the parallel school for children with disabilities. The challenge is to build cultural change through school. For the time being, we cannot see any transformations of the formal strategies. A positive evaluation of the experience will depend not only on complying with the formal activities, but also on the slow but steady transformation of other education entities.

The authors' evaluation during the five-year period of USAER 8's work states that it has been able to influence favourably the learning and family processes of approximately 40 children. As for most of the parents, they claim not to know about USAER's work.

The persisting difficulties are mainly twofold. One aspect is that the social and historical representation of people with disabilities is still marked by prejudice, stigmatisation and discrimination. The other aspect is that there is a parallel education structure for education services, where the basic education system has an operating logic, evaluation methods, resources and a stimuli system that do not correspond with special education re-orientation.

The step towards the future

The challenge is for school to incorporate the model and make it its own, liberating USAER from the responsibility of inclusive education. The first changes are seen in the education aspect. Teachers are surprised by the achievements of children with disabilities. Therefore, inclusion in the school environment is something that cannot be imposed by official mandates.

Inclusion does not mean erasing, disguising or denying differences but understanding the space in which they belong. In other words, advances might occur in response to an intended reflection. Gradually, teaching groups to work for the group and achieve a collaborative effort is essential for the future development of an inclusive education.

USAER 8 is showing through its systematic efforts that we can work towards enhancing education processes and transform, at least slowly, the mentality of small school communities. However, the execution of this policy faces obstacles at structural and institutional levels in the realms of economy, politics, society and culture that even today, more than a decade after reform, cannot be overcome.

Case Study 3
Intelligent Classroom for Migrants[12]

What does the Intelligent Classroom represent for you and your team?

"Our initiative comes from the recognition that most of the migrant children in our State have a level of education that is far behind that of their peers. However we know this is due to the incapacity of education structures to respond to their needs, given that all these children are very capable of learning and already have good levels of knowledge. This mismatch is the consequence of multiple and complex factors.

The Intelligent Classroom is not a multi-grade classroom, our conception is very different from it being just a space where children from different grades can come together to learn. The reports and the transversal analysis give an idea, but do not reflect all the different components of our initiative. This may be in part because this is a recent initiative, thus there is a requirement for careful follow-up over a longer period of time."

What would you expect after participating in this OECD initiative?

"We hope this project will encourage a national policy that would support these types of initiative and that the general education system could learn from us, since we provide an example of paying real attention to this vulnerable population. In particular, some changes in school organisation and systems of accreditation should take place, along with better dialogue between the federation and the regional state authorities."

Patricia Inzunza-Rodríguez and Berta Gómez-Elías[13]
Local leaders of Case 3

---

[12] The complete report was written by: Francisco Benavides (OECD-CERI Analyst), Alfonso Noriega (Education Researcher), Teresa Rojas (Researcher Professor of National Pedagogical University).

Origins and context

In Mexico the educational policies and programmes oriented to respond to the specific educational needs of the children of *internal migrant agricultural workers*[14] have been fostered specifically since 1976 with limited results.[15] These migrant workers are usually from different very poor regions within the country, which in general are also zones where indigenous populations are concentrated. They and their families migrate every year to those agricultural states where there are job opportunities and where they stay for several months before going back to their homeland. Sinaloa is the main producer of agricultural goods and is the state that receives the highest number of migrant workers per year – between 160 000 and 300 000.

The federal government is currently trying to strengthen basic education for the children of these migrants through the Programme of Basic Education for Migrant Children (PRONIM), through co-ordination strategies with state governments to propitiate the development of a pedagogical and curricular proposal that is relevant for this population's basic education. Despite the effort made, the achievements are still modest.

The strong temporary or definitive affluence of migrant laborers has transformed the various states' structures. The greater presence and precariousness of the families and their increasing sedentariness have generated, among other things, an increasing educational demand. The young immigrants are children coming from families with social, ethnical, cultural and linguistic characteristics that are generally different to those of the region's inhabitants; there are also differences among themselves as they come from different regions and ethnic groups. Most of these migrants are victims of strong social exclusion and live in precarious conditions on the farms.[16]

---

[13] Bertha Gómez-Elías is the co-ordinator of the *Programa de atención a niños y niñas migrantes*. Patricia Inzunza Rodríguez was Head of the Department of Technical Pedagogic Support for Basic Education in 2004 and is currently Academic Coordinator of Basic Education in the Ministry of Education and Culture in the State of Sinaloa.

[14] In Mexico this worker is known as: *jornalero migrante* = migrant worker, usually working in farming-related tasks.

[15] Mainly through different initiatives from the federal Ministry of Education (SEP) and the National Council of Educational Development (CONAFE).

[16] Farms are usually owned by big agro-industrial companies and/or groups and they possess or rent large extensions of land.

The Intelligent Classroom project started formally in 2004 as part of the latest effort of a team of public servants at the Sinaloa Ministry of Education and Culture to respond to the complex educational deficits and needs of the populations. Under the leadership of Patricia Inzunza-Rodríguez, they have developed a psycho-pedagogical mechanism to support those migrant students living and studying on the farms (where their family live and work) who are in an "educational risk situation". Thus its target population was defined as i) all students on the farms who have a strong deficit in the acquisition of language (writing and reading) and mathematic competencies; ii) older students; and iii) girls and boys with different learning special needs and capabilities. The purpose is to prevent the migrant population falling behind and therefore prevent educational failure.

Operation of the Intelligent Classroom

The Intelligent Classroom attempts to create educational environments that are more relevant and adequate for the population, while respecting the differences of migrant boys and girls. Thus, school failure is not centred on individual (in)capacities and learning is based on the acknowledgment of the following principles: i) all students are persons capable of learning; ii) they learn *de facto* and possess a lot of knowledge that is not formally acquired in school; and iii) to obtain the expected results, they require more educational attention. "*It should be an intelligence capable of perceiving the educational needs of migrant students*".[17]

The Intelligent Classroom has been implemented on those farms that already have a school and in which the manager supports the initiatives (see more about this below). Following different mechanisms of selection (which include direct observations from teachers, evaluation from the person in charge of the Intelligent Classroom, assessments and discussions with the students and parents, etc.), those students in "traditional" classrooms who are in an "at risk" educational situation (as described in the previous point) are sent to the Intelligent Classroom.

The Intelligent Classrooms are multi-grade groups, where children study during an unspecified period of time (some older children spend nearly three months there), which concludes when they reach the objective of acquiring basic reading/writing and mathematics skills. Each Intelligent Classroom usually has three staff members: one titular teacher, one psychologist and one expert on special education. Their activities in the classroom are

---

[17] "Project: Psycho-pedagogical intervention for basic education for migrant students in a school risk situation. Sinaloa case", p. 5, SEPyC, Sinaloa, México, December 2005.

supported externally by the educational centre's director and a school consultant. In terms of main infrastructure, the participants of the Intelligent Classroom use a room within the school with similar conditions to the other "traditional" classrooms.

The teacher is the person who co-ordinates and leads the different didactic strategies together with the other two professionals. These strategies are previously decided collaboratively among the three of them and in accordance with the needs of the group. Three students are normally organised in small subgroups (with an average of 5-7 students each) around three different tables, according to their conceptual development and reading/writing levels, as well as their age gap in connection with the expected level. They also create different resources (games, drawings, etc.), taking into account the heterogeneity of the group. The intention is to give more "personalised" and "*ad hoc*" attention to each student. These elements impact the high levels of participation and interaction.

Generally speaking, we can see that this mechanism of educational attention creates an intermission in the school path of these children, thus subordinating the "contents race" in order to encourage activities that foster the process of acquisition of basic competences.

The reduced number of students in the Intelligent Classroom (an average of 5-8 per teacher) is a positive aspect. It is worth questioning if this is the main factor that ensures the key to its success. The children's comments clearly reflect the notion of **personal achievement**; they are also capable of referring it to an experience of their own. Furthermore, one can perceive a feeling of comfort and a playful and protected atmosphere in the classrooms. This result is of extraordinary value.

Some results

However, although the Intelligent Classroom is a very recent experience, the quantitative and qualitative results it appears to have shown when this report was written are eloquent. In the 2004-2005 school period, the number of students at risk of having to repeat the course integrated in the nine Intelligent Classrooms then operating stood at 111. Of them, 91% (101) were able to pass the school year.

Most of the actors involved evaluate it as being very positive. Staff mention that the children have not only overcome their basic initial deficiencies, but they have also reached a level of knowledge and competence that makes them capable of integrating into upper education grades (for example, a 12-year-old child taking courses in the second year of elementary school, would be able to integrate into 5th or 6th grade after passing through the Intelligent Classroom).[18] **Parents** suggest that their children are better because they receive more personalised attention.

The actors as motors

The **technical team** that supports this initiative is part of the government and their leaders have a high level of schooling (masters and doctorate studies), as well as experience in the field and in administration. They have contributed to the creation of links between Sinaloa's various sectors (universities, companies, agricultural associations, professional networks, etc.), thus securing the project's continuity. The Intelligent Classroom is also an initiative that is part of the different efforts they have led for several years to try and respond to migrant children's educational needs.

On the other hand, the **professors** have been able to adapt to the difficult context in which they work and have made the project their own: "because we see that it works and the children need it". To them, the Intelligent Classroom represents a more flexible space where they can be more creative and more "useful".

The **companies** that support the Intelligent Classroom are successful in economic terms, with a pro-active vision that promotes (at least in its discourse) improvements in working conditions. The Intelligent Classroom allows them to present a positive image of the company externally (the media, the government, international clients), providing a better service to their workers and training a potential future workforce. These companies assign an **administrator** for the agricultural fields who manages the services provided in the camp and plays a key role in the implementation or non-implementation of these initiatives.

The **connector** is also an important factor. This is the mediator between migrant families and the companies' owners, since he contacts the workforce in their place of origin, at the same time operating as representative of the migrants and as overseer (representative of the employer) in the camps. He uses the Intelligent Classroom as a persuasive argument in order to attract more workers.

---

[18] One of the problems identified during the visit was that of the administrative impediments faced by the educational centre's authorities to integrate into a higher grade those students who, after studying in the Intelligent Classroom, had tried to progress to a superior school grade. Recently, the project's leaders have informed CERI that these difficulties are being overcome and that most of the children that leave the Intelligent Classroom have made several "leaps" towards higher levels.

INNOVATING TO LEARN, LEARNING TO INNOVATE – ISBN-978-92-64-04797-6 © OECD 2008

Scope, limitations and survival

There is strong pressure on behalf of the market to increase the number of agricultural workers during certain periods of the year. The companies are tempted to **hire minors** in a clandestine manner. Some families encourage this too, because of their economic needs. Despite the efforts of several organisations, this is a danger that must be considered, since school desertion can very often become very attractive, if it means being able to enter the labour market more quickly. In general, social workers in one of the camps were able to conclude that almost 15% of the children (under 14 years old) who live in the camps do not attend school which presents the probability that most of them are working in the fields.

Another problem is that most of the parents, as well as the connectors, **do not clearly understand** what the Intelligent Classroom is or what are the other didactic mechanisms that have been implemented. In addition to this, most of the teachers and school consultants have contracts that are neither permanent nor continuous. Many teachers work twice the standard labour hours in order to increase their salary and must constantly adapt to the agricultural seasons and migrations of the population. It is worth mentioning that the agricultural cycle and migration of the workforce this implies do not coincide with the official school cycle; therefore the number of children (and professors) in those educational centres visited significantly fluctuates throughout the school period.

The Intelligent Classroom, despite being financed by the state and some company owners, is at risk of depending too much on the latter. Besides, not all company owners are willing to co-finance the initiative; therefore the Intelligent Classroom, as it currently operates, only benefits some people and does not appear to change the existing dynamics of inequality (and indeed, perhaps aggravates it).

The reinsertion, accreditation and certification of the students that have been part of the Intelligent Classroom constitute an important problem that needs urgent solutions. Moreover, some teachers of the "traditional" classrooms perceive the work of the Intelligent Classroom as being distant or alien. This is also demonstrated in the attitude of some of the students in the traditional classrooms, who have a negative opinion of those who attend the "Aula de los burros" (the idiots' classroom).

The future: the proposals

The Intelligent Classroom promises change and allows children to participate in a qualitatively distinct learning experience. The truth is that minors are receiving a service that the educational system in their places of origin would probably not be able to offer. In qualitative and quantitative terms the results seem very stimulating. This justifies its existence, but does not justify the incapacity of the general education system to give a quality and integral response to the educational needs to all migrant children.

On the other hand, it is not possible to affirm with certainty that this mechanism can be useful in any other context. Different adaptations would have to be implemented from its conception (objectives, goals, tools, pedagogical and intervention strategies, etc). Nevertheless, the need that justifies the existence of the Intelligent Classroom in agricultural camps also appears to be valid and urgent in other "regular" contexts.

From a pragmatic point of view, the future of the Intelligent Classrooms greatly depends on (the financing and commitment of) the industry and the state's educational agents. The administrators seem to be willing to continue supporting the programme as long as "it keeps having good results". Moreover, the total investment cost on behalf of company owners is relatively low. Thus the increasing demand of migrant workers and the struggle of authorities and civil society to avoid minors being hired to work, guarantees to a certain degree, the spaces for the Intelligent Classroom to continue.

The state's government agents seem to want to strengthen the institutionalisation, programme and organisation of this initiative. This may demonstrate clear benefits (recognition, more official resources, etc.) but also some risks (losing the capacity to innovate, bureaucratisation, etc.). In order to obtain more autonomy with regard to the companies, new financing sources – from the state or otherwise – should be looked for. The federal government should also demand the existence of this type of initiative (and maybe their financing through trusts or other transparent and autonomous entities) of all company owners.

Case Study 4
Ayuujk Polyvalent Integral Community High School
BICAP[19]

This community high school project emerged as a result of the need to integrate the Ayuujk-Mixe culture and language into education and to co-ordinate all types and levels of education within the municipality under the same principles. The model favours the knowledge exchange of the community and different institutions, in order to foster sustainable development and employment and at the same time, consolidate cultural values. This is achieved by including training in practical manual arts following the teacher-apprentice model and overcoming traditional school limits by expanding the task to include the direct instruction of producers and development of community leaders. Thus, BICAP is part of a series of local educational initiatives[20] that have been set up inconsistently as integral projects under different administrations.

The concept of the BICAP high school is innovating because the cultural and educational values of the Ayuujk community constitute the project's philosophy and pedagogical action. Family and community knowledge is considered a value and a link with universal knowledge, thus the community relationship forms are revalued and the student is responsible for his/her own learning. The educational institution becomes a catalyst of social cohesion generated by the search for consensus.

---

[19] The complete report was written by: Marcela Tovar-Gómez (co-author of Chapter 6; National Pedagogical University), Juana Mª Sancho-Gil (co-author of Chapter 6; University of Barcelona) and Natalia Edith Tenorio-Tovar (Analyst, Ministry of Education).

[20] The Ayuujk Polyvalent Integral Community High School (BICAP – Bachillerato Integral Comunitario Ayuuk Polivalente), the Musical Training Centre (CECAM – Centro de Capacitación Musical) and the Technological Institute of the Mixe Region (ITRM – Instituto Tecnológico de la Región Mixe) were integrated into the Mixe Community Integral Education project (EDICOM – Educación Integral Comunitaria Mixe), between 1994 and 1999.

The project's local management was initially established as an alternative to the state's centralised model and as an answer to the wear and tear on the educational policy's vertical structure and inefficiency. Federal and state initiatives have been perceived as impositions that respond to the needs of an elite, which lack values and are distant from strong traditional ethics. Based on this context, the position held is that education must correspond better to community needs than to international standards. Thus, education is monitored by the community and needs to be sufficiently flexible and rooted in local values, along with being normal and coherent with the community logic.

Historical and social context

Cultural diversity in the state of Oaxaca is the broadest in the country.[21] Many of its inhabitants come from different indigenous peoples who live in territorially grouped locations that maintain their own government structure, based on the honorific and solidarity participation of its members. All services are organised through this mechanism, except the areas of health and education, which are in the charge of the federal government. Santa María Tlahuitoltepec is located in the state's northern sierra. It is a Mixe community, poor and with a low level of educational development, but it has educational coverage on all levels and most of its teachers are bilingual members of the community.

The relationship between the local government structure and the central government has significantly evolved in the past few years. During the 1990s there was a change in the state's conception, when the validity of bilingual education and of "uses and customs" was acknowledged. During this period, formal demands were expressed for the formal and unlimited issue of public policies in the areas of decision making and school budgets, as well as the elimination of discrimination against students because of their identity and culture. Thus, this project's driving force is part of the reconstitution of the identity and culture of indigenous communities and of an autonomous conception of power.

Planning for BICAP started at the end of the 1970s, within the context of revalorisation of indigenous cultures and rights. It was founded by local university graduates in the 1990s and in 1996 it was established as a pilot

---

[21] According to National Institute of Statistics and Geography (INEGI) statistics, there are 14 different indigenous peoples and 37% of the population over five years old speak an indigenous language. Out of 570 municipalities, approximately half (298) of them have 30% or more indigenous inhabitants.

project that received official recognition from 1999 onwards. It is currently integrated into the General Direction of Technological Education (DGETA) and abides by its regulation, trying to maintain its particular characteristics.

Educational proposal

Education through BICAP results in the awarding of the title of Technician in Community Integral Development. Besides high school, it offers the creation of productive projects and craftsmanship workshops: sewing, jewellery, blacksmithing and ceramics. Education lines include Ayuujk traditions and culture, management of natural resources, farming and animal husbandry activities and community health. In this way, this programme complements the official programmes.

The learning model follows the Ayuujk educational conception, which promotes collective and family dialogue and includes the obligation of being useful to the community. Direct contact with the community is maintained through group work. The school must advise and protect, as well as coach and guide; the basic principle of education is the example. Culture and identity are favoured through the use of the Mixe language and culture, respect for community values, along with a social and political involvement that produces confident performance in the students, the valorisation of their culture and the construction of an "ethnical citizenship". In sum, education has a strong basis in communitarian and social strategies.

The objective of the model's educational foundations is to improve life conditions from a student-focused perspective. In order to achieve this, previous knowledge and experience are valued and individual and teamwork capabilities are stimulated. Professors are considered active and committed members of the community, who participate in permanent training and who collaborate and work as a group. They are perceived as consultants who teach both others and themselves how to learn. The union of local and universal knowledge – and of theory and practice – is fostered during training. To that effect, the concepts of integration, functionality, transformation capacity, social construction and generation of knowledge action are stressed. Learning is based on experience and evaluation is considered an integral part of it.

The learning method combines explanatory classes, which include the search for information, exercises and the questioning of contexts. This is done within extended schedules. In the morning, subject matters and curricular courses are covered and in the afternoon, students work on research and development projects, as well as in craftsmanship workshops. During the whole process, particular emphasis is placed on creating a working ethic of their own: *education is based on examples* and *knowledge and virtue are combined.*

Adult education offers basic management and technical training tools, as well as personal and community human development resources. Thus, it results in productive projects originated by promoters who travel in that area. Up until now, as a result of the incrimination of training and a change in mentality, environmental and productivity improvements have been verified. Gender equity has been reinforced, ecological conscience has been fostered and the population is dignified and has acquired more confidence. All this has produced more self-management and has reduced emigration.

Results, challenges and perspectives

The BICAP project has been active for over ten years.[22] The community now appreciates the benefits and has strengthened the certainty that they can achieve development following their own cultural model. The number of students is growing, identity and ecological conscience have now been consolidated and self-esteem levels and capabilities have increased.

Low performance and deficient academic quality are still some of the main obstacles faced by the project. Follow-up is hampered by lack of evaluation and statistics about results. The lack of resources, salaries and positions has prevented the incorporation and training of new teachers according to the proposed pedagogical programme. Thus, in practice, the pedagogical model is not implemented in a thorough manner and this is demonstrated by the contents, which are not consistent with the curriculum, as well as by lack of motivation.

The discrepancy between official programmes and the project is evident in the cultural aspect, when individual and community notions and the indigenous and Spanish languages are opposed, as well as when the customs and rules of the community relationship are ignored. It is necessary, then, to understand and integrate the local cultural identity within the global context. In practical terms, a collateral convergence between central and local curricula is required. The lack of autonomy, the inflexibility of central administrative structures and excessive bureaucracy have created dependency on personal favours granted by high-level authorities, because this is not part of an integral project specifically designed for this reality. Sometimes the project has evolved rather accidentally, due to the discontinuity of institutional projects. Therefore, the success and possibility

---

[22] 324 students signed up for the 2004-05 academic courses; the institution's staff is composed of 25 teachers and 13 administrative employees.

of transference of this educational model rest on the community's capacity to sustain these initiatives and on the survival of its nature when it is integrated into the structure of the central institutions.

OECD PUBLICATIONS, 2, rue André-Pascal, 75775 PARIS CEDEX 16
PRINTED IN FRANCE
(96 2008 09 1 P) ISBN 978-92-64-04797-6 – 56513 2008